HOPE FOR RWANDA

HOPE FOR RWANDA

Conversations with Laure Guilbert and Hervé Deguine

André Sibomana

Translated and with a Postscript by Carina Tertsakian

Foreword by Alison Des Forges

Pluto Press

LONDON • STERLING, VIRGINIA

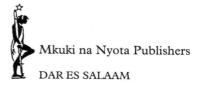
Mkuki na Nyota Publishers

DAR ES SALAAM

First published by Desclée de Brouwer, Paris,
as *Gardons espoir pour le Rwanda*, 1997

English-language edition first published 1999 by Pluto Press
345 Archway Road, London N6 5AA
and 22883 Quicksilver Drive, Sterling, VA 20166-2012, USA
and by Mkuki na Nyota Publishers
6 Muhonda Street,
Kariakoo, PO Box 4246,
Dar es Salaam, Tanzania

British Library Cataloguing in Publication Data
A catalogue record for this book is available from the British Library

ISBN 0 7453 1561 5 pbk (Pluto Press)
ISBN 0 7453 1566 6 hbk (Pluto Press)
ISBN 9976 973 61 6 pbk (Mkuki na Nyota Publishers)

Library of Congress Cataloging in Publication Data
Sibomana, Andre, 1954–
    [Gardons espoir pour le Rwanda. English]
    Hope for Rwanda : conversations with Laure Guilbert and Hervé
Deguine / André Sibomana, translated by Carina Tertsakian.
        p.   cm.
    Includes bibliographical references (p.   ) and index.
    ISBN 0–7453–1566–6
    1. Genocide—Rwanda—History—20th century. 2. Rwanda—Ethnic
relations—History—20th century. 3. Guilbert, Laure Interviews.
4. Historians—France Interviews. 5. Deguine, Hervé Interviews.
6. Journalists—France Interviews. I. Guilbert, Laure.
II. Deguine, Hervé.
DT450.435.S5313   1999
967.57104—dc21   99–35170
                                                                   CIP

Designed and produced for Pluto Press by
Chase Production Services, Chadlington, OX7 3LN
Typeset from disk by Stanford DTP Services, Northampton
Printed in the EC by TJ International, Padstow

Contents

Foreword by Alison Des Forges   ix
Chronology   xv
Abbreviations   xxv
Preface: André Sibomana, or faith against the odds
             by Laure Guilbert and Hervé Deguine   xxvii

Part I: The Committed Priest   1

1   The Gifted Child from Masango   3
2   Choosing the Path of God   10
3   The Journalist and Human Rights Activist   18

Part II: On the Edge of the Abyss   33

4   A Cry in the Wilderness   35
5   Lord, Where Were You During the Genocide?   54
6   Words Fail Us   77

Part III: Time is Against Us   99

7   The Duty of Justice and the Duty of Memory   101
8   The Role of the Church: Guilty or an Incriminating
    Witness?   121
9   Rwanda Caught in an Impasse   137

Conclusion: We Must Not Give Up Hope   153
Postscript: What Future for the Defence of Human
             Rights in Rwanda? by Carina Tertsakian   158
Select Bibliography   173
Human Rights in Rwanda   180
Index   183

When I despair, I remember that all through history, the way of truth and love has always won. There have been tyrants and murderers and for a time they seem invincible, but in the end, they always fall – think of it, always.

Mahatma Gandhi

I thought it was commendable to lend a voice, however weak, to those who do not have the right to speak. Have I managed to make their voices heard? Not always. Those who live without chains, without constraints, those who have enough to eat every day make such a deafening noise on their own behalf that they do not hear the moans that rise from below. If you ask them for a moment of silence, they reply that they cannot afford it. They do not believe that it is their duty.

Albert Londres

Acknowledgement

I wish to thank Roger Clark for his patience and care.

Carina Tertsakian

Foreword
Alison Des Forges

When I first went looking for André Sibomana in August 1994, shortly after the end of the genocide in Rwanda, I had trouble finding him. Even at Kabgayi, the centre of the diocese, no one seemed to have seen this well-known priest or his readily recognizable vehicle. I went from one to another of the many buildings, scattered over the extensive grounds. Finally a sister who had known me for sometime indicated that he was lodged in a room in the interior courtyard of the convent.

I sat down on a bench in the arcade and studied the flowers still blooming in the untended garden. The sister knocked at the door of a room across the garden and spoke briefly once the door had opened a crack. I had heard that Sibomana wanted no visitors and that he felt his life was in danger. Still I was surprised that he hesitated so long before deciding to come out.

He greeted me with no warmth but did sit down next to me. We had hardly begun to talk when a journalist pushed his way in the gate and presumed to begin interviewing Sibomana. Perhaps out of sympathy for a fellow journalist, the priest agreed to answer a few questions. After a brief discussion, the journalist asked his age. Sibomana replied that he had lived forty years and that was one year too many. With an angry scowl, he refused to talk further and the journalist left.

I didn't stay much longer since I found no way to respond to Sibomana's obvious anguish. The next day I went back. This visit went no better, although Sibomana let down his guard enough to talk of some of the horrors he had seen during the genocide and of his own efforts to save people. As we sat on the bench he mused about the human capacity for evil and voiced a desire to become a monk and withdraw from the world. He readily agreed that Rwanda needed courageous leaders more than ever before, but insisted that he no longer saw himself playing such a role.

Just before I left, he remarked that there were still bodies scattered in the nearby woods, both Tutsi slain during the genocide and Hutu killed by soldiers of the Rwandan Patriotic Front (RPF) who had driven away the genocidal assailants. I wanted to investigate the site. Sibomana refused to go with me, saying 'I've seen enough dead bodies.'

Sibomana had come to prominence as editor of *Kinyamateka*, the most important independent newspaper in Rwanda. As a crusader against official corruption, he had been prosecuted for his reports in 1990 but had won acquittal after presenting well-documented proof of his conclusions. Working behind the scenes as well, he had fashioned a powerful statement, issued by the clergy of the Kabgayi diocese, which criticized the close links between the church hierarchy and the government. Spurred by his unrelenting anger against injustice, Sibomana had helped mobilize the Rwandan human rights movement and had ensured that the massacres that presaged the 1994 genocide were documented.

The genocide had transformed Sibomana's anger to anguish and sapped his driving energy. He was overwhelmed not just by the sheer, incomprehensible horror of the slaughter but also by the betrayal of some of our human rights colleagues. Most had been so overwhelmed by fear that they had retreated into silence, although some did try to save lives more privately. Worse still, some had chosen to support the genocide, echoing the government's explanation that the killing was a necessary form of self-defence. One human rights activist even went so far as to describe the effort to exterminate Tutsi as normal.

When I came to see Sibomana a third time, I was looking for information about a report of RPF soldiers killing civilians. Once more we took our places on the bench in the sun and I pressed him for what he knew about the massacre. It was not the midday sun that caused the sweat to form and stream down his face. We sat a few minutes in silence, gazing out at the flowers in the calm courtyard. Then, without looking at me, he started to relate what he knew of the incident where soldiers had gunned down unarmed civilians.

Deciding to take up his work again, Sibomana had to confront not just intimidation and threats from authorities – accustomed hindrances to his work – but also a new enemy: his own despair. In his very hesitation and turmoil, he offered the best model to others who had been similarly devastated by the genocide and who could no longer cheerfully hope to save the world.

His decision to keep on trying led him to recount his personal journey through suffering to hope. Readers of this book have a chance to share his journey and, as they deepen their understanding of the Rwandan tragedy, to renew their own commitment to the ideals of justice, peace, and reconciliation that fired the spirit of André Sibomana.

Alison Des Forges
New York City
May 1999

Map of Rwanda

Chronology

From conquest to social revolution (1894–1959)

1894	German explorers discover Rwanda.
1900	Creation of the first White Fathers mission.
1916	Belgium takes over Rwanda and relies on the traditional elite to govern the country.
1922	The League of Nations puts the kingdom of Urundi (Rwanda–Burundi) under the trusteeship of Belgium.
1931	The king is deposed by the Belgians and replaced by his son Rudahigwa, who is more conciliatory. The Belgian administration imposes an identity booklet in which each person's ethnic origin is specified.
1932	Creation of the newspaper *Kinyamateka*.
1952	Creation of the first representative council, the Superior Council, composed mainly of prominent Tutsi.
1957	Publication of a 'Note on the social aspect of the racial problem in Rwanda', later known as the 'Manifesto of the Bahutu'. In this document, the Hutu denounce the 'feudal regime' and domination of the Tutsi.
1958	Inter-ethnic tensions increase. The Belgians become wary of signs of a desire for independence among their former Tutsi allies; they get closer to the Hutu.

The Social Revolution, independence and the Kayibanda regime (1959–73)

1959–62	The 'Social Revolution'. With the support of the Rwandan Roman Catholic Church, the emancipated Hutu elite takes power. The Belgian trusteeship administration withdraws its support from the Tutsi, many of whom are massacred. Several thousand Tutsi flee to Uganda, Burundi and Zaire.
1961	Declaration of the Republic of Rwanda, following the death of the king. Grégoire Kayibanda is elected president (1961–73).

1962	Declaration of independence (simultaneous declaration of independence in Burundi).
1972	More than 200,000 Burundian Hutu – the intellectual class – are massacred by the Tutsi-dominated army. Thousands of Hutu flee to Tanzania and Rwanda.
1973	Hutu extremists in Rwanda push the Kayibanda regime in a more radical direction, exploiting fears of Tutsi provoked by the massacres in Burundi. Public salvation committees organize a 'Tutsi hunt'. More massacres; another exodus.

The early phase of the Habyarimana regime (1973–90)

1973	The Chief-of-Staff of the armed forces, Juvénal Habyarimana, takes power following a *coup d'état* (1973–94).
1978	New Constitution. Single party state: *Mouvement révolutionnaire national pour le développement*, MRND (National Revolutionary Movement for Development).
1979	Creation of the Rwandan National Union (RANU) in Kenya, representing Rwandan Tutsi refugees.
1987	Creation of the Rwandan Patriotic Front (RPF) in Uganda. *Coup d'état* in Burundi.
1988	Massacres of Tutsi in Burundi. Repression by the army leads to tens of thousands of deaths among Hutu peasants and provokes another exodus to Rwanda.

The democratization of the regime and the war (1990–94)

1990

September	Visit of Pope John Paul II. Trial of *Kinyamateka* journalists.
October	The RPF attacks Rwanda from Uganda. Thousands of Tutsi and opponents of the Habyarimana government are arrested on suspicion of complicity.
November	First signs of democratization of the regime (development of freedom of the press, *de facto* creation of opposition political parties). Juvénal Habyarimana announces the suppression of the mention of ethnicity on identity cards.

1991

January–March
　　　　　Massacres of Bagogwe (a group of Tutsi pastoralists).

| April | A multi-party system is recognized. |

1992

March	Creation of the *Coalition pour la défense de la République*, CDR (Coalition for the Defence of the Republic), an extremist Hutu party. Massacres of Tutsi in the Bugesera region.
April	A transitional government is formed, headed by the leader of the democratic opposition, Dismas Nsengiyaremye.
May	RPF offensive in the north of the country. More than 350,000 peasants are displaced by the fighting.
June	The democratic opposition meets RPF representatives in Brussels with a view to forming a united front against the Habyarimana regime.
July	Ceasefire agreement between the government and the RPF.

September–December
Extremist militia begin organizing.

1993

January	Signature of a protocol agreement to form a broad-based, transitional government. An independent international commission of inquiry denounces large-scale human rights violations.
February	The RPF resumes fighting in the north of the country and arrives on the outskirts of Kigali. Between 800,000 and 1 million Hutu peasants are forced to flee and live in a camp for the internally displaced, where they suffer from starvation. A French military intervention prevents the RPF rebels from taking control of the capital and forces them to resume peace negotiations.
June	Creation of a new provisional government. Dismas Nsengiyaremye is forced to flee. Agathe Uwilingiyimana takes over as prime minister. She will remain in this post until she is killed on 7 April 1994. General elections in Burundi: for the first time in the country's history, a Hutu, Melchior Ndadaye, becomes president.
August	Signature of the Arusha peace accords, which put an end to hostilities and provide a power-sharing agreement between the MRND, the democratic opposition and the RPF.

October   *Coup d'état* in Burundi. Melchior Ndadaye is
            assassinated by extremist Tutsi soldiers. Massacres of
            Tutsi; repression by the army and massacres of Hutu;
            700,000 Hutu flee to Rwanda, fuelling fear of Tutsi
            among Rwandan Hutu peasants.
December   French soldiers of Operation Noroît leave Rwanda and
            hand over to UNAMIR (United Nations Assistance
            Mission for Rwanda).

1994
January   The Arusha accords are blocked. The broad-based
            transitional government cannot be set up.
February   Assassination of Félicien Gatabazi, leader of the *Parti
            social démocrate*, PSD (Social Democratic Party), and
            Martin Bucyana, leader of the CDR.
March   Atmosphere of civil war in Kigali. Incidents occur on
            a daily basis and lists of people to be eliminated are
            drawn up.
April   Juvénal Habyarimana goes to Dar es Salaam
            (Tanzania) for a regional peace summit. 6 April: he
            is assassinated as he returns, along with Burundian
            President Cyprien Ntaryamira. 7 April: Prime Minister
            Agathe Uwilingiyimana and several other ministers are
            killed. Massacres of Tutsi and Hutu opponents begin
            in Kigali and several other areas. 8 April: creation of
            a provisional government made up of Hutu extremists.
            9 April: France and Belgium fly in troops to evacuate
            European expatriates. 21 April: the UN Security
            Council votes to withdraw UNAMIR.
May   The United Nations votes to adopt an arms embargo.
            The Human Rights Commission asks its Special
            Rapporteur, René Degni-Ségui, to investigate ongoing
            massacres.
June   16 June: France considers a military intervention in
            Rwanda. 22 June: the Security Council authorizes
            the despatch of a 'humanitarian force'. 23 June: start
            of Operation Turquoise and creation of a safe
            humanitarian zone in the south of the country. 28 June:
            René Degni-Ségui describes the ongoing massacres as
            'genocide'. The International Committee of the Red
            Cross estimates that between 500,000 and 1 million
            Tutsi and Hutu government opponents were killed
            during the genocide.

| July | 4 July: the RPF takes control of Kigali. 10 July: creation of a government of National Unity. 13–14 July: fearing the advances of the RPF, 1 million Rwandan Hutu – many of whom were heavily involved in the genocide – flee to eastern Zaire, in the Goma region. In the following two weeks, 50,000 of them die of exhaustion and cholera. |
| August | 22 August: end of Operation Turquoise. |

Rwanda since 1994

1994

September–December

The reconstruction of Rwanda begins. Pasteur Bizimungu is President of the Republic. Paul Kagame is Vice-President and Minister of Defence. Of the 7.5 million inhabitants in Rwanda before the war, almost 1 million have been killed, 2 million are living in camps for the internally displaced (mainly in the south of the country, in the former safe humanitarian zone) and 2 million in refugee camps (mainly in Zaire and Tanzania). Nearly 600,000 Tutsi, most of them descendants of Tutsi who were forced into exile between 1959 and 1990, return to Rwanda.

1995

April	22 April: massacre of displaced persons at Kibeho by RPA (Rwandan Patriotic Army) soldiers.
August	Break-up of the government of National Unity. Prime Minister Faustin Twagiramungu and Minister of the Interior Seth Sendashonga flee the country.
September	The UN Security Council creates a commission of inquiry to investigate supplies of arms and military equipment to the ex-FAR (*Forces armées rwandaises*) (Rwandan Armed Forces).

1996

| July | *Coup d'état* in Burundi. Sylvestre Ntibantunganya - Cyprien Ntaryamira's successor – is overthrown by Major Pierre Buyoya who is supported by the Burundian army. Regional trade sanctions imposed on Burundi. |
| August | Adoption of a new law on crimes of genocide. |

October   Clashes between the Banyamulenge (a Kinyarwanda-speaking Zairian Tutsi minority) and the Zairian Armed Forces (FAZ) in the Lake Kivu region. Rwandan refugees and part of the civilian population support the FAZ against the Banyamulenge. The revolt of the Banyamulenge, supported by RPA soldiers from Rwanda, becomes a regional war led by the head of the Alliance of Democratic Forces for the Liberation of Congo–Zaire (AFDL), Laurent-Désiré Kabila. First massacres of Hutu refugees.

November   Success of the rebellion which controls large parts of Kivu. The UN considers a military intervention to save Hutu refugees who have been deliberately deprived of food by the rebels. Just as the arrival of an international force seems imminent, the rebels organize the voluntary or forced return to Rwanda of half the refugees. The other half (around 500,000 refugees) are pushed back into the Zairian forests.

December   Forcible closure of the refugee camps in Tanzania. Hundreds of thousands more refugees return to Rwanda.

           End December: first trials in Rwanda for crimes of genocide. Almost 100,000 Rwandans have been arrested since 1994.

1997

from January onwards

           Armed conflict escalates in the northwest: groups of former Rwandan soldiers and *interahamwe* militia launch frequent attacks and the RPA retaliates in counter-insurgency operations. Civilians are massacred by both sides.

January   The rebellion in Kivu turns into a Zairian civil war. Laurent-Désiré Kabila's rebels advance towards Kisangani.

February   4 February: five employees of the Office of the United Nations High Commissioner for Human Rights are killed in southwestern Rwanda.

March   The AFDL, which controls half of Zaire, denies access to humanitarian organizations. 15 March: fall of the town of Kisangani.

April   The UN Security Council expresses concern about reports of massacres of Rwandan refugees by AFDL forces.

May   8 May: the UN Secretary-General, Kofi Annan, accuses the AFDL of 'killing by starvation' the Rwandan Hutu refugees who have been surrounded to the south of Kisangani and expresses his 'shock and horror at the absence of humanity of those who control eastern Zaire'. The European Union Commissioner responsible for humanitarian affairs, Emma Bonino, denounces this 'major carnage'. An estimated 200,000 Rwandan refugees are reported to have disappeared. 17 May: President Mobutu flees. A few hours later, AFDL forces take Kinshasa. Zaire becomes the Democratic Republic of Congo (DRC). Laurent-Désiré Kabila becomes President.

July   10 July: in an interview with the *Washington Post*, Rwandan Vice-President and Minister of Defence Paul Kagame acknowledges the active participation of RPA troops in the conquest of Zaire, claiming that the AFDL forces were 'not capable' of winning the war on their own.

          12 July: the UN publishes the report of the team which investigated massacres of Rwandan Hutu refugees in Zaire between September 1996 and May 1997. The report denounces 'crimes against humanity' systematically committed by AFDL troops and their Rwandan Tutsi allies. A further mission will determine 'whether a genocide had been planned'.

          18 July: the International Criminal Tribunal for Rwanda (ICTR) arrests a dozen senior officials responsible for the genocide, in exile in Kenya, including the former Prime Minister Jean Kambanda and the director of the *Kangura* newspaper, Hassan Ngeze.

August   Following the AFDL's obstructions of an UN investigation in April into massacres committed in eastern Zaire in 1996 and 1997, the UN Secretary-General sends out a new investigative team. This team is also repeatedly obstructed by the new Congolese authorities.

October–December

          The northwest of Rwanda is in state of civil war. More killings of civilians by insurgents and RPA troops.

December   The Belgian Parliament publishes the report of its commission of inquiry into the genocide.

1998

January–April
            Armed conflict and massacres of civilians continue in the northwest, spreading to parts of Gitarama.

January   31 January: assassination in Kigali of Croatian priest Father Vjeko Curic.

March   9 March: Death of André Sibomana.
            25 March: US President Bill Clinton visits Rwanda and acknowledges that the international community bears a share of responsibility for the genocide by failing to respond to the massacres.

April   24 April: 22 people are executed in public in the first executions of people sentenced to death for participation in the genocide.

May   1 May: Jean Kambanda, Prime Minister of the interim government at the time of the genocide, pleads guilty at the ICTR in Arusha.
            7 May: the government suspends the operations of the UN Human Rights Field Operation in Rwanda after expelling its spokesperson.
            16 May: assassination in Nairobi of Seth Sendashonga, former Minister of the Interior in the first government formed by the RPF.

June   Report of the UN Secretary-General's Investigative Team on massacres in the DRC in 1996 and 1997. Some of the massacres committed by the AFDL and its allies, including the RPA, are described as crimes against humanity, some of which could amount to genocide.

July   Departure of the UN Human Rights Field Operation for Rwanda after the Rwandan government asks for its monitoring work to end.

August–December
            2 August: war breaks out again in the Democratic Republic of Congo. Fighting between a predominantly Tutsi rebel alliance, the *Rassemblement congolais pour la démocratie*, RCD (Congolese Rally for Democracy), and their former allies, President Kabila's Congolese armed forces. Massacres of civilians by both sides. The RCD takes control of large parts of

	the Kivu region. The war becomes increasingly regionalized as several foreign countries intervene. Kabila's forces are supported by troops from Zimbabwe, Angola, Namibia and Chad; the RCD is supported by Rwanda, Uganda and Burundi.
September	2 September: Jean-Paul Akayesu, former *bourgmestre* (local government official) of Taba commune, is found guilty by the ICTR of nine charges including genocide and crimes against humanity.
	4 September: Jean Kambanda is sentenced to life imprisonment by the ICTR.
October	2 October: Jean-Paul Akayesu is sentenced to life imprisonment by the ICTR.
November	the UN commission of inquiry set up in 1995 to investigate ongoing arms supplies to the ex-FAR publishes its final report.
December	Publication of the report of a French parliamentary investigation into the role of France in the genocide.

1999

January	Minister of Justice Faustin Ntezilyayo resigns and leaves the country.
end January	Trade sanctions lifted on Burundi.
February	5 February: Omar Serushago, *interahamwe* leader in Gisenyi, is sentenced to 15 years' imprisonment by the ICTR after pleading guilty.
January–March	War continues in the DRC. Various regional heads of state attempt to mediate, without result.
March	UN Secretary-General Kofi Annan announces an inquiry into the role of the UN in the genocide in Rwanda in 1994.

Abbreviations

ADL   *Association rwandaise pour la défense des droits de la personne et des libertés publiques* (Rwandan Association for the Defence of Human Rights and Public Liberties)

AFDL   *Alliance des forces démocratiques pour la libération du Congo-Zaïre* (Alliance of Democratic Forces for the Liberation of Congo-Zaire)

AJR   *Association des journalistes du Rwanda* (Association of Journalists of Rwanda)

AJRE   *Association des journalistes rwandais en exil* (Association of Rwandan Journalists in Exile)

ARDHO   *Association rwandaise pour la défense des droits de l'homme* (Rwandan Association for the Defence of Human Rights)

AVP   *Association des volontaires de la paix* (Association of Peace Volunteers)

CDR   *Coalition pour la défense de la République* (Coalition for the Defence of the Republic)

CLADHO   *Collectif des ligues et associations de défense des droits de l'homme au Rwanda* (Collective of Human Rights Leagues and Associations in Rwanda)

DRC   Democratic Republic of Congo

FAR   *Forces armées rwandaises* (Rwandan Armed Forces)

FAZ   *Forces armées zaïroises* (Zairian Armed Forces)

ICRC   International Committee of the Red Cross

ICTR   International Criminal Tribunal for Rwanda

LIPRODHOR   *Ligue rwandaise pour la promotion et la défense des droits de l'homme* (Rwandan League for the Promotion and Defence of Human Rights)

MDR   *Mouvement démocratique républicain* (Democratic Republican Movement)

MRND   *Mouvement révolutionnaire national pour le développement* (National Revolutionary Movement for Development), later *Mouvement républicain national pour la démocratie et le développement*

	(National Republican Movement for Democracy and Development)
NGO	Non-governmental organization
ORINFOR	*Office rwandais de l'information* (Rwandan Information Office)
PARMEHUTU	*Parti du mouvement d'émancipation Hutu* (Party of the Movement for Hutu Emancipation).
PSD	*Parti social démocrate* (Social Democratic Party)
RANU	Rwandan National Union
RCD	*Rassemblement congolais pour la démocratie* (Congolese Rally for Democracy)
RFI	*Radio France Internationale*
RPA	Rwandan Patriotic Army
RPF	Rwandan Patriotic Front
RTLM	*Radio Télévision Libre des Mille Collines* (Free Radio Television of the Thousand Hills)
UDPR	*Union démocratique du peuple rwandais* (Rwandan People's Democratic Union)
UNAMIR	United Nations Assistance Mission for Rwanda
UNDP	United Nations Development Programme
UNHRFOR	United Nations Human Rights Field Operation for Rwanda

Preface
André Sibomana, or faith against the odds

André Sibomana was born in 1954 into a modest family in the commune of Masango, in Rwanda. In 1974, this brilliant pupil was admitted into the major seminary of Nyakibanda. He was ordained as a priest in 1980. After six years of pastoral work, he went to France to study journalism. In 1988, he became the editor of the only private newspaper in Rwanda, *Kinyamateka*. In 1991 he created a human rights organization, ADL, which denounced the abuses of the Habyarimana regime. In the months leading up to the genocide of 1994, he desperately tried to alert international public opinion to the imminence of large-scale massacres: in vain. He managed to escape the killings, as well as several assassination attempts. After the war, he resumed his work as editor of *Kinyamateka* and replaced the Bishop of Kabgayi who was killed in 1994. In the columns of his newspaper and at the head of his diocese, he undertook an active policy of reconciliation. Constantly threatened by extremists on all sides, he rejected both exile and silence. His actions were symbolic of a certain conception of faith, human rights and public life.

André Sibomana impressed us from the first time we met him, a few years ago. All those who come into contact with him cannot fail to admire him for his spiritual and worldly commitment, the physical and intellectual risks he takes, his rigour, his tolerance and his generosity. At the same time, they are intrigued by his austere personality, which may seem inaccessible and almost secretive. We had the opportunity to work together on several occasions, in France and in Rwanda, sometimes in tragic circumstances, always with a sense of urgency. But we did not have many opportunities to talk freely. As our curiosity increased, we eventually decided to hatch a plot.

So last summer, we invited André Sibomana to spend a few days in Israel, a country which we know and like. He was attracted by this well-earned holiday and did not see the trap we had set for him. Each morning, before taking him to the shores of Lake Tiberias or through the backstreets of Jerusalem, we subjected him to several hours of interviews. In the Kfar Ha'khoresch kibbutz, under the cool shade of the olive trees, we made this defender of faith talk about himself and tell us the secrets of his youth (Part I). We asked him to help us understand why and how Rwandans prepared and carried out a genocide (Part II). He explained to us how difficult it is to continue living 'afterwards' and the need to hold on to faith and hope, against the odds (Part III). This book is the result of these informal discussions.

Laure Guilbert
Hervé Deguine

PART I

THE COMMITTED PRIEST

1 The Gifted Child from Masango

André Sibomana, you are the son of two orphans?

Yes. I was fortunate from birth: when I was born on 21 July 1954, I was welcomed by a father and a mother who were waiting for me with joy and impatience. My mother was not so fortunate. Her name was Cécile Mukamihigo. In my country, the first name is a Latin name, but what you call the family name is like another first name for us; it expresses a proverb or a wish in Kinyarwanda, our national language. Mukamihigo means 'the wife of Mihigo', or 'she for whom one wishes a life like Mihigo's'. This led my mother to believe that Mihigo's life must have been sufficiently good for the same life to have been wished upon her. That was all she knew about her origins. I loved her and I am still saddened by her death in 1991.

My father was not brought up by both his parents either. His father and brother died when he was still very young, so he ended up almost an only child. His name, Mushenyi, means 'gatherer of dry wood'. Is that why he devoted his life to working with wood? I don't know. In any case, he continued sculpting wood which he gathered on the hill or which people from our village brought to him until he could no longer do so because of old age. My father was talented and he inspired respect. People appreciated his work. He would create sophisticated kitchen utensils out of old sticks, as if by magic. For years he made a living from selling milk jugs, bowls and all sorts of wooden objects which he made by hand.

Did he teach you his trade?

Of course. He started by teaching me to gather wood, that is to open my eyes to find what I was looking for. One piece of wood always looks like another. Yet each piece is different. The gatherer must be able to tell the difference at first glance between the raw material and firewood. Later on, when I was twelve or thirteen years old, I started making ladles and mortars, under his supervision. My father never told me that my work was good, but I was pleased to

3

see that he did not throw away the objects I made and that he sold everything he took to the market ...

I struggled as I learned this demanding trade. It requires dexterity, courage and perseverance, as well as discipline. For example, it is forbidden to drink alcohol while you are sculpting because every movement must be precise and the craftsman must retain complete self-control. Mistakes are not allowed. Should the sculptor miss a stroke, he will either waste wood or injure himself. And in our rural areas, a gash on the hand can quickly lead to poverty for the whole family.

My father had experienced poverty at first hand. The memories of his youth were painful. He rarely talked about the past, but we could always sense the weight of those difficult years when he spoke. Nevertheless, in his misery, he was fortunate to encounter generosity. Some friends who recognized in him a capable and hard-working young man lent him a plot of land. He put it to good use and cultivated it so well that he still has use of it up to this day. He called this field his 'Egyptian exile', both because the living conditions there were rough and because this plot of land was his salvation. He would spend entire days and nights there, hoping for a better future. My father planted a sacred tree, a coralbean, to mark the site of the shack where he lived until he got married; the tree is still there.

Then his salvation came, proving that one must never lose confidence. He traced a branch of his family on his father's side and reclaimed the land which was owed to him, at Wimana, in Kirwa sector, in Masango commune.[1] That is where my parents built the family home and where I grew up, along with my brothers and sisters. We were five children. Two sisters were born before me, which was why my parents were so impatient to have a boy. In Rwanda, as in most traditional societies, parents passionately wish for a son among their children. It is like a sign of respectability. This is because for centuries, the birth of a son would guarantee a family's economic survival and sustain its social rank and lineage.

When my mother was expecting me, jealous neighbours began to speculate on the probable disappearance of our young family. It is true that my parents' situation was precarious, but they did not doubt that, once again, luck would be on their side. When I was born, my father acquired the certainty that neither his own life

---

[1] Masango is located in the south of the country, near Kabgayi, which is considered the capital of Christianity in Rwanda.

Translator's note: Rwanda is divided into regions known as *préfectures*. Each *préfecture* is divided into communes, which are divided into sectors.

nor that of his children would depend on the fate predicted by malicious people, but on that which God had chosen for him. That is what my name, 'Sibomana', means: 'it is not (Si) they (Bo) who guide my life, but God (Mana)'.

My two elder sisters live in Gitarama. One of them was arrested in early 1995, then released without any explanation. In 1994, my younger sister became a refugee in eastern Zaire. I have not heard from her since war broke out again in the region in October 1996.[2] My only brother died in 1995, a week before Christmas.

How did you spend your days?

Our day-to-day life was very basic. Our house had two rooms and a yard. My parents slept in the main room, near the entrance. Their bed was made up of a few planks above the hen-house. My brothers and sisters and I slept on the floor, huddled up against each other on a straw mat, with a piece of plaited matting as a blanket. In the other half of the room, our goats slept at our feet.

I was never fast asleep, as it was my duty to watch over our herd during the night. That is how I became used to sleeping lightly, always alert and ready to respond. Later, during the genocide, this faculty of 'listening' in my sleep saved my life more than once.

Each morning, my father woke up at the first cockcrow, at around 3 o'clock, and started going about his work. My mother and the rest of us were up from about 5 o'clock, at the second cockcrow. Each of us knew what we had to do. The girls cleaned the house or fetched water. They helped my mother with the housework. My brother and I looked after the yard and our two cows, which needed a lot of care. A cow must always be kept clean, not only for reasons of hygiene, but because the family's honour depends on it. In our culture, a cow is more than just an animal. It is a proof of social status. Each cow has its own history and its origins reflect strong social links. We had two cows and people in our village knew it. This made them respect us. I also looked after the goats; we had about twenty of them.

We had few opportunities to play. There was one game which we found very exciting but which my father did not approve of. We would 'ski' on the stalks of banana leaves. We skied like this in secret because it would spoil our clothes and it could be

---

[2] André Sibomana's sister was repatriated from Kisangani (in the Democratic Republic of Congo, formerly Zaire) in 1997. Her husband and one of her children had disappeared in eastern Zaire in 1996; she now lives in her father's house in Muyunzwe.

dangerous; our parents had forbidden us to play this game. We spread out grass or banana leaves on the steepest hillside and slid down, standing up straight on our makeshift 'skis', egged on by cries of encouragement from our friends.

In the evening, other chores awaited us when we came home from school. I checked the herds while my sisters fetched more water or made baskets. Rwandans are very skilled at basketwork: every European who visits us goes back home laden with woven baskets, without fail.

The routine never changed: we never tired of repeating the same tasks every day of the week, all year round, year after year. Except on Sundays: Sundays were devoted to rest and prayer.

We received a strict and very religious education. Our parents brought us up to respect human beings and to love God. My mother was devout. She would pray often and saw to it that we were instilled with a deep Roman Catholic education. Our father also followed our education closely, despite his work. He was austere and demanding; that was his way of loving us and supporting us. Our life was not easy, but we were sustained and protected by our parents.

I remember the second wife of my grandfather Nicodème, my father's uncle; she was called Cécile Kankindi. When Nicodème died, I was sent to stay with her so that she would not be alone in the house. In the evenings, she would tell me stories. There was one story which made a lasting impression on me. It was the story of a man who had to attack a king in Zaire. He had to overcome many obstacles to accomplish his mission: there were traps scattered in the forest, he would come across young girls and beer along the way, and a thousand other temptations. But the hero of the story never succumbed to these distractions and managed to reach his goal. Such tales were part of our culture and formed our character.

Were you the only one of your brothers and sisters who studied?

We all went to primary school, which was unusual even at that time. My parents had not studied but they understood the importance of education. They invested all their savings in our education: by paying our school fees, they were banking on our personal development and professional success.

I was admitted into secondary school. I was shy and reserved and did not talk much. But I loved learning and I had an excellent memory. There was only one dictionary for the whole school. I would borrow it and memorize the words. That is how I learned

French. My father quickly realized that I was more skilled at using language than at working the land. So instead of sending me to the fields, he encouraged me to attend the minor seminary at Save. This new phase marked a decisive turning point in my life. Access to school had already ensured that we were different from other children in the village. Entering the minor seminary at Save was like penetrating the heart of the tiny lay and ecclesiastical educated elite, which would be called upon one day to play a leading role in the country. It also enabled me to get closer to the religious vocation which was beginning to take shape in my mind. I derived great pride from this situation, but I also sensed the full weight of this new responsibility. I carried the honour of my family, my closest relatives and friends, and the people of my village. This was in 1968; I was 14 years old.

Didn't this create jealousy around you?

There was one regrettable incident which served me well in the end, despite the pain it caused me at the time. The Roman Catholic Church enjoyed a virtual monopoly on primary and secondary education and the minor seminary played the role of a secondary school for those who did not have access to other forms of education. Not all the students there intended to go into priesthood, far from it. Neither were all the teachers model saints.

One of them tried to make me leave the seminary on two occasions, for reasons which I prefer not to try to explain. Maybe he considered that my origins did not warrant my claim to study the lessons which he had taught my predecessors. Whatever the reason, this teacher seized upon a minor incident to demand that I leave the seminary. I was absent from the class when he asked for the exercise books to be handed to him. A well-meaning classmate took one of the exercise books which he found in my locker. Unfortunately, he made a mistake and handed him an exercise book of rough drafts. The teacher claimed to have been insulted; he summoned me and prohibited me from returning to Save.

The injustice of this punishment was so blatant and its consequences were so dramatic for my future that I categorically refused to accept them. I sat down in the courtyard and refused to move. I must stress that this kind of behaviour on the part of a teenager was highly unusual and incongruous. I stayed in the courtyard for several hours until a female teacher, a *Muzungu* (a 'white person'), came to ask me the reason for this sit-in. I explained to her what had happened and was allowed back into the school. Later, the same teacher tried to keep me out again, in similar circumstances, but thankfully without success.

This incident taught me two things: that injustice is unacceptable and that the fight against injustice will always win. In this respect, I would like to tell you about another, much more serious event which left a lasting impression on me. It was in 1973, a few weeks before the fall of the Kayibanda regime.

Grégoire Kayibanda was the first president of Rwanda after independence. He was deposed by Juvénal Habyarimana, his Chief-of-Staff, on 5 July 1973. During the months which preceded this *coup d'état* – which, according to some, had been orchestrated by France and the United States – the Kayibanda regime drifted into policies of an increasingly ethnic character. In 1972, Hutu in Burundi had been the victims of a selective genocide during which more than 200,000 intellectuals were killed – almost all the Hutu who held positions of responsibility or simply those who were literate. Politicians from Gitarama, in the centre of Rwanda, exploited the fears of the Tutsi which these events had revived. They made up Kayibanda's entourage and had grabbed all the levers of power. They were supported by influential elements within an army composed primarily of people from the north (Ruhengeri and Gisenyi). These extremists sparked off a campaign to drive Tutsi out of schools, out of the administration, out of the army and elsewhere. Several thousand Tutsi were killed and tens of thousands are estimated to have fled.

I was 19 years old at the time and I remember this period very well. We were acutely aware of what was politically at stake during these events; people's different reactions were highly significant. Just think that those who govern the country today were also 20 years old at that time. It would be interesting to ask them where they were then and how they behaved.

A group of students at the educational establishment of Butare had created a Committee of Public Salvation; its main agenda was to drive Tutsi out of the schools and out of public or private employment. One of the leaders of this group was Ferdinand Nahimana, a character whom we will have the opportunity to talk about later.

So the Tutsi were driven out of the school. At the minor seminary of Kansi, we – the Hutu – rejected this policy of discrimination. We protested and expressed our solidarity towards the Tutsi. But those in charge of the establishment preferred to close the seminary temporarily. So we went home. After a few weeks, only the Hutu were allowed to return to school; the Tutsi had been forced to flee to Burundi or elsewhere. It was nearly the end of the year. We found out that the teachers were planning to expel some of us, claiming that we were 'racist'. That was when we decided to launch a protest strike against this injustice. We appealed to the Bishop of Butare to intervene so that none of us would be expelled from the establishment and so that we would all be admitted into the following year. Some teachers tried to discourage us or to dissuade us with moralizing speeches. We responded by stamping our naked feet – an act which is viewed as an expression of deep contempt. Bishop Jean-Baptiste Gahamamyi came in person to witness the gravity of the situation and eventually agreed to all our demands.

This experience proved to me that determination is the key to success in politics, in the broadest sense of the word. You don't need many resources to make your voice heard when you are defending a cause you believe to be just. This does not mean that you will succeed in every case. But at least it is possible to influence decisions and obtain very concrete results through dramatic actions. In this case, we managed to ensure that a whole class of students was admitted into the following year. It was a drop in the ocean in the context of the events of 1973, but that drop was within our reach and we had the duty to take it on.

2 Choosing the Path of God

Why did you become a priest?

Because I chose to. Or rather because I never imagined that I could choose anything else. According to my parents, when I was three years old, I announced that I wanted to become a priest. Since then, I always believed it, and those around me did not expect anything else. At every age I adopted the behaviour which matched this commitment, and each stage of my life flowed on from there. In this sense, it really was a vocation.

My father and mother were profoundly Christian. This might explain my family's sense of pride when I was ordained; but it does not explain my commitment. Nor am I able to name any priest or anyone else who might have been a role model and whom I might have wanted to imitate.

I don't have a rational explanation for what always seemed like a natural path to me. I don't believe in predestination, nor do I consider myself to have been 'chosen'. But it's a fact that this orientation which determined the course of my life simply imposed itself. Deep down, I felt that the only way I would find happiness would be to devote my life to others, to give myself unreservedly so that they would find happiness. It seemed to me that priesthood was the best path to that goal.

What was your daily life like at the major seminary of Nyakibanda?

The day started at dawn, at 5.30 a.m., with a cold shower! After meditation, prayers and mass, we were given breakfast, which we thoroughly enjoyed. At the start of the cycle, there were around 30 pupils in each class; two-thirds of them would complete the training which lasted six years. We all knew each other and we knew that our paths would cross throughout our life.

The lessons were very varied. We learned psychology, accountancy or foreign languages, alongside theology and philosophy. My favourite subjects were metaphysics and theology. Historical criticism of the Bible was stimulating, both for our intellect and for our faith.

Some of the time was spent on sports. I hated team sports and I was never a member of any team in competitive sports. However, I was quite good at running. Sometimes I would run about 20 kilometres early in the morning, before dawn, to keep fit. This served me well later: when I became a parish priest in Muyunzwe, I had no means of transport and I used to run from parish to parish so that I could be wherever I thought I needed to be. Sometimes I covered more than 40 kilometres in half a day. The sight of a priest running around like that made people laugh: it was unusual.

In the afternoon, after lunch, we returned to the classroom. The teaching methods were quite classical. Most of our teachers were Rwandan priests supported by religious officials from Europe. There were two priests who enriched my thoughts greatly. From being my teachers for a long time, they became my close friends. I respected them and sought their advice.

One was called Pierre de Schatzen. He was a rigorous man. He made me work hard and forced me to search the depths of my thoughts. He lent me the books which I asked for, but in return he asked me for a report on what I had read. Reading had to be more than just a pleasure; I was expected to learn lessons from what I read. He worked as a priest and steward at the diocese of Kabgayi for a long time, then eventually retired in Belgium.

I also owe a lot to Félicien Muvara. Throughout my studies, like all my co-disciples, I was a boarder at the major seminary. My room happened to be just opposite his. In the evenings, after our lessons, I used to go and see him and we would have long discussions. He taught me to analyse problems in the light of the Gospel. I admired his calm in the face of hardship, his wisdom and his certainty in life. He was an upright man, with great integrity, which caused him a number of problems. He was very poorly thought of by some circles in the ecclesiastical hierarchy. President Habyarimana himself was openly hostile towards him. On the eve of his ordination as an auxiliary priest in the diocese of Butare, a plot was hatched against him – as often happens in Rwanda, unfortunately. He was made to stand down.

Félicien Muvara was killed right at the beginning of the genocide, around April 1994. He was in Butare when the massacres started. He knew he was at risk, not only because he was a Tutsi but also because his presence was an embarrassment to those who did not have such a noble soul. He immediately understood the scale of the danger and tried to find safety in Burundi. Unfortunately, militiamen were waiting for him along the way. They killed him before he could reach the border.

Which books or authors impressed you most?

I didn't read much religious literature; I have never found it very inspiring. Instead, Pierre de Schatzen introduced me to some French writers that I particularly like, such as Albert Camus and Antoine de Saint-Exupéry, who is still my favourite author. What I like in Saint-Exupéry is the combination of a spiritual search with a commitment to the real world. Action didn't get in the way of his meditation. On the contrary, action enabled him to test and perfect the moral values he had adopted. Antoine de Saint-Exupéry gave all he could to search for the truth.

I also like Gabriel Marcel. This philosopher – now almost forgotten in France – converted to Roman Catholicism in 1929. He was one of the Christian existentialist thinkers. Like Emmanuel Mounier, the founder of personalism, he reflected deeply on the problems of commitment in the context of modern life. Gabriel Marcel sought the right words to denounce materialism and selfishness. His philosophical and literary writings were possibly old-fashioned in Europe at the time that I was reading them, but they corresponded to the situation I was experiencing in Rwanda in the mid-1970s. What particularly struck me was his taste for freedom and his refusal to give in to pessimism.

I used to read a lot; I also wrote. My articles were regularly published in the bimonthly Roman Catholic newspaper *Kinyamateka*. I was not a journalist and it had not occurred to me to become one. But I published columns, opinion pieces or commentaries under various pseudonyms. *Kinyamateka* was the only newspaper which was independent of the government and it was a vehicle for ideas which could not be expressed elsewhere.

I stopped writing at the end of my first year at the major seminary when I became seriously ill. I still don't know what disease struck me, but within a few days I lost all control of my body. This very rare illness, the name of which I have forgotten, was terrible. My body started rotting. I lost all my strength and I couldn't eat. My skin was falling off in shreds, my scalp was separating from my skull, my teeth were falling out one by one. Within a few days I became a skeleton.

The sight of me, which was quite revolting, alarmed those who had agreed to look after me after having overcome an understandable initial sense of repulsion. I spent two months in intensive care and, after several days in a coma, I survived, against all expectations. That was when I first met the Bishop of Kabgayi, André Perraudin, whom we will talk about later. He had been told about the disease which was destroying me and he came to visit me to encourage me to overcome this challenge. That is what I did. Medically, the after-effects of this disease were insignificant, although to this day I take care to avoid certain foods. However, on a personal level, I acquired a taste for fighting. We have to fight to live. We have to try everything, always. No effort is useless, even if it is not successful. Each effort requires another, then another, then another. Gradually we regain confidence, we try harder and, finally, we manage to win. There is always a door waiting to be pushed open somewhere: it's just a question of finding it. I was saved by the belief that everything is possible if you have hope.[3]

Incidentally I also acquired some very valuable medical knowledge. From that time onwards, I became the medical orderly at the major seminary. I had quite a reputation! Even now, I occasionally give advice to friends who are ill.

Your life as a seminarian was quite austere. Did you never think about leading a more comfortable life, about getting married and bringing up a family?

But I am bringing up a family! I have adopted seven children; they are refugees from the war, orphans like my father and mother. I see to all their needs, I watch over their education, I guide them – this is no small responsibility. I can assure you, these children are a serious matter. They give me more satisfaction than worries.

Roman Catholicism means that you have to make a choice. I have always chosen priesthood as my vocation, which has meant accepting chastity and giving up the idea of marriage. You could say that I am married to a community which is broader than a couple and that my family is the Church. These are not just words; it is a reality which I take on every day. Nor is it a sacrifice. I give a lot, but I also find my own happiness in this life which I devote to others. And there are some advantages. For example, being single means that I can be available without any restrictions. It allows me to be free to take risks which the head of a family can't take and to live through my commitment to the full.

---

[3] Translator's note: it was this same rare illness, eventually diagnosed as Lyell's Syndrome, which struck André Sibomana again in early 1998 and caused his death on 9 March 1998 (see Postscript).

Don't you feel lonely?

Never. I always feel that I belong to a group. I support it and it supports me. I admit that this is a particular kind of relationship which does not suit everybody. Some of my friends at the seminary found the vow of celibacy too distressing. They gave up and got married, and we remained friends. I respect their choice and I think they were rewarded for their sincerity. In Europe, the question of celibacy is the subject of debate because celibacy is viewed as an ordeal. That's not the case in Rwanda. At least not for me. The hardest aspect of my life as a priest has not been to accept celibacy but to live through situations where I have felt totally powerless and unable to fulfil my mandate. My vocation is to preach the good news. But what does that mean when parishioners come to church armed with machetes dripping with blood? As you can imagine, this kind of question makes many other concerns seem a lot less important.

Not only do I not feel lonely, but I don't feel isolated either. Faith gives me strength and enables me to see beyond physical appearances. I am convinced that a believer is never alone and will never die. A believer struggles for life, for justice, for peace, for love, for selflessness. A believer receives grace for carrying out those things he must do and struggles for life within Christianity. I believe this wholeheartedly; otherwise, I would be incapable of doing what I do and taking the risks to which my choices lead me.

I was ordained as a priest on 27 July 1980 by Bishop Perraudin, who was Bishop of Kabgayi at the time.[4] I can't mention his name without providing some explanations.

Having devoted his life to Rwanda, Bishop Perraudin returned to Switzerland in 1994. He settled there for his retirement. Nowadays he is the object of fierce criticism: he is criticized for having contributed to the transfer of power from the Tutsi to the Hutu and for having been responsible, in a sense, for the fall of the monarchy and the demonization of the Tutsi. He is accused of having written a letter in 1959 entitled 'Charity comes first' in which

---

[4] Bishop Perraudin arrived in Rwanda in 1955 and was appointed Bishop of Kabgayi. His private secretary was Grégoire Kayibanda, a young seminarian whose political education he helped form. Later, he made him editor of *Kinyamateka* (1956–58). It was during this period that Kayibanda wrote and published the Manifesto of the Bahutu in his newspaper (see Part II, Chapter 6). Instead of continuing a religious vocation, Kayibanda chose a political career. He became the leader of a movement known as Parmehutu, which took the opportunity of the social revolution of 1959 to seize power, and became president of Rwanda when the country first declared its independence in 1962. Bishop Perraudin played a prominent role throughout this period, because of the all-powerful role of the Roman Catholic Church in Rwanda and the moral and spiritual influence he had over Kayibanda.

he described the reality which he had seen with his own eyes: forced labour for the master, beatings, the practice of tying (men had their arms tied behind their backs so that they could be beaten more easily or held as prisoners), the torture of those who tried to resist, people being fed to the vultures, the hanging of 'criminals' ...

I am not saying that Bishop Perraudin was not a victim of outbursts, nor that there weren't any points to be criticized in his public statements. But he had the courage to speak the truth at a time when silence was the rule. I owe him a great deal. He taught me to turn my attention first and foremost towards the peasants, towards people who are destitute and without protection. He took on the role of a father during my ordination and I am proud to have been ordained by Bishop Perraudin. Some elements in the press accuse me of being his 'ideological son'. I wouldn't mind, but it's actually wrong: the ideology was not Perraudin's, it was Christ's.

The ceremony was moving. It was one of those official occasions in life when you find yourself watched by your family, your friends and all those close to you; all the inhabitants of my village had come. More than 5,000 people attended my ordination. I was 26 years old. That day, I experienced a moment of great grace.

The day after my ordination, I celebrated my first mass in the village where I was born, to honour my family. It was a way of paying tribute to all those who had loved me and provided me with food and education. The whole village gathered around 'its' child. I was – and still am – the only priest to have come from this village, where life is tough and human relations are difficult. I had the feeling that for the people who lived on that land, I had become a source of pride and compensated for their misery. Many seemed to live through me the life they had been denied or the life which they had given up hoping for for their own children. Once I became a priest, it was my duty not to disappoint them. I often think of them. They don't know it, but I know that I owe them a great deal. Their trust gives me courage and strengthens my faith.

Soon afterwards, I received a written notification of the authority to hear confessions. The power to hear a man's or a woman's confession is a huge responsibility. It is not easy to enter their intimacy, to go to the depth of their soul to try to find good.

Then, after a few days' leave, the bishop appointed me vicar at Kabgayi, at a time when the young priest Sylvestre Ndaberetse[5] was due to go to a seminary in Burkina Faso. There were hardly any other priests in this cathedral parish so, from the start, I took

[5] Sylvestre Ndaberetse was killed on 5 June 1994 by a squad of the Rwandan Patriotic Front (RPF).

on substantial responsibilities. But this was the start of the life to which I had always aspired. I had left the cows and goats in the family yard in order to look after my fellow creatures and to become a shepherd in the service of God. In all respects, this was the life I had always imagined and wished for.

Then, one fine morning, at breakfast time, Bishop Perraudin called me to his office and said: 'The priest of Muyunzwe has to leave his post and you will replace him.'

'But Muyunzwe is where I was born!'

'You will start next week.'

I got cross. 'Do you know what you're doing?'

'Yes.'

'Are you prepared to pay the price for any damage?'

'There won't be any.'

When the conversation ended, I was furious. Unusually for me, I jumped into the Beetle which belonged to the bishopric and drove around Gitarama several times at top speed to calm down.

Then, of course, I settled down in Muyunzwe. I stayed there from 1982 to 1986.

Why such anger?

Because Muyunzwe was well known as a difficult parish, riven by conflicts. What's more, this was the first time that a priest was being assigned to his parish of origin. I felt very young to be taking on such a responsibility – I had only been ordained for two years. Although I must say, it was also a great sign of trust.

During my first mass, I immediately set the tone. I warned my new parishioners that I had not come there as a leader to impose my authority, but as a pastor anxious to help them find God. I remember that sermon very well. I told them, 'God has given me this parish and I am accountable to Him for the fate of its parishioners.' I added that my success in the parish would depend on the success of each of them, as I had grown up there before becoming its guardian and its ambassador. I ended by saying that I no longer recognized among them a father or a brother, a friend or a neighbour, but that all parishioners were equal before the priest. I quickly acquired the reputation of being a strict man.

They called you 'the wild animal'.

Yes, they called me 'the wild animal', but in Kinyarwanda, the precise translation is 'the wild animal which does not devour, does not crush the crops and does not do harm'.

It's true, I had to be very hard to put an end to the lies. As soon as I arrived in the parish, I spent three days and three nights reading all the files, searching for details of the various 'incidents' between parishioners, so that they could not take advantage of my youth or my inexperience. If someone lied to me by omission, I would plug the gaps in their memory from what I had read. It didn't take long to shatter the illusions of those who thought they could benefit from the situation. But I always took care to reward truth. I believe I was especially attentive to the needs of those who had been left out in the cold: the most destitute and the sick.

When I left the parish four years later, people came to see me to ask me to stay.

'So now you want me to stay, me, the wild animal?'

'Yes, because you protect us from danger.'

3 The Journalist and Human Rights Activist

How did you make the move from the sacristy of Muyunzwe to the editing room at Kinyamateka?

By pure chance. One Sunday, I was attending the ordination of two friends, Michel Murenzi and Jean-Baptiste Ruzigana[6] when, out of the blue, Bishop Perraudin asked me to translate into Kinyarwanda a sermon which a Swiss preacher had just delivered in French. He hadn't given me any warning but, because I had listened to the sermon carefully, I was able to reconstruct it almost completely, much to the astonishment of the assembly. I think Perraudin was trying to put me to the test. He asked me, 'Do you want to go to Europe to learn journalism?'

I replied that I didn't know anything about journalism and that I would have to think about his suggestion. A few days later he asked me the same question again, 'Do you want to study journalism?'

'No.'

'Think again.'

A week went by. Perraudin asked me again, 'Have you thought about it?'

'I said no.'

'That means you haven't thought about it properly.'

'I want to be a preacher, not a journalist.'

'But you can also be a preacher with a pen and paper. The Pope wants the Church to develop its social communication and you're capable of doing it.'

So one morning in 1986, a delegation from the diocese took me to the airport at Kanombe, near Kigali. I was going to France for two years. It was a new challenge and, once again, I knew that I could not afford to be a disappointment on my return.

After two short stops in Brussels and Paris, I arrived in Lyon. It wasn't my first trip to Europe; I had already been to Rome with a

---

[6] Jean-Baptiste Ruzigana was killed by *interahamwe* militia in 1994, during the genocide.

Rwandan delegation four years earlier. But this time, I was alone when I landed in this town; all I knew about it was its name. I took a taxi and we drove towards Rillieux-la-Pape; I was completely lost and didn't have a penny in my pocket. By chance, when we arrived, a priest, Martial Bonnet, the former national chaplain of the *Jeunesse ouvrière chrétienne* (Christian Workers' Youth) in Kigali, happened to be standing on the steps of the presbytery. He saved me from this embarrassing situation and paid the taxi fare.

I spent two years studying at the law faculty of the Catholic Institute of Lyon. There were around fifty students in my year, including four compatriots. All of them now hold senior positions: one is working at the Ministry of the Environment, another is the Permanent Secretary of the Minister of Social Affairs, another was *préfet*[7] of Cyangugu until recently.

The course broadened my mind. I discovered a new way of thinking and learning. Rwanda is a small and very isolated country. Until then I had only lived in villages or in a small town. I was not familiar with urban life, let alone modern life. I was like a provincial person coming from an obscure rural area. Lyon was like a capital of initiation, a breath of fresh air. I discovered another society there, which was much more open to the outside world, a society with a capacity for communication, where people expressed themselves freely, without fear for their future or for their life. At the university, we moved in fairly closed circles but I made the effort to reach out to French society: I learned a lot.

I acquired the basic skills of journalism, even though it transpired later that there was much more to discover. The course included three months' training at the offices of a newspaper. That was how I ended up at *La Vie nouvelle*, the Roman Catholic weekly, in Chambéry. In fact it was more like a real job than a training course. I was not allowed to sit back and watch the others work. It was at the time of the Olympics in Albertville and the region was under the media spotlights. Politicians had made numerous promises in the hope of being re-elected or persuading people to accept the inconvenience caused by the Games. But the promises were rarely fulfilled. What was worse, in order to build the necessary infra-structure for the sports or for the roads, they had to proceed with a number of evictions, and some property owners felt cheated or abused. I learned how to carry out contradictory investigations, to compare statements by witnesses and trace back sources of

---

[7] Translator's note: each *préfecture* of Rwanda is governed by a local civilian authority, the *préfet*.

information. I discovered how to be a journalist on the job and I soon acquired a taste for investigation techniques. I owe a lot to Philippe Revil, the editor of *La Vie nouvelle*. Nor will I ever forget Jacques Raymond, the office manager, who showed me how it is possible be both a journalist and a priest while remaining faithful to one's commitments.

After studying for two years, did you go back to Rwanda?

In the early summer of 1988, I returned home with my diploma. I felt I had earned it, but I didn't know what was in store for me. The Church had been wanting to launch a private radio station; it needed staff with experience of audiovisual techniques.

There weren't many openings for a journalist. In the late 1980s there was no freedom of the press in Rwanda. We were living in a single-party state and only the MRND was allowed to express the truth.[8] The state media had a monopoly on information through the national radio and television station, the official press agency, the daily government newspaper *Imvaho* and the weekly *La Relève*.

There was one exception to this monopoly: *Kinyamateka*. *Kinyamateka* had been created by the White Fathers in 1933; it belonged to the Episcopal Conference and was the Church's main vehicle for social communication. It was the oldest newspaper in the country and had a certain standing. Before becoming the first president of the Republic of Rwanda, Grégoire Kayibanda had been its editor, from 1956 to 1958. *Kinyamateka* reached out to the whole population. That is why it is written in the national language and is distributed widely in the countryside, through the parish network.

Some of the bishops wanted me to take the leadership of *Kinyamateka*; this had been the purpose of sending me to Lyon. But I found out later that others opposed this idea. They understood the strategic importance of a publication like *Kinyamateka* and were afraid of losing control.

The newspaper was at the heart of an intense political struggle. In 1980 *Kinyamateka* was run by Father Sylvio Sindambiwe, who had just finished his studies at the college of journalism in Lille. Father Sylvio set up a team of experienced journalists – Tharcisse

---

[8] The MRND was in power from 1973 to 1994. It started off as the *Mouvement révolutionnaire national pour le développement* (National Revolutionary Movement for Development), then became the *Mouvement républicain national pour la démocratie et le développement* (National Republican Movement for Democracy and Development).

Urayeneza, Philibert Ransoni, Anastase Seruvumba[9] and Théodore Simburudali – and adopted a very critical line towards the Habyarimana regime. The Episcopal Conference, chaired by Archbishop Vincent Nsengiyumva,[10] withdrew its approval. Father Sylvio had a lot of information about the abuses of the regime. He was talented and passionate. His investigations hit their target every time. He was made to resign in December 1985. He narrowly escaped several assassination attempts, including one in the offices of *Kinyamateka*. Finally, on 7 November 1989, a lorry crashed headlong into his car ... he was killed on the spot. When the Belgian journalist Colette Braeckman interviewed President Habyarimana soon afterwards, the president replied with a jovial and cynical smile, 'In your country, there are also plenty of car accidents every weekend.'

He was replaced by Bishop Innocent Gasabwoya, the former vicar-general of Bishop Perraudin, for whom I had worked in Kabgayi in the early 1980s. But he was an elderly and sick man. He didn't safeguard the newspaper's independence, nor its cohesion. There was a lack of dynamism in the editorial team. The quality of the articles had dropped. Information was no longer cross-checked. Practices which hardly conformed to the ethics of journalism began to take hold. I should also say that in the meantime, with Sylvio's departure, several journalists had preferred to choose a different professional career.

A well-known businessman in Kigali, Silas Majyambele, used to buy whole pages in *Kinyamateka* to publish updates on his wrangles with the law. Readers started complaining and the number of subscribers dropped within a short time. The situation absolutely had to be rectified. I believe this is what prompted my appointment as the head of *Kinyamateka* in October 1988.

At the beginning it was difficult, because my aim was to put an end to this complacent form of journalism. I wanted to put into practice what I had learned at *La Vie nouvelle* and promote an authentic form of investigative journalism. I wanted to search for facts, ask awkward questions, check information and, above all, publish the truth. I didn't know anybody in Kigali and I had to set up a network of contacts. At the start, people didn't trust me. Then they saw that I was serious in my work. Soon the long speeches

---

[9] Anastase Seruvumba was killed by *interahamwe* militia on 29 April 1994 in Kigali.
[10] Vincent Nsengiyumva, who had been Archbishop of Kigali since 1973, was well known for his close links with the Habyarimana regime and in particular with those close to the president's wife. He was assassinated by an RPF squad on 5 June 1994.

became redundant: all they had to do was read *Kinyamateka*. Gradually people started sending me spontaneously information on what was going on around the country. Not all of it was interesting or true, but gradually, through practice, this informal network of correspondents improved and became very useful.

I had to regain control of the editorship. The most difficult task was to break bad habits, so I decided to accompany journalists when they covered a story and correct their mistakes one by one. I wanted to improve the quality of the newspaper, but that improvement had to be the result of each person's contribution. I tried to avoid engaging in useless polemics as much as possible, but I made ruthless decisions whenever I thought it necessary. The work of some employees at *Kinyamateka* was not up to scratch; others didn't do their work or were simply dishonest. Once it became clear that some of them would not change their behaviour, I decided that they had to leave.

The newspaper's style changed. There was one story which attracted particular attention. In 1989, a terrible famine struck the south of the country. There was a natural explanation for this phenomenon, but the authorities did nothing to improve the situation. Worse still, I had evidence that part of the government's assistance which was intended for the population at risk had been diverted. It was a scandal. I decided to publish this information. We were threatened and we were called liars, until I published photographs which were overwhelming.

This had an immediate effect. Readers wrote in to express their satisfaction: at last the truth was being told. In 1988, *Kinyamateka*'s print run had dropped to 7,000 copies. It stopped dropping, stabilized then started rising again as subscriptions multiplied. We received 1,000 subscriptions each year until 1994. These numbers may seem low for a country of 7 million inhabitants. But as a point of comparison, the daily government newspaper *Imvaho* had to struggle to sell 2,000 copies.

Were there political struggles in the editorial team?

Kinyamateka was not a general information newspaper, but a vehicle for social communication. Having said that, we gave a high priority to political news. And as in any editorial team, there were different political sensitivities and differences of opinion.

These differences turned into a conflict with those who did not respect the ethics of the profession. A journalist called Manzi, whom I had sent to the north of Rwanda to report on the infiltration of soldiers coming from Uganda, produced an article in which he stated that they were just bandits crossing the border to steal cows. Everyone knew this was wrong and that these were the first incursions of the soldiers of the Rwandan Patriotic Front[11] (this was a few months before the start of the war). There could be different opinions about these incursions, but you couldn't lie to the readers by denying that they were taking place. Journalists are not supposed to know everything, but their duty is to provide information on the basis of what they do know, not to conceal information, or dress up the truth for political ends, which is even more serious. The atmosphere was very tense. I preferred to get rid of that journalist; I don't know what's happened to him since the genocide of 1994.

Another journalist, Gaspard Gasasira, was involved in fraud. He would steal equipment which belonged to *Kinyamateka* or falsify articles. After several attempts at conciliation, I eventually had to dismiss him in 1993.

Nevertheless I don't believe that political involvement is incompatible with the profession of journalism. It's a question of professional conscience. The vice-president of the *Union démocratique du peuple rwandais* (UDPR), the Democratic Union of the Rwandan People, Sylvestre Nkubiri, was a journalist at *Kinyamateka*. I only ever had one argument with him, right at the beginning. The rules were clarified and I never had cause to complain again. He was an excellent journalist and he knew how to make the distinction between information and his own opinions. His death[12] was a great loss for all of us and also for the newspaper; we all miss him.

What kind of relations did you have with the Catholic hierarchy?

Bad, very bad. I'll give you an example: throughout the time that I was in charge of the newspaper – from 1988 until this day – *Kinyamateka* didn't receive a single franc of subsidy from the

[11] The Rwandan Patriotic Front (RPF) was created in 1987 in Uganda by former Tutsi refugees. Its objective was to secure the return of refugees to Rwanda, whether by negotiation or by force.
[12] Sylvestre Nkubiri was a Tutsi. He was killed on 12 April 1994 by *interahamwe* militia in Kigali. His wife, Athanasie Uwamariya, managed to protect their two daughters, Carine, aged five, and Aurore, aged four. All three of them survived the genocide. After the war, Athanasie was accused of denouncing a Tutsi neighbour to a group of militiamen. She was arrested on 25 February 1995 and detained in Kigali Central Prison, where she died on 12 September 1997. An aunt took care of the children who now live in Canada.

Roman Catholic Church of Rwanda to finance its work. The newspaper only had one advantage: printing on credit. But what about the salaries? the overheads? the costs of maintaining our offices and our only vehicle? We never received any help and this didn't make the work any easier. Having said that, our financial independence turned out to be very useful.

The newspaper belonged to the Episcopal Conference, and still does. Legally, the real head of the newspaper was the Archbishop of Kigali, Archbishop Nsengiyumva, who was in charge of the Committee for Social Communication. But the links between Archbishop Vincent Nsengiyumva and those close to the head of state were notorious. Nsengiyumva had even been a member of the central committee of the single party in power, the MRND, until the Pope demanded that he resign from it, just before his visit to Rwanda.

One day, towards the end of 1989, Archbishop Nsengiyumva summoned me to the bishops' palace. He was furious. He had just seen the president. The head of state had complained about an article published in *Kinyamateka* which accused him of involvement in drug trafficking along with his son. According to Archbishop Nsengiyumva, the president's wife, Agathe Kanziga, had even underlined in red the parts of the article which she considered to be offensive lies.

Nsengiyumva ordered me to disclaim the article. I refused. I took out of my pocket a letter of thanks from the president's wife to a Gabonese businessman called Barry. This document, which was very embarrassing for the president, provided the evidence to support the facts reported in *Kinyamateka*. Nsengiyumva tried to destroy the letter but I warned him that it was just a copy and that the original was safely stored away. Our meeting ended without another word being said.

Two days later, Nsengiyumva summoned me again. This time, his tone was completely different, quite charming. He gave me an invitation from the head of state who wished to meet me 'over a drink' to 'get to know me'. It was a classic trap, which many people had fallen into. During such meetings, offers were made – a post in the administration, a sum of money – in order to buy silence or subservience. 'I'm sorry, I don't want to have a drink with that man', I told him. Since that day, and until his fall in 1994, Nsengiyumva never spoke to me again and never dared look me in the eye.

There is another incident which illustrates the atmosphere of the time. I had been editor of *Kinyamateka* for three years and my term was due to expire in 1991. Vincent Nsengiyumva was no longer chairing the Committee for Social Communication; Thaddée Nsengiyumva [no relation] had replaced him. But before his departure, Vincent Nsengiyumva had made certain that my mandate was not renewed. When Thaddée Nsengiyumva came to tell me that I was no longer editor of *Kinyamateka*, I explained to him the likely consequence of this decision in terms of public opinion. After the trial in which I had confronted the highest government authorities, the decision to replace me could only be interpreted as an act of desertion. Three hours after that short conversation, I received a letter renewing my contract for three years.

Which trial was that?

Between June and December 1989, we published a series of articles denouncing the large-scale embezzlement of public funds by government authorities. Rwanda was a country which still had the reputation of being well run, ruled by a sort of 'enlightened despot', Juvénal Habyarimana. But you don't become an honest man just by knowing how to quote French poetry to President Mitterrand. Juvénal Habyarimana and his people were plundering the country while the peasants were starving. We had evidence that he or his wife were diverting funds allocated to buying food for the population to import luxury items instead, for example televisions which were sold at vastly inflated prices. We also had information on drug trafficking.

A priest is not a politician; neither is a journalist. But as a priest, it was my duty to fight injustice and as a journalist, it was my duty to provide information. I knew that I was taking a risk by publishing these articles. It was at that time that Father Sylvio Sindambiwe was killed and it was difficult not to make a link between these two events. I also knew that I was exposing the whole of the editorial team to possible retaliation. We accepted these risks.

The state dragged us to court. I won't pretend that we weren't worried. But we were determined. We had several advantages: the support of public opinion and especially of several international human rights organizations, like Amnesty International, Human Rights Watch, the *Fédération internationale des droits de l'homme* (International Federation of Human Rights) and the Committee to Protect Journalists. These organizations sent letters of protest to the authorities. This had a disastrous effect on the government, because Rwanda was extremely sensitive about its international image.

Our trial took place on 18 September 1990 at the high court of Nyamirambo, a poor district of Kigali. Crowds of people gathered around the court. Three of my journalists had been charged along with me: Sylvestre Nkubiri, Antoine Rwagahilima and Gaspard Gasasira. We were accused of publishing articles described as 'seditious'. According to the prosecution, we had discredited 'senior authorities' in the country by claiming that they had accumulated wealth at the detriment of the rest of the population and that they were putting themselves above the law in order to carry out abuses.

The purpose of the trial was to intimidate and ridicule us. But as the hearings proceeded, I opened my files and kept producing more evidence to support the accusations we had published. I was carrying a huge bag stuffed full of documents and I was prepared to read them all, one by one, all night long if necessary. The session soon turned into an embarrassment for those who wanted to silence us. Passions were aroused among the crowds who were watching the trial or who were waiting outside; they were outraged by my revelations about massacres, torture, and various kinds of trafficking. In the general confusion, the prosecution decided that the hearing should be cut short. They still called for a six-month sentence, but we were acquitted on 26 September.

The same day, I was on trial in another case brought about by *La Centrale*, a powerful food import company run by Séraphin Rwabukumba, one of the brothers of Agathe Kanziga, the president's wife. We were criticized for an article published in November 1989 in which I denounced the abuses of this company in obtaining import licences. But the judge was worried that the trial would degenerate like the previous one and that I would use the courtroom as a platform. The trial was adjourned to a later date on the basis that the legal representative of the newspaper, Archbishop Vincent Nsengiyumva, was out of the country. It was never followed up.

Did this case affect the newspaper?

Of course. We had adopted an attitude of resistance to all those in power and we hadn't given in. The trial strengthened our reputation. From that time onwards, the fact that *Kinyamateka* was on the side of the opposition, that is on the side of the weak, could no longer be disputed. I have always kept the newspaper on that side of the divide, and that is still its position, even though many people don't like this.

I don't want to give the impression that *Kinyamateka* was only a political and polemical newspaper. We listened to our readers and tried to meet their expectations. For many Rwandans living in the countryside, *Kinyamateka* was the only source of written information, the only publication which would bring news into their lives every other week. People used to wait for *Kinyamateka* in the villages and in the hills. They read it out loud in the evenings. Generations of children, and even adults, learned to read with *Kinyamateka*. We always took care not to disappoint them in their expectations.

That is why we outdid ourselves when Pope John Paul II visited Kigali in September 1990. His visit was the object of great anticipation. The country was in a bad state, people were suffering, we couldn't see the light at the end of the tunnel. Naively, we believe that the Pope's visit would change things. We decided to mobilize everybody at *Kinyamateka* to try to cover the event as thoroughly as possible. You should have seen the atmosphere! For four days, our bimonthly newspaper turned into a daily. Those who are familiar with the very conservative mentality of Rwandans will appreciate that this sudden break with routine was a true revolution.

I strengthened the editorial team as well as the number of photo reporters. At any one time we had at least two people at the location where the Supreme Pontiff happened to be. The teams of reporters worked at top speed. They had to write their articles on the spot and bring them to the office straight away. Each issue was finalized at around midnight. An hour later, I was shown the proofs. At 2 o'clock in the morning, I gave the go-ahead to print. The editors went off to sleep, but only for a few hours.

During that time, the printers were working to their full capacity to meet the demand which was increasing day by day. At 5 o'clock, dozens of volunteers collected the first copies fresh off the printing press and started distributing them. We didn't skip a single issue.

Unfortunately, the outcome of the visit failed to match our expectations. The Pope kept repeating: 'A thousand hills, a thousand problems, a thousand solutions.'[13] His speeches, which were very dense, seemed to have been written in advance and did not correspond to what we wanted him to see during his visit.

---

[13] Translator's note: Rwanda is often described as the country of a thousand hills (*le pays des mille collines*), because of its landscape.

As for President Habyarimana, the visit gave him great pride. It was as if he had been knighted by the Pontiff's visit. Maybe this influenced his attitude later on.

Soon after the Pope's visit, in late September 1990, you helped set up the Association rwandaise pour la défense des droits de la personne et des libertés publiques *(ADL) (Rwandan Association for the Defence of Human Rights and Public Liberties). Why did you want to add human rights work to your pastoral commitment and your work as a journalist?*

Because the situation required it. Since the end of 1989, the country had entered a period of political turmoil. Opposition to the Habyarimana regime was expressing itself more and more openly. Illegal political parties were being formed in a more or less clandestine way. A number of very virulent private newspapers were appearing and were harassing the government, often very cleverly.

President Habyarimana and his followers reacted by attacking on all fronts, but with a single objective: to hold on to power. Officially, the regime was becoming more democratic. It had to impress France after the speech at La Baule during which François Mitterrand had expressed his wish to link development aid to democratic progress. But on the ground, the first signs of the radicalization which led Habyarimana to his downfall were already apparent. Political violence had never ceased to exist, but it was taking on new proportions.

Before ADL was created, there was only one human rights organization in Rwanda, ARDHO (Rwandan Association for the Defence of Human Rights). I was one of the founding members of that organization. But like many others, I felt uncomfortable with the fact that ARDHO's president, Alphonse-Marie Nkubito,[14] was also the Public Prosecutor. Furthermore, it struck me as dangerous that there was only one organization taking action in such a complex and sensitive field.

When the historian Emmanuel Ntezimana[15] came to my office at *Kinyamateka* to put to me his plan to create ADL, I agreed with

---

[14] Alphonse-Marie Nkubito was seriously injured in a grenade attack in 1993 and narrowly escaped the 1994 massacres. He was appointed Minister of Justice in the government of national unity in July 1994 but was forced to resign in August 1995. He died on 13 February 1997, in circumstances which remain unclear [see Postscript]. The following day, the President of the Council of State and Vice-President of the Supreme Court, Vincent Nkezabaganwa, was assassinated, casting further doubt over the circumstances of the death of the former Minister of Justice.
[15] Emmanuel Ntezimana died in Brussels in 1995, following a long illness which was attributed to poisoning.

the idea straight away. We started up the organization without any resources or any support, and in spite of hostile rumours. For several weeks there was even a rumour that I was trying to create a subversive political party. Eventually, on 11 September 1991, we adopted our statute during a constituent assembly held at the Christus Centre at Remera.[16] Technically, ADL was founded on 7 December 1991.

What kind of work were you doing in ADL?

We had a very practical approach to the question of human rights. ADL has never been interested in issuing solemn statements or organizing prestigious gatherings, some of which have no immediately obvious purpose. We published reports and news releases. But that was only the visible aspect of our work.

In the early 1980s, when I was in charge of the parish at Muyunzwe, I had devoted my time to looking after the sick and the destitute, those who didn't have the strength to call for help. But I had also discovered other categories of people whose despair was just as great, even though it was less visible.

Muyunzwe is in the *préfecture* of Gitarama, President Grégoire Kayibanda's region of origin. When he was ousted from power by his Chief-of-Staff, Juvénal Habyarimana, Habyarimana ordered the assassination of many political officials who had been close to Kayibanda. These men left behind widows and orphans who had real difficulty surviving. We had to provide guidance to these people, help them assert their rights, obtain pensions and death certificates when their husbands disappeared. We had to fight to intervene with the Ministry of Justice against the intrigues of local civil servants who were trying to get their hands on the pensions. That was my first struggle for human rights and it provided me with the inspiration to organize the work at ADL.

ADL's aim was to document systematically the facts relating to human rights violations and record them in a public report. We wanted to let Rwandans know that we understood their problems. It was important for the diplomatic community and the international press to be informed. This work would also help create pressure on those in power by showing that they could no longer commit abuses without disgracing themselves through exposure to public opinion.

[16] André Sibomana succeeded Emmanuel Ntezimana as president of ADL.

So we launched very precise investigations in the field. The results turned out to be overwhelming. I remember in particular some graves which we discovered in a remote forest, at Nasho, in Kibungo *préfecture*. It was a terrifying sight. There were hundreds of skulls and skeletons. Who were the dead? Who had killed these people? The ground was covered with bodies. An American woman who worked for Human Rights Watch, Alison Des Forges, took part in this investigation; she can testify to what I am saying. We questioned the authorities and demanded an explanation. The response was staggeringly flippant: we were told that these were just old bones. I went back to the site, picked up a skull which was only partly decomposed and showed it to anyone who wanted to know the truth. These remains were those of victims who had been killed recently. Why had these people died and why hadn't anyone seen or said anything? We decided to set up a network of informers: from then on, we had to prevent such crimes or alert public opinion if they occurred again.

ADL trained a team of investigators and built up a network of volunteer correspondents in each region. The task of these correspondents was to gather information and send it to the ADL office. They also organized meetings to raise awareness of tolerance and peace, thus helping opposition political parties to reject extremist propaganda, wherever it came from.

We were offering a form of grassroots activism: we taught the population to refuse to allow itself to be crushed by those who held the reins of power. Even today, there are still people in my country who believe that military or police officials have the right to beat them. There are military and police officials who in good faith cannot imagine exercising their authority without using violence. With infinite patience, ADL explained to one and all that violence is prohibited and that men have inalienable rights.

Men, and women too.

Domestic violence was one of our concerns. Thanks to ADL, women discovered that they, too, had rights, particularly the right to be treated with respect by their husbands. We helped them organize themselves to defend these rights more effectively.

Rwandan women have an unenviable status. They are completely subjected to the authority of their husband and of their community. They do the bulk of the domestic work and work on the land. They often seem to carry life on their shoulders and in their bodies like an unbearable burden. We tried to emancipate them from this apparent fatalism and help them regain their independence and dignity. As far as I know, the servitude of women is not prescribed in the Gospel.

The meetings we organized were just a small contribution, but they helped a lot of people. Sometimes we managed to change the relationship between Rwandans and the authorities. The vast majority of illiterate peasants who live in the countryside live under the moral guidance of chiefs. These peasants are completely stripped of any responsibility and follow orders blindly, whatever they might be, without any detachment and without the slightest thought of criticism. You cannot imagine the power of submission of Rwandan peasants. They literally sign up to the authority of the chief, for better or for worse. 'I was following orders', 'All I did was obey', 'I am not responsible': I have heard these explanations a thousand times from the lips of those who participated in the massacres in 1994. Unfortunately I believe that these peasants are sincere and that they don't feel responsible for the crimes they committed through submission to the authorities. Some try to dilute their responsibility in a greater collective responsibility, which is less heavy to bear. But others feel no remorse or regret. They are at peace with their conscience because all they did was follow orders!

We had just started teaching the notion of resistance to official authority. Some remembered this during the genocide. We needed time to take this further, but time was against us.

All the same, you were a priest, a journalist and a human rights activist: aren't these three functions incompatible sometimes? Are you sure that you are not confusing the roles?

Absolutely not. These three roles are completely complementary. As a priest, I preach the Gospel and I look after the soul. Christ was sent to bring the good news to the poor and to cure the sick. A priest carries this message forward. A journalist echoes the message further. The profession of journalism enables the Christian community to have access to information which should be used for pastoral work. Through *Kinyamateka* I could inform the public about the misery in the country and the massacres which were about to happen. Unfortunately, writing is not always enough. Sometimes you have to engage with your audience to convince them. That's when the human rights activist steps in. I went round the embassies and the United Nations agencies carrying ADL's reports and explained to them over and over again where our country was heading. None of the diplomats who were in Rwanda at that time can claim that they didn't know what was about to happen.

PART II

ON THE EDGE OF THE ABYSS

4 A Cry in the Wilderness

Observers who have followed events in Rwanda over the last few years find it difficult to understand what happened between 1990 and 1994. As you have said, in the late 1980s the Habyarimana regime was looking weary and there were signs of political turmoil. Some people felt that Rwanda would follow in the footsteps of many other African states at the time and make a commitment to a democratic future. Four years later, Habyarimana was killed and the regime he had founded was destroyed, having committed genocide in the meantime. What happened?

Rwanda has a complex history. Were it not so bloody, it could be likened to a game of chess. Someone who hasn't followed the game from the outset and doesn't know the moves can't follow the subsequent stages.

There are immediate causes for the crisis which engulfed the Habyarimana regime in the late 1980s, but there are also structural causes which are much more ancient and deep-rooted. It was not only the Habyarimana regime, but also the republic, declared in 1961, and the whole of Rwandan society which were built on antagonisms which had been concealed for a long time but never disappeared. I will come back to these contradictions which blocked social development, but I want to make clear at this stage that the events which occurred between 1990 and 1994 provide only part of the explanation. What were these events? I will mention at least four of them.

First of all, in the early 1990s, Rwanda entered a phase of economic recession while demographic pressure was at its height. The collapse of the price of coffee and tea, for example, deprived the country of its main sources of income just as the International Monetary Fund and the World Bank were demanding draconian readjustment plans. Unemployment was continually rising, affecting whole swathes of society and fuelling overall discontent. Life in Rwanda had always been expensive; it became unafford-able. In normal times, peasants living in the countryside barely had enough to eat; now they were beginning to starve. No one was fooled any longer by the image of balance and prosperity which the government projected abroad: everyone knew that the country was sick.

Secondly, it would be an understatement to say that the government could not handle the situation. Habyarimana and his followers did nothing to save the country. On the contrary. Power became concentrated in an increasingly restricted family circle, centred around the President's wife, Agathe Kanziga, and the *akazu*, the 'little house'.

It is not possible to overstate the harm inflicted on Rwanda by those who grabbed power. For example, Pascal Simbikangwa, who worked in the intelligence services and drew up lists of people to be killed; Séraphin Rwabukumba, director of the company *La Centrale*, who lent out vehicles to transport militiamen or to transport bodies; Protais Zigiranyirazo, who was one of the brains behind the *réseau zéro*[17] and the death squads; Michel Bagaragaza, director of the national tea agency, who extorted tea from our peasants to exchange them for arms in Egypt – the same arms which would bring about their death. And many others besides.

These people did nothing to try to restore prosperity; they were too busy plundering our meagre resources. The scandals which we exposed in *Kinyamateka* and which earned us that trial in 1990 were just the tip of the iceberg. The collusion between the higher circles of the state and several big dealers and traffickers was notorious. Corruption had completely eaten into the wheels of the state: anything could be bought, anything could be sold. Even the army was completely corrupt – apart from a few exceptions – and it's no coincidence that it ended up losing the war.

Rwandans lost confidence in a government which could not provide them with any guarantee of a future, or even of daily subsistence. The population's increasing disaffection towards the Habyarimana regime explains in large part the success of the opposition. The press – to its credit – also played an important role in this process. I wrote articles in *Kinyamateka* which President Habyarimana did not like at all.

One day, during an interview he gave to the national committee for the creation of a national television station – of which I was a member – someone pointed me out to him. He came over and asked me, 'So you're Sibomana?' I nodded. He said, 'I had imagined you taller.' What he really meant was 'I thought you were a Tutsi', the stereotype of a Tutsi being someone who is physically tall and sys-

---

[17] The *réseau zéro* (Network Zero) – Z for Zigiranyirazo - was a clandestine organization charged with eliminating opponents.

tematically hostile to power held by a Hutu. Before walking away, he added, 'Thanks to your editorials, the population no longer believes my official speeches.'

For one must remember that, in the beginning, people believed in Habyarimana. He had graduated as an officer with flying colours and had been named Chief-of-Staff in 1965. In 1973, he was seen as the one who would lift the country out of its misery, which he succeeded in doing, to a certain extent. Many Tutsi believed in him at the beginning and felt that he would not manipulate ethnic sentiments to consolidate his power. Unfortunately, these illusions were short-lived.

The disaffection of the population and the internal disintegration of the state do not provide the only explanations. There were also external causes.

The first of these was the emergence of increasing international pressure – although in my opinion, this pressure was insufficient. The fall of the Berlin Wall in 1989 and the end of communism in Eastern Europe created a belief in a new international order. Many believed that this would be the era of pluralist democracies and that the model of Western democracy would gradually spread across the planet. As I said, during the Franco-African summit at La Baule, President François Mitterrand stated that, from then on, French development aid would be linked to democratic progress. This seems like a joke in the light of subsequent events and the role that France played in supporting this despicable government. But at the time, people believed in these new policies.

Much has been written about the relations between France and Rwanda and the friendship which developed between François Mitterrand's son, Jean-Christophe, the former special adviser to the French presidency on African affairs, and Juvénal Habyarimana's son, Jean-Pierre. There were also suggestions that President Habyarimana was close to François Mitterrand, that the French president had succumbed to his charms and saw in Habyarimana a refined intellectual, someone who could be trusted. I don't want to take a position on this very polemical subject because ultimately we don't have much information about it. But what I did notice was that President Habyarimana agreed to make concessions and that, in return, he secured the support of France until the end.

What motivated France to support this regime?

I have no idea. Specialists have offered all kinds of explanations: a policy based on the lesser of two evils, a wish to preserve or extend

France's colonial patch in Africa, rivalry between the Francophone world and the Anglophone world (the so-called 'Fashoda complex'), the desire to hold a strategic position in the event of an implosion in Zaire ... Questions could also be raised about the various kinds of trafficking which were going on in Rwanda – drugs, arms,[18] etc. – and about the role of certain lobbies and elite circles. It is a fact that France committed itself to supporting Habyarimana, but was there a real political strategy behind this support? I don't know.

In any case, it enabled a political opposition to emerge. Parties began organizing secretly. Then they acquired newspapers, offices and programmes. Eventually – within a short time and still without any legal status – they started holding public meetings. The government was forced to follow suit and during the summer of 1990, there was talk of a 'political aggiornamento', of separation between the state and the single party and of a multi-party system. The content of the programmes and the real ambitions of the leaders didn't matter – in some cases, their ambitions were purely personal and they saw politics as a convenient way of getting their hands on power and wealth; others had a real sense of state; what mattered more was the emergence of public opinion where for years there had only been pro-MRND propaganda.

On 24 September 1990, Juvénal Habyarimana appointed a 'national synthesis committee' responsible for 'identifying what the concept of democracy meant to the majority of Rwandans'.

The last element, but the most decisive in upsetting the Rwandan chessboard, was the attack launched on the northeast of Rwanda on 1 October 1990 by soldiers of the Rwandan Patriotic Front (RPF) based in Uganda.

Who were these soldiers and what did they want?

They were descendants of Tutsi who had fled Rwanda at the time of independence, between 1959 and 1962. Around 100,000 Tutsi, who had been ousted from power and had become victims of persecution, had chosen the path of exile and settled in refugee camps, mainly in Burundi and Uganda. At the time, they believed that their exile would be short-lived. The reality was different. In fact, new waves of refugees came to join them during the 1960s

---

[18] Kigali Airport was allegedly used as a hub for French arms dealers who were secretly supplying Iran.

and 1970s. Taking into account the natural population growth, the number of Tutsi living in exile by 1990 was estimated at 600,000.

The government in Kigali was not in a hurry to negotiate the return of these refugees: the country was already overpopulated and could not accommodate this additional population. Overpopulation is a critical problem in Rwanda. The relief of the country, which is aptly called 'the country of a thousand hills', does not help. The land is rich, but scarce, and the population doubles once every 20 years. Observers all agree that the country is suffocating under the weight of its population. Rwanda and Burundi are the only two countries in Africa where there isn't a single wild animal left, apart from a few gorillas: the entire land is occupied by human beings. But there were other motives for refusing to find a solution. If they returned, these Tutsi – many of whom had once been masters of the land and allies of the colonial powers – would be likely to want to take back power, as well as the wealth they had had to abandon and which others had claimed.

So these refugees, who were facing increasing resistance to their presence in Uganda, ended up organizing themselves and created the RPF. Officially, the aim of this political structure was to represent the entire refugee population and negotiate its return with the government in Kigali. But at the same time, the RPF was building up an underground army with a view to waging a war of national liberation should this prove to be necessary.

What sparked off the war in October?

This question is still the subject of much controversy. Officially, from the RPF's point of view, the failure of negotiations justified opening a military front. Every means of pressure had to be exerted on the government to force it to accept an agreement; military pressure was just one of several levers.

Critics of the RPF, however, believe that the negotiations were just an alibi for the armed struggle. They claim that, from the start, the intention of the RPF was to regain power by force, at any cost, to avoid having to share it. As for the timing, that was imposed by the rapid pace of events in Rwanda. If the process of democratization had been successful, it would have deprived the RPF of some of its legitimacy. Because, inside Rwanda as well as on the international scene, the RPF did not just claim to be the party of an oppressed minority; it claimed to be acting in the name of all those who were struggling against the dictatorship of General Habyarimana. In a way, it was being overshadowed by the democratic opposition growing inside Rwanda. Even the relationship between the RPF and the parties which were implicitly close to it was ambiguous.

In addition, even if the government was not in a hurry to see the refugees return, negotiations were under way and were likely to produce a result. As Colette Braeckman rightly points out in *Terreur africaine* (African Terror), 'They were never as close to reaching a negotiated solution as on the eve of the outbreak of hostilities.' In this hypothesis, the RPF lost its *raison d'être*. It had to act quickly because, as the saying goes, 'history does not offer second helpings'.

Militarily, the offensive ended in failure.

The attack was carried out in a hurry. The RPF bore many casualties. An estimated 1,800 fighters out of a total of 2,500 to 3,000 are thought to have been killed or taken prisoner. The rebels' Chief-of-Staff, Major Fred Rwigyema, was among the victims. The exact circumstances of his death have never been explained. The fact remains that Paul Kagame, the current Vice-President and Minister of Defence of Rwanda, who was being trained at the American military college, took over the leadership of the RPF. He organized the guerrilla movement and expanded the ranks of the RPF. The RPF was able to mobilize significant human and financial resources, thanks to his military successes, but also thanks to his prestige among the Tutsi diaspora and the sympathy he soon attracted through the Western media – a national liberation movement fighting a dictatorship is always a popular cause, especially if it is born out of an oppressed minority. Young Tutsi came from Burundi, Tanzania, Zaire and even from Europe or the USA to join the RPF. Many Tutsi in Rwanda also crossed the border. They wanted to participate in what they saw as a liberation war. The RPF helped them by organizing underground recruitment networks. The initial military mistakes were corrected. That is how the RPF gradually took control of the region of Byumba, in northeastern Rwanda.

The regular army, the Rwandan Armed Forces (*Forces armées rwandaises*, FAR), were caught off guard. Everyone knew that a conflict was imminent; incursions and border incidents had become more and more frequent in the months which preceded the start of the war. But the FAR did not prepare themselves appropriately and their reactions were not effective.

The army was corrupt. The headquarters' staff ranks included notoriously incompetent men who owed their nomination to dishonest deals. The soldiers who were sent to the frontline were most often Hutu from the south, who were badly payed, badly equipped, not respected by the hierarchy which was from the north, and not at all motivated. The FAR were incapable of countering single-handedly the attack launched in October. It took the intervention of the *Division spéciale présidentielle* (the Special Presidential Division) sent by Mobutu and the French army to restore order. Even then, they failed to drive the RPF back completely over the border.

Officially, the French army intervened in Rwanda in 1990 to guarantee the security of French and European nationals in the country. This intervention took place in the context of Operation Noroît. How was the French army affected by the fighting?

There was a difference between the official mandate of the legionnaires who landed in Kigali on 4 October 1990 and what they really did in the country until their final departure three years later. These soldiers spent three years there, whereas the 400 Belgian parachutists, who arrived at the same time, only stayed three weeks; this certainly wasn't because they were slow in action! It was an open secret that the French army had come to help the FAR. Not only did they supply them with arms and ammunition but they also placed military advisers within the ranks of the FAR.[19] One of them, Lieutenant-Colonel Chollet, was the military adviser to the Chief-of-Staff of the FAR; he might as well have been leading our national army. Some people claim – although without convincing evidence – that the French sometimes participated directly in the fighting. It may be true, I don't know. Anyway, it is likely that if the French army had not intervened in February 1993, the RPF would have taken Kigali at that time.

One thing is certain: the war claimed a greater number of civilian lives than military ones. Soldiers on all sides behaved outrageously. Human rights were totally ignored. Some FAR units behaved towards the local Hutu population like an army of occupation, looting, raping, killing with total impunity – let alone slaughtering the Tutsi population: for example on 8 October 1990, several

[19] In accordance with a military cooperation agreement between France and Rwanda signed in 1975, France provided military assistance to Rwanda worth 5 million francs a year until 1990. This assistance increased to 55 million francs in 1993. During the first three months of 1994, they provided a further sum of approximately 6 million francs. According to the French government, this aid was suspended when the Security Council adopted the resolution on the arms embargo.

hundred Hima Tutsi from the Mutara region were massacred simply because they were Tutsi. The presence of these soldiers who had come to defend the border against the invaders was a calamity for local people of all ethnic groups. Discipline seemed more rigorous among the ranks of the RPF. Apparently, any failure to obey orders, any theft or looting was punished severely. It's possible. But it's difficult to know the truth because the press hardly ever had access to that side of the front line. Nevertheless, large numbers of Hutu peasants – as well as Tutsi civilians – were massacred in areas controlled by the RPF. Incidentally, access to these regions is still today denied to United Nations human rights observers and to the international press. We should question why access is prohibited.

The RPF guerrilla war also had political consequences.

It was a political rather than a military war. Obviously the military results were significant. As I said, without the intervention of the French army, Kigali could have fallen to the RPF. But until 1994, the RPF's political gains were much more decisive that its military successes. There was no comparison between the impact of the political defeat of the Habyarimana regime and the danger inflicted on the country by the rebels' assaults.

Before going any further, I would like to clarify an important point. I don't want to give the impression that, had it not been for the RPF attack, the Habyarimana regime would have become a democratic government and that it was the rebellion which ruined everything, dragging Rwanda into a cycle of violence which reached its climax during the genocide of 1994. The Habyarimana regime had embarked on the path of democracy under pressure. But there was strong resistance within the state, and it was not at all certain that those who held the power and wealth would have allowed the movement to develop.

Nevertheless, the October war was a gift to the government. It derived a new legitimacy from the real or imaginary threat which the war had cast over the country. The argument of national defence was over-exploited; in the name of the greater interest of the country, public liberties were suspended, opponents were imprisoned, human rights were ignored. The government deliberately created an atmosphere of confusion, turning every opponent into an accomplice of the rebellion and turning every Tutsi into a secret RPF soldier.

During the whole of October, alleged accomplices (*Ibyitso*) of the rebels were arrested. In order to justify accusations of 'sabotage' against them, a fake battle was organized in Kigali in the night of 4 to 5 October. Gunfire was heard all over town, but there wasn't a single casualty ... Six or seven thousand men were detained, half of them in Kigali, because of their 'suspicious' activities. Nine out of ten were Tutsi; that was their only crime. Sylvestre Nkubiri, a journalist at *Kinyamateka* whom I mentioned earlier, was among the detainees.

This wave of arrests disturbed public opinion and the diplomatic community protested. On 18 October 1990, government officials organized a visit to Kigali Central Prison, where the prisoners were gathered. They wanted to show that the detainees were well treated. I took part in the visit, but I had my own informers. Once we got inside the prison, I left the official delegation and visited the detainees who had been carefully hidden away by the authorities. Under a blanket, I discovered a pile of bodies; some of them were motionless, others had been mutilated. Innocent people had been beaten, their backs had been slashed with bayonets. Some had deep cuts on their arms from being tied up. I took photos which we then published in *Kinyamateka*. The scandal this provoked was extremely embarrassing for the government and probably contributed to hastening the release of the detainees between April and October 1991.

The Habyarimana regime had become politically fragile because of increasing internal demands for democratic reform; it was at risk militarily since the opening of an armed rebellion on its northern border; it was beginning to lose favour on the international scene. Economic and social tensions were increasing and political violence was spreading. How did you experience these changes, as a journalist and a human rights activist?

I'll start with my work at ADL. From October onwards, I was constantly writing public statements and letters of protest, calling meetings of our members and raising public awareness. We were all acutely aware of the gravity of the situation and of the infernal wheels which had been set in motion by cynical or irresponsible people. Here is an example of an extract of a statement which we distributed soon after the start of the war and which sums up our state of mind at the time:

> The organization condemns this war [the war of October 1990] unre-
> servedly. This war is claiming an increasing number of innocent victims
> and constitutes a major obstacle to attempts to open up the political

system in Rwanda. We are appealing to all the protagonists to do all they can to end it. The organization strongly supports the democratization process on which Rwanda has embarked and hopes that it will come to fruition. However, we condemn the entrenched attitude of some of those in power who do not appear to have the national interest at heart. We openly condemn the violence and intimidation against opposition parties and members.

In particular, ADL denounces the fact that some political authorities are fostering the confusion between the actions of opposition political parties and those of the RPF *inkotanyi*.[20] We are appealing to the judiciary to fulfil its duty to ensure that the truth is known and to put an end to this climate of suspicion which is being deliberately sustained. On the particular subject of justice, we deplore the way in which those who should be ensuring respect for the law appear to have abdicated their responsibilities.

Since October 1990, people have been killed, others have disappeared, others have been subjected to all kinds of abuses [...] The membership of ADL strongly denounces the torture, illegal detentions and threats which have become common practice [...] This situation and these practices are unacceptable and unbearable in a so-called law-abiding country. Our country is committed to a democratic system and this is not the time to allow certain hardline elements to reduce it to a weak state [...]

As a journalist, once again I discovered that 'truth is the first casualty of war'. The state tried to muzzle the press. The director of ORINFOR, the Rwandan Office of Information, organized a meeting of all the journalists to explain to them the importance of uniting and supporting the state through these difficult times ... He wanted to make us sign a kind of motion of support to the government. In an effort to ensure success, he even made the ORINFOR drivers participate! We refused and left the room. Later, we met again in the offices of *Kinyamateka*, where we decided to create our own organization, the *Association des journalistes du Rwanda* (AJR) [Association of Rwandan Journalists]. I became its president.

Kinyamateka maintained a strong line towards the government. *Kinyamateka* doesn't have any political bias or enemies, but the newspaper fights those who do not respect human rights or who indulge in corruption. That is how we came to oppose the MRND.

You also adopted a very hard line towards the RPF.

We did. It has never been a secret, even though some people pretend to have discovered this only recently. I always considered

---

[20] Kinyarwanda word meaning 'fighter', commonly used to refer to RPF soldiers.

the RPF rebellion as an additional obstacle to Rwanda's evolution towards peace and democracy. The situation was difficult enough without creating new problems. I said it and I wrote it at the time, whether in *Kinyamateka* or in the ADL statements; it wasn't an original opinion. The private press and independent human rights organizations – I'm not talking about the RPF propaganda agencies – expressed the same opinions.

The fact that you are attacking a dictatorship – the Habyarimana regime – does not mean that you have the right to do whatever you like. Fighting a government which tramples on human rights does not entitle you to use the same methods. That is why we denounced the crimes committed by the RPF since October 1990. Many opponents of the Habyarimana government criticized us for playing into its hands by denouncing an opposition force like the RPF. They didn't realize that they were the ones who were playing into the hands of the dictatorship by turning a blind eye to this movement which was using the same methods as the government it was fighting, and furthermore, which was more interested in taking its place than in destroying its bases. There was a strong consensus on this point within the editorial team.

Political killings started becoming more frequent. Were you personally threatened?

We were all personally threatened, all those who spoke out, those who wrote, those who took part in meetings, but also all those who did nothing but had the misfortune of belonging to the wrong ethnic group or who happened to be in the wrong place at the wrong time. Insecurity increased as the months went by. It was cleverly sustained by extremists on all sides: the climate of terror which they had succeeded in creating enabled them to spread their influence over the whole society. Rwandans were already an anxious people; they became paranoid.

Having said that, I did receive specific threats on several occasions. After the assassination of Sylvio Sindambiwe, I had good reason to take them seriously.

Can you give an example?

One day, in February 1992, I received a letter from a man who was unknown at the time but who later acquired a sinister reputation as an extremist. His name was Jean-Baptiste Hategekimana. This is what he wrote to me: 'You shouldn't be alarmed by the fact that the security forces have allowed you to endanger national security but you should worry about the consequences because you have become like a bull which does what it pleases. Those you have attacked [...] have decided to confront you directly [...] In the context of self-defence[21] these people have decided to pay you back in kind [...] No one will be able to counter our objective of saving the country by getting rid of undesirable elements.'

This is a typical, ordinary example but it was altogether serious. The people who were threatening us didn't even try to hide because they knew they could act with impunity. When the genocide started, they leapt into action quite naturally: I would say they were psychologically and materially ready and had just been waiting for an opportunity to act.

Recently I re-read a report which the president of CLADHO,[22] Alphonse-Marie Nkubito, had addressed to the diplomatic community in December 1993. He himself had just narrowly escaped an assassination attempt so he knew what he was talking about. In this report he had drawn up a list of people who, according to him, were especially at risk. I'll read you the paragraph about journalists and I'll point out what has happened to the people to whom he referred:

> Some journalists are under threat in their daily lives because they dare to criticize the government or because of the ethnic group they belong to: for example, Marcelin Kayiranga [killed in April 1994] and Vincent Rwabukwisi [killed in April 1994] of *Kanguka*, Obed Bazimaziki [killed in April 1994] and Adrien Rangira of *Le Flambeau*, Sylvestre Nkubili [killed on 12 April 1994] and André Sibomana of *Kinyamateka*, André Kameya [killed on 15 June 1994] of *Rwanda Rushya*, Edouard Mutsinzi [victim of an assassination attempt on 29 January 1995], Sixbert Musangamfura of *Isibo*, Elie Mpayimana of *L'Ere des libertés*, Louise Kayibanda of Radio Rwanda ...

As you can see, the toll is overwhelming. The press was in the vanguard of the struggle against dictatorship and for democracy: it was made to pay the price.

But the press didn't just support the struggle for public liberties. There were also journalists who broadcast the propaganda of the regime and others who incited ethnic hatred.

---

[21] The state incited the population to organize itself to ensure its own security. Within a short time, these self-defence groups went on the offensive.
[22] CLADHO is the umbrella organization of Rwandan human rights organizations. ADL is a member of CLADHO.

There is no doubt about it and, unfortunately, I am familiar with the problem. As president of the Association of Rwandan Journalists, I participated in many seminars where we tried to lay down rules for a professional code of ethics in order to counter this worrying trend.

The extremist newspapers which were fuelling ethnic hatred presented the war as the only solution to Rwanda's problems. *L'Echo des Mille Collines, Interahamwe, Kamarampaka* or *La Médaille-Nyiramacibiri* had a disastrous impact on public opinion. The worst one was called *Kangura*. It was run by Hassan Ngeze.

What about RTLM?

The *Radio Télévision Libre des Mille Collines* (Free Radio Television of the Thousand Hills) appeared later. It began broadcasting during the summer of 1993. This radio station was the extremists' counter-attack to the negotiations which were under way between the government and the RPF. A successful conclusion to the negotiations was imminent. But the agreement which was eventually signed in Arusha in August 1993 provided specifically for the parties to share the airwaves of the national radio station, Radio Rwanda, which up until then was controlled by members of 'Hutu Power' (the extremist Hutu wing). The extremists were afraid of losing control of an instrument of propaganda which was crucial in reaching a population which was 90 per cent rural and illiterate; they set up their own radio station, with support from the highest levels. Part of the money was provided by Félicien Kabuga, a businessman whose daughter had married Jean-Pierre Habyarimana, the president's son.

Who worked at the radio station?

Contrary to what many people think, the journalists who worked at RTLM were excellent professionals, people who had had a good education and had been hand-picked. The director of programmes was Ferdinand Nahimana (see Chapter 7). He was a brilliant historian. He had written a thesis at the university of Paris-VII on the Hutu royalty of the north of Rwanda and had been the director of the Rwandan Office of Information (ORINFOR). The chief editor was Gaspard Gahigi. The other journalists were 'Hutu Power' party activists, among them Valérie Bemeriki, Kantano Habimana (a famous reporter, trained at the most prestigious school of journalism at Saint Petersburg in the former Soviet

Union), Noël Hitimana (a popular sports commentator) and Georges Ruggiu.

Isn't it paradoxical that the government was secretly encouraging an extremist press while it was busy negotiating peace with the RPF and a democratic transition with the opposition?

It would be naive to believe that a government speaks with one voice. Like Janus, it always has at least two faces. Officially, the government was negotiating a power-sharing arrangement and a return to peace. Eventually opposition parties were legalized and gradually became official parties to the dialogue. A first ceasefire was agreed with the RPF in Arusha in July 1992. It provided for the refugees' right to return and for the inclusion of the RPF in a transitional government. But at the same time, it was preparing for war. Just like the RPF, which launched a surprise offensive in January 1993 which led it right up to the gates of Kigali.

Did you have evidence of these government activities?

There was no shortage of evidence – nor of real-life illustrations either, unfortunately. I'll give you an example. In March 1992, the extremists carried out a most cynical experiment: they tested the effectiveness of calls to murder on the radio by sacrificing the Tutsi who lived in the Bugesera.

Until the early 1960s the Bugesera was an underpopulated region which had an unfavourable reputation. Tutsi who had been driven away from more fertile land had been made to settle there soon after independence. Through hard work and ingenuity, they managed to turn it into a habitable and even a prosperous region. Then many Hutu came to settle there under the weight of demographic pressure. Some of them soon began coveting the land which had been made profitable by the Tutsi. The propaganda exploited this envy, against a backdrop of poverty.

As soon as the radio gave the signal, the manhunt began. An Italian woman who lived at Nyamata was there at the time. Antonella Locatelli only just had time to sound the alarm by telephone: she warned the Belgian embassy, RFI and the BBC and explained what she was witnessing. The next day, she was killed by a squad sent straight from Kigali. But thanks to her, the events were now known and the gendarmerie was obliged to intervene and put an end to the killings. In the meantime, between 300 and 400 Tutsi had died, many of them in appalling conditions.

It may seem incredible now, but all these events were unfolding before us and we were perfectly aware of what they meant. No one can claim that they didn't know what was happening or that they didn't know what was being prepared. Since you're asking for evidence, here is an extract from a speech I gave on 7 December 1992 at the French Cultural Centre in Kigali, in the context of a week in support of tolerance organized by ADL:

> On 3 March 1992, a Radio Rwanda journalist, Jean-Baptiste Bamwanga, read out on the air a statement signed by a certain Innocent Mutangana, jointly with a number of unknown organizations, denouncing a so-called programme of the 'new wave RPF'. Among other things, the statement claimed that Tutsi women would be used in operations to assassinate the main Rwandan political leaders. The Liberal Party was especially targeted. Two days later, the Bugesera went up in flames. The provisional count on 10 March 1992 was 300 dead and more than 15,000 displaced [...]
>
> [Some media justify this behaviour, trivialize it and make it seem normal.] About this trivialization: when a communicator decides to broadcast a piece of information to the public, however minor it may seem, it is never a gratuitous act. Through a game of repetition, drop by drop, the media build moral and cultural constructs which eventually become permanent features [...] Lists of grenade attacks and murders diminish the tragedy of death or grave injuries or turn them into empty words. Gradually, the public which is targeted moves from the horror of the first killing to a state of immunisation against the drama which each and every killing represents. In the end, the readers or the listeners say to themselves: killings happen, they're tolerable.
>
> At that level, we move from trivialization to normalisation. It's the transformation from 'trivial' to 'normal' and from normal to prescriptive. It's a smooth transition, of course. After the killings which took place in Butamwa commune, we were astonished when a woman told us, 'They killed one of ours, next time we will kill one of theirs!' The short circuit in human conscience starts like this: this happens – this can happen – this must happen ... We will not go into the details of the almost unconscious process of conditioning of behaviour by the media, but we believe that each communicator should be responsible for ensuring that the public is not injected with the virus of prehistoric behaviour.

And what did we see in 1994? A return to prehistoric behaviour. Violence was trivialized. Murder became normal. You had to be completely lacking in goodwill not to understand the mechanisms which were being put in place. But that was not all. Here is the rest of the speech:

> We have a responsibility to think about when and how we disclose information. Regarding the actual situation in Rwanda, unfortunately

we have to recognize that all the circumstances conspired to ensure (deliberately or not) that our main media did not rise above the situation of those who were out to create dissent. With a few rare exceptions, the organs of the press [...] became tools for trouble-makers who were serving the interests of regional, ethnic and ideological intolerance. Indeed, the regular selection and broadcasting of information suggesting or reporting ethnic or regional clashes or conflicts between various political groupings, without any commentary or note of caution, tends to contribute to the awakening of warlike instincts and primary reactions of vengeance based on ethnic or party divisions [...]

We believe that this failure of responsibility on the part of officials in the media has contributed significantly to fuelling a climate of intolerance and turned them into agents of destruction of Rwandan society. Whether deliberately or not, our communicators had a share of responsibility in teaching Rwandans to kill each other, not to tolerate or appreciate their differences. And when this right to difference is not recognized, cohabitation becomes impossible[...]

I deeply regret that this speech, like many others, had no impact. It may have provoked some questioning or increased awareness. But the situation on the ground did not change at all. The whole of 1993 was marked by massacres, killings, abductions and all kinds of odious crimes. The extremists continued preparing and training for war under the very eyes of UNAMIR, the United Nations Mission which was deployed in Rwanda from November and whose mandate consisted in supervising the implementation of the peace accords signed at Arusha.

Are you referring to the militia?

Absolutely. These militia have a terrible history. In the late 1980s, the public meetings organized by the former single party, the MRND, would often end with sports gatherings. The young people who participated in these gatherings later created supporters' groups. When opposition parties began emerging, these supporters' teams gradually turned into a kind of police force. They were given uniforms. The young people who were members of these militia no longer had anything to do with the world of sports and sometimes asked to be paid for their 'services'. They were often drunk or under the effect of drugs. Each time, they went a bit further. Eventually the groups that became known as the *interahamwe* militia ('those who attack together') were given para-military training. Along with the *ipuzamugambi* militia ('those who share the same aim', the militia of the *Coalition pour la défense de la République*), they went on to become the spearhead for the genocide.

These preparations received substantial coverage in the opposition press. Here is a quote from a statement published by the newspaper *Le Flambeau* on 17 December 1993:

> Military sources have confirmed [...] that 40,000 *interahamwe* have just completed their training in several centres in the Akagera park (in the east of Rwanda). [They] are about to carry out a plot which the instigators will portray as a civil war [...] The fascists of Rwanda and their leader have decided to apply the 'final solution' to their compatriots who are seen as enemies of the regime.

It couldn't have been any clearer. Shortly before he was killed, the Minister Félicien Gatabazi also denounced these plans. In a letter dated 12 December 1993, a group of senior FAR officers who did not want to participate in these massacres alerted General Dallaire, the UNAMIR commander. But the United Nations forces, like the international community, did not react to these warnings. I don't know why.

Once again, everyone knew what was being prepared; those who claim the opposite are lying. Although it's a bit long, I would like to read you an extract from another speech I delivered as ADL president, on the occasion of the 45th anniversary of the Universal Declaration of Human Rights, on 10 December 1993 – less than four months before the start of the genocide. The points of view expressed in this text are not my personal opinions; they are the result of the brave, persistent and dangerous work undertaken by all the members of ADL. It is important to know that human rights organizations did not fail in their duty and that they did all they could within the limits of their resources to alert those who had the power to break the cycle of violence:

> [...] We are celebrating the 45th anniversary of the Universal Declaration of Human Rights just one week after 16 schoolchildren were killed in Taba commune. This is the first time that the organization of killers which is operating in this country with complete impunity has chosen to attack children.
>
> We cannot remain silent or stand by idly when faced with this revolting cruelty [...] which comes on top of other recent killings of peaceful peasants in Kirambo *sous-préfecture* and Mutura commune. We are also celebrating this day while thousands of Rwandans, crammed into [refugee camps] like a flock penned into a cemetery, with death hanging over them as they graze, are marking the third anniversary of their misfortune and misery.[23] Taking into account the current political

---

[23] These were people from the northeast of Rwanda who had fled the war and were living in precarious conditions, transferred from provisional camps to transit camps.

situation, characterized by the search for personal profit to the detriment of common good, by a disorganized administration, paralysis in the Rwandan judiciary and deliberate sabotage of the peace agreement signed at Arusha, there is little hope for happy days ahead in the near future [...]

Every day in this country, human beings are killed. They are dying because they expressed a political opinion, because they belong to a particular community or region, or simply because they are guilty of being poor [...]

These violations are the logical consequence of a system based on injustice and inequality, which has been set up and strengthened, skilfully and deliberately, through a series of political, social and economic measures [...]

ADL is appealing to the Rwandan people to say no, to revolt against a situation where their rights are ignored and trampled upon – a phenomenon which has led to barbaric acts against which human conscience would revolt in normal conditions [...]

Matching our words with actions, we distributed our second annual report on this occasion. It was full of specific examples. This is how I introduced it:

ADL's report [which we are publishing today] takes you on a tour around the country of a thousand hills to show you that it is also the country of a thousand schemes, drowning in blood and misery. Whichever direction you take, you cannot help but reach the same conclusion: 'People are killing each other! Yes! People are killing each other!'; and some authorities responsible for protecting the population are prepared to distort reality by blaming others for these killings. They often try to create confusion about the identity of the killers and portray them as civilian or military delinquents who have managed to escape the control of the authorities. However, there are many indications that these groups often operate in close collaboration with the state, and may even be acting as a cover for certain agents of the state.

What more could we do? It was as if we were left to cry in the wilderness. I personally visited many representatives of the international community to alert them to the gravity of the situation. I distributed documents which described the preparations of the genocide. I was distressed by the reactions I encountered. After a long discussion with the Senegalese Amadou Lee, a representative of the United Nations Development Programme (UNDP), he looked me straight in the eye and just said, 'Rwanda's problems will only be solved by Rwandans.' What a nice way of putting it! I remember going to the American embassy several times to talk to the ambassador, David Rawson. I told him, 'You have come here to undo what you created 20 years ago. Please use the most peaceful means available.' I spent many long evenings talking to his first counsellor, Joyce Leader, who was very interested in what I was saying but didn't believe me. After the war, I saw her again in Kabgayi. At least she had the decency to apologize for not having taken what I had told her seriously.

What about France?

I didn't have any contact with the French embassy. Even if I had, what could I have learned or expected from the country which was the most open supporter of the Habyarimana regime?

5 Lord, Where Were You During the Genocide?

On 6 April 1994, Juvénal Habyarimana was killed on his way back from Dar es Salaam, in Tanzania, where there had been an international conference aimed at resolving 'the Rwandan stalemate'. Why was he killed? Who killed him? What were the consequences of this attack?

The peace accords signed in August 1993 in Arusha, which provided for gradual power-sharing between the MRND, opposition parties and the RPF, had broken down. The hardliners in the regime were refusing to give up any share of power. Rumours of a *coup d'état* were becoming increasingly frequent. According to one rumour, the most extremist elements had started to consider Habyarimana, if not as an enemy, then at least as a man who would no longer be an obstacle to the Arusha process.

There were good reasons for believing this. Rwanda was sinking and Habyarimana could no longer run the country without foreign support. But the Secretary-General of the United Nations, Boutros Boutros-Ghali, was not happy. He was threatening not to renew UNAMIR's mandate. The head of the World Food Programme was also tired of the government's lack of goodwill and of the massive diversion of food aid intended for refugees, while around 800,000 Rwandans faced the threat of famine. France – the regime's main foreign backer – was showing signs of impatience. The president had no choice: in Dar es Salaam he was obliged to give in and to agree to implement the peace accords.

In the evening, he left Arusha for Kigali on board his Falcon plane. He knew he was threatened by the extremists around him. Apparently that was why he requested one of them, Elie Sagatwa, to accompany him. That was also supposedly the reason he offered to accompany Cyprien Ntaryamira – the Burundian president who participated in the conference – back to Bujumbura, in the belief that his presence on board the plane would discourage the perpetrators of any attempted attack. The Rwandan president was on his guard; he protected himself with as many guarantees as possible.

At around 8.30 p.m., the presidential plane began its descent towards Kanombe Airport, 20 minutes away from Kigali, when one or two missiles hit the aircraft head on: according to witnesses the presidential jet was blown to pieces. There were no survivors.

Who carried out this attack?

Some people know the answer, but the truth has not been disclosed. The killers have not been found and speculation has centred mostly around the identity of those who ordered the attack. The press carried out investigations and several hypotheses were put forward. Some claim that responsibility lies with Hutu extremists who wanted to get rid of a president who was getting in their way. The 6 April attack was a kind of signal to begin the massacres of Tutsi and government opponents. Others, on the other hand, have implicated the RPF, on the grounds that the implementation of the Arusha accords was not in its interest, as they would only entitle the RPF to a small share of power, whereas its ambition was to run the country without sharing power. Both theses are credible and are backed by valid arguments, but neither is based on irrefutable evidence. Three years after the attack of 6 April, we still don't know who killed President Habyarimana.

Yet we need to know the answer. The thesis which blames Hutu extremists supports the point of view that the regime was beyond reform, that it was based on ethnic exclusion and that it had to be brought down at any price as soon as possible. It legitimizes the guerrilla war waged by the RPF. It reinforces the thesis of a genocide which was premeditated and planned; according to this thesis, the 6 April attack did not set off the genocide; it was its first act, according to a plan formulated in advance. It is worth noting that the death of the president of Burundi, who was on board the same plane, did not start a similar genocide or any massacres in Burundi, even though the conditions were propitious.

The other thesis, which implicates the RPF, would have wide-ranging consequences if it proved to be true. The RPF would have to take on a large share of responsibility for the genocide which was planned to a certain extent, but which might not have reached the scale that it did if Habyarimana had not been killed. Many books have been published about the genocide, but few provide specific information on the way it was planned. We know for certain that it was conceived and executed according to plans drawn up by Hutu extremist circles close to the government or within the government. But we don't know when these plans were drawn up, by whom, with what degree of precision and on what scale. Investigations have yet to take place.

Given the stakes, each side tried to produce evidence of the other side's guilt in the attack, without success. I honestly can't say that I support one thesis over the other. However, what we can assert without hesitation is that the attack was carefully planned. A document dated 14 January 1994 stated: 'The intensification of the security of Habyarimana did not change the plans nor deter the members and supporters. We examine with our advisers how to destroy his aircraft [...] The Hutu who lived overseas, especially in North America, are conducting activities to stop our plan. You are urged to initiate some actions against them and to transmit us their names and those of their family members.' I do not dare disclose the signatory's identity at this stage.

As for the consequences of the attack, they are incalculable. From April to July, Rwanda lived through the hundred darkest days of its history. From the evening of 6 April, *interahamwe* militia, then members of the Presidential Guard, gendarmes and FAR soldiers set up scores of 'roadblocks'.

What is a 'roadblock'? This seemingly banal word hides a reality which sends shivers down your spine. A roadblock is a small pile of stones in the middle of the road and a big pile of bodies on the side of the road. At the roadblocks a handful of militiamen, drunk or on drugs, watched as pedestrians and drivers approached, cheered on by onlookers, women and children who had come to encourage them. Each person had to show their identity card – a sentence of death for those whose documents contained the word 'Tutsi'. It was also a sentence of death for those who pretended they didn't have one or who had genuinely lost it. And a sentence of death for those whose documents bore the precious inscription 'Hutu' (or 'Twa'), but whose skin was a bit too light, who were a bit too tall or whose necks were a bit too long. Soon it became a sentence of death for anyone who looked suspiciously at the militiamen, for those who didn't pay up, for children who were wandering around aimlessly and whose existence was useless in the eyes of a militiaman. As you can see, the word 'roadblock' became synonymous with hell.

As the days went by, roadblocks appeared all over the country. Sometimes 'spontaneously'. People had been prepared for this, both in psychological and material terms. The army had organized 'civilian self-defence groups'. In a document dated 29 September 1991, an officer at the staff headquarters, Colonel Nsabimana, wrote: 'Civilian self-defence forms an integral part of a credible defence policy.' But those who were manipulating the crowds soon perverted these defence groups and turned them into an additional strike force. Very soon, from April onwards, it was not so much a question of self-defence, but rather a question of anticipating possible attacks. Anticipating in the broadest and most horrific sense imaginable: there were mass killings of children, because 20 years on, these children could become fighters for the RPF cause!

Across the countryside and in the towns, people had been given machetes, training, moral support and political assurances. They took this unexpected opportunity to let out all the hatred which they had bottled up inside and which propaganda had channelled against the *Inyenzi* ('cockroaches', the word used to describe Tutsi). At other times, they had to wait for Kigali to send detachments from the Presidential Guard for the massacres to begin. The population was then dragged into the killings under the influence of money or beer, or under threat.

This was the case in Butare, for example, in the south of the country. The south was the stronghold of the opposition. Hutu from the south often felt closer to Tutsi from the south than to Hutu from the north. For various reasons, they had a different concept of society. The *préfet*, Jean-Baptiste Habyarimana [no relation to President Habyarimana], devoted his energy to calming tensions and preventing massacres. Then, on 19 April, the president of the interim government set up on 8 April, Sindikubwabo, came to deliver an inflammatory speech. He dismissed Jean-Baptiste Habyarimana, who was perceived as too passive, and appointed in his place a notorious extremist, Sylvain Nsabimana. On 23 April, a plane flew from Kigali into Butare: the provisional government was sending a detachment of soldiers and militiamen to 'raise awareness among the population of the danger they were facing' and to incite them to 'work' (*gukora*, in Kinyarwanda, is an ambiguous term used to mean 'kill'). One of the first victims was the former *préfet* himself: no doubt he was seen as unfit to organize the massacres.

Soon it was not even necessary to encourage the population to kill. Violence feeds on violence, like a fire. People went mad and lost all points of reference. They killed and killed and killed. Or rather, they stopped killing to 'work'. They weren't crushing skulls with their rifle butts any more; they were stamping on vermin. The meaning of words changed and language adjusted to this new concept of life which identified different levels in the human species. Tutsi and their Hutu accomplices were really no longer viewed as human beings, but as things, dirt which had to be eliminated, poisonous snakes which had to be destroyed, whatever their age.

Who was killing, who was being killed, where, when and how?

The killers are well known. It was the Presidential Guard, 'elite' troops who were very well equipped and very well paid, composed of around 1,500 soldiers, all from Gisenyi, the birthplace of the presidential couple. Alongside them there were large numbers of soldiers of the Rwandan Armed Forces, the FAR. Some soldiers fought the RPF invasion because they believed it was their duty to defend the country's borders but they refused to take part in the massacres. But this attitude was very rare. Overall, the FAR distinguished themselves by cruel and ignoble acts rather than by acts of courage or bravery. The *interahamwe* militia, of course, constituted what I would call the 'living strength' of the genocide.

These young men – some of them very young – recruited all those who were old enough to carry a weapon. Their appearance was truly terrifying: bare-chested, covered in dried banana leaves – like traditional dancers – they shouted, sang and killed with a kind of jubilation and unbelievable fury. In addition to these groups, there was the gendarmerie, the *préfets*, the *bourgmestres*,[24] as well as many other people who joined the hordes of killers, whether willingly or unwillingly, whether by force or for pleasure. It would be an exaggeration to say that the entire population took part in the massacres, but those who resisted were rare and those who had conceived the genocide left no stone unturned to involve as many Rwandans as possible in their crime.

As usual, there were exceptions. Reports have occasionally mentioned testimonies of individual soldiers, gendarmes and even militiamen who saved a Tutsi or a Hutu opponent. These testimonies are not just convenient stories; they are real. Just as it is true that the same man could hide a Tutsi friend in his home and kill his Tutsi neighbour. It is no use looking for logic in this illogical and inhuman behaviour.

Much has been written about the supply of arms to Rwanda before and during the war. I denounced it myself, so I know that the trafficking was going on and that the grenades which were thrown into the churches where people who had had time to flee their homes had sought protection had not been produced in our country. But the fact is that most of the massacres were carried out

---

[24] The *bourgmestres* are local government officials, at the level of the communes.

using much more basic weapons: machetes, knives, axes, hoes, hammers, spears, bludgeons, or clubs studded with nails (known as *ntampongano* or 'without pity'). I don't need to dwell on the horror of these deaths, the frightful noise of skulls being smashed in, the sound of bodies falling on top of each other. Every Rwandan still has these sounds etched deep in their memory, and will do for a long time: the screams of people being killed, the groans of the dying and, perhaps worst of all, the unbearable silence of death which still hovers over the mass graves.

Everywhere, people were killed. First at the roadblocks, as I've explained, and in houses where Tutsi were known to be living. Then, when the districts had been 'cleaned out', they attacked settlements where gendarmes had encouraged the future targets to gather, under the pretext of providing protection: barracks, administrative centres, industrial warehouses, churches, convents ...

At the technical school in Murambi (in Gikongoro *préfecture*), where the gendarmerie had gathered all the Tutsi who had survived a first wave of massacres, the carnage lasted a whole night, from 22 to 23 April. The next day, at dawn, looters came to help themselves from the dead bodies and finished off any survivors. The bodies were left there until the *bourgmestre*, who had been warned of the arrival of French soldiers of Operation Turquoise on 7 July, paid the very same people who carried out the killings to scatter the bodies in various mass graves. Later, after the genocide, United Nations investigators uncovered 27,000 bodies in one of these graves.

At Kibuye, Tutsi were made to gather at Gatwaro Stadium. The International Committee of the Red Cross (ICRC) estimated that 14,000 people were there on 16 April when soldiers took up their positions on the terraces and opened fire. A few managed to escape before the stadium was completely closed off. None of the others survived.

Yet it is likely that most of the victims were killed in very small groups, if not one by one, in the countryside, along small paths, in the forest. The suffering and despair experienced by these thousands of unfortunate victims will never be known as their bodies were buried immediately: they disappeared for good from the world and the memory of the living. Others were thrown into lakes or rivers. A CNN team, returning from South Africa where Nelson Mandela had just been elected, stopped off in Kampala (in Uganda) and filmed the mouth of Lake Victoria. The water was red: 50,000 bodies, most of them dismembered, were floating on the surface.

There were three events which put an end to the genocide. First, there was military defeat. The FAR were too busy killing and looting; they were incapable of driving back the offensive launched by the RPF on 7 April to take control of Rwanda. There were very few head-on battles between the FAR and the RPF; the battle for Kigali, which lasted from 12 April to 4 July, was the exception. Overall, around the country, the war was waged essentially against the civilian population.

The second factor was the creation of the safe humanitarian zone by the French army. Before going any further on the subject of Operation Turquoise, I must remind you that the countries which make up the international community and which, on several occasions, expressed their indignation and concern at the tragedy which had struck the people of Rwanda, did absolutely nothing to help us. We were completely abandoned and handed over to our killers.

Do we need to remind ourselves of the unspeakable attitude of UNAMIR? It is the done thing to say that the soldiers acted heroically but that their UN mandate did not allow them to do anything other than leave. With your permission I will express a different opinion. Nearly 2,500 heavily armed peacekeepers were present in Rwanda when the massacres started. My first observation is that they – or at least their leaders – did very little to prevent the massacres. My second observation is that, as soon as the first shot was fired, they left. Some left of their own accord. Much has been said about the death of the ten Belgian peace-keepers who were protecting the prime minister and who were killed by members of the Presidential Guard. These ten deaths meant that Belgium could disengage from UNAMIR unilaterally and pack up its arms and belongings without giving the impression that it was completely destabilizing what was left of UNAMIR and abandoning to the killers all the Tutsi who had sought protection in UN camps. On 27 April, the UN decided to end the mandate of UNAMIR and cleared out all its men and materials, while Rwanda sank into chaos.

Who did they think they were fooling when they claimed that they couldn't do anything? Between 10 and 15 April, the French and the Belgians organized Operation Silver Back to repatriate their expatriate citizens. A team of 1,500 men came to take back their own people and left, preferably without the burden of any Rwandan refugees. Who can look a survivor in the eyes today and explain that despite the presence of 2,500 peacekeepers and 1,500 Belgian and French parachutists, it was impossible to save any of them? I

am not only accusing those who were there at the time: I am
pointing the finger at all those countries which spend vast amounts
of money maintaining professional armies which they only deploy
when there is oil to protect, like during the Gulf War, and who won't
move to save people like us.

To come back to Operation Turquoise, on 22 June 1994 the
Security Council adopted Resolution 929 which authorized France
to deploy 3,000 men for two months to 'restore security' in the
southwest of the country. The RPF was fiercely opposed to this
intervention, fearing that the French might take control of part of
the country and stand in its way. Paul Kagame told the French
government explicitly that his soldiers would use arms to fight the
presence of Operation Turquoise soldiers. This did not stop the
French from setting up a safe humanitarian zone in southwestern
Rwanda.

The third factor was the massive exodus of the killers and of the
people they had taken hostage. In May, there had already been a
mass flight of soldiers and militiamen to Tanzania; in a matter of
hours, they created the largest refugee camp in the world, Benaco.[25]
In mid-June, hundreds of thousands of peasants were on the roads,
completely at the mercy of the fighting. They were following the
orders of the provisional government which was using them as a
human shield. The UN High Commissioner for Refugees, fearing
the disastrous consequences of this huge population displacement,
even intervened to persuade RTLM to stop broadcasting messages
calling on the population to flee the advances of the RPF. By
around 14 July, 1 million refugees crossed into Zaire and settled
around Goma, in the disastrous conditions which we all know
about.

So when a government of national unity was created in Kigali
on 19 July, the war and the genocide had ended. But not the
massacres.

*We'll come back to that. But first, let's go back to 6 April 1994. Where
were you when President Habyarimana's plane was shot down?*

I had spent the whole day at my office at *Kinyamateka*. I had just
finished drafting a letter of protest denouncing the specific threats
which had been made for several days against Monique
Mujawamaliya, the secretary of ADL. Her life was increasingly at

---

[25] Almost 300,000 Rwandan Hutu became refugees at Benaco. They were forced
to return to Rwanda in December 1996.

risk and we needed to act fast. I had finished the letter; it was to be typed the following morning and sent to government authorities and members of the diplomatic community. The letter was never sent but Monique managed to escape. At the end of the day, I left my office and went to the Centre Saint-Paul, where I was living, about 50 metres away from the *Kinyamateka* office.

I heard the news of the attack that same evening on RTLM. The national radio station did not confirm the death of the head of state until the following morning, at dawn.

So you used to listen to Radio Télévision Libre des Mille Collines, *the extremist Hutu radio station?*

Of course! Everyone used to listen to RTLM, even the Tutsi. It is best to know what your enemies are thinking.

What did you do?

What could I do? I was sure that massacres were about to take place. The climate of hatred and violence which had spread across the country over the preceding months left no doubt about it. In fact, that same evening, we heard the first sounds of gunfire. Militiamen started setting up roadblocks and taking over the town. Soon it became impossible to move around. For several months we had already been avoiding going out after dark. We knew that something terrible was about to happen. Lists of names had begun circulating. We didn't need any more information: it was obvious that it was not wise to go out. I spent the night at the Centre Saint-Paul; I was very worried.

The following morning, on 7 April, I tried to reach the *Kinyamateka* office, in vain. I really wanted to recover the important files I had left in my office. After three unsuccessful attempts – a sniper was systematically opening fire – I gave up once and for all.

Refugees began flooding into the Centre Saint-Paul. A first group of six or seven people turned up at the gate. I ordered the guard to let them in.

The Centre Saint-Paul was run by Father Leopold Vermeersch, an elderly Belgian priest, who did not immediately understand the gravity of the situation. He did not want to let the refugees in because he thought they were just peasants who had come from the countryside. He wanted to send them to the parish of Sainte-Famille, which was usually responsible for receiving them. Sainte-Famille was located about 20 or 30 metres away, but the road was almost impassable: shots were being fired from every side. I got a bit cross and told him off for making light of such a serious situation. I persuaded him to let all the refugees in. Along with Father Célestin Hakizimana, we took on the responsibility for looking after them.

Where did they come from?

From everywhere. People did not have time to get organized. They were caught wherever they happened to be; those who managed to escape the bullets and the machetes sought protection in the nearest shelter. At first we hid the refugees in the cellar of the main building, but very soon, we ran out of space. People settled wherever they could. The centre served as a shelter for a total of around 2,000 people, excluding children. It was a relatively protected place.

At first the militiamen hesitated before coming to the centre: they knew that there was nothing to loot. Then they came, several times, armed to the teeth. They looked at the faces of the people who were in the compound, then they went away without a word. They came back a bit later, showing so-called arrest warrants for opponents they had identified previously. They took these people away and killed them a bit further along, on the side of the road. Around 60 refugees died in this way.

Did you witness these events?

No, I had already left the Centre Saint-Paul. On 12 April, the Archbishop of Kigali asked the priests to evacuate the town with the bishops' escort (it so happened that most of the bishops, who had been due to fly to Rome, had been gathered in Kigali since 5 April). I had no intention of joining that procession. But at the same time, RTLM announced that 'an important accomplice' was hiding in the Centre Saint-Paul; I presumed that they were referring to me. I fled in my own car, at 11.30 a.m. The militiamen came to arrest me at 2 p.m.

There were four of us in the car; I took with me two Tutsi nuns and a priest called Valens (all three of whom survived). We tried to leave Kigali on the road going south. Everywhere along the road, we saw dead bodies. Men, women, children, old people, they were lying there, in clumps, killed in groups or individually. Some bodies were dismembered. The militiamen were laughing, drunk on beer or under the effect of narcotics. For them, it was a celebration: they killed and looted without restraint. We took advantage of the general confusion to drive through several roadblocks. But we were stopped by militiamen at the roadblock at Nyabugago. A young woman whom I didn't know – and who was with the militiamen – came towards me and warned me, 'Father, they're after you, they're going to kill you.' We forced our way through but we had hardly driven 50 metres than the militiamen started catching up with us. And another roadblock appeared ahead of us, at Giticyinyoni. We were in a panic; we were sure that we would not come out of this ordeal alive. At that moment, we had a stroke of luck: a military official that I knew, Colonel Léonidas Rusatira,[26] arrived on the scene and helped us get through.

Later that day, after several other hurdles, we arrived at Kabgayi. When I went to the bishopric to inform the bishop of my arrival, I saw that members of the Presidential Guard – the same ones who had already tried to kill me – had occupied the place. The Presidential Guard was on its way to Gitarama, where the provisional government had decided to withdraw. I left immediately and went back to the village where I was born. I hid in Muyunzwe for a while, in my father's house. Then I changed my hiding place regularly. No place was safe.

How did you spend your days?

The days seem both short and long when you're in hiding. I had to take precautions every time I moved, which didn't leave me much spare time. At the same time, the hours went by very slowly. What could I do in the face of such an outbreak of violence?

Until 20 April, the region remained relatively calm. I used this period to 'pacify' the people in my parish, to persuade them by every means to refuse to resort to violence. Then the war caught up with us. Apparently money and machetes were distributed in the village. In any case, the massacres which started then were not at all spontaneous. From that moment onwards, it became impossible to live normally – and very difficult to survive. In my own parish, at Muyunzwe, I almost died from drinking poisoned communion wine.

---

[26] Colonel Rusatira was one of the rare Hutu officers who deserted the FAR and joined the ranks of the RPF. However, in 1995, he was forced to go into exile after being threatened by elements within the RPF.

When you were talking about the locations where massacres took place, you mentioned churches and convents.

Not only were the churches not spared, not only were many of them destroyed through shelling or burnt down, but often in the most horrific circumstances they became graves for Tutsi who had sought protection there. Those who were fleeing the massacres had the same reflex as their ancestors in 1959, 1964 and 1973. Sometimes encouraged by gendarmes, they sought protection in churches, convents and all sorts of religious establishments where they believed that the killers would not dare attack them. They thought they would be safe in these holy sanctuaries. This is how many had survived in the past; they hoped that they could do the same. Alas, the reality was quite different.

At the beginning, the militiamen did refrain from intervening as they were too busy looting the houses of those who had fled. They gave the Tutsi time to group together and to hope. But when they were all gathered in one place, they surrounded the churches and began massacring them. It was the same scenario everywhere. Between 10 and 15 April, around 15,000 Tutsi had sought protection at the church at Kaduha (in Gikongoro *préfecture*). On 19 April, the *interahamwe* tried out several small attacks to test their resistance. On 21 April, they attacked on all fronts: there were no survivors.

Six thousand refugees had gathered in the parish of Mibirizi. A first attack left only 2,000 survivors. For days on end, the militiamen – some of them 14 or 15 years old – came back to kill 10, 20 or 100 people, at random, for no particular reason, just because they had time on their hands. They stopped killing when they found something interesting to loot or when they became too tired. Their behaviour was incoherent and completely inhuman: they came to take life away in the same way that people might clear a wood of trees.

The church in Kibuye was attacked for the first time on 16 April. The assailants, who were armed with guns and grenades, were driven back by refugees who threw stones at them. But a fresh attack was launched on 17 April: of 4,000 Tutsi who were there, around 300 survived. One of the survivors owed his life to the large number of corpses which hid his body from the eyes of the killers. He stayed there for 15 days, from 17 April to 1 May, lying face down. He decided to leave only when the stench of decomposing bodies became utterly unbearable.

At Ntarama, 3,000 Tutsi had gathered in the church and the parish centre from 15 April. They fought back the assailants with spears and bows. But they came back in large numbers and eventually massacred all of them; I think only four or five people survived. It was the same thing at Nyamata and in several other churches. At Nyarubuye, near the Tanzanian border, the *bourgmestre* personally ensured that, in their frenzy, the assailants did not damage the convent where the unfortunate people had piled in. People were killed with machetes and hammers, leaving the building intact. You can go and see for yourself: the bodies are still there.

You mention that people fought back attacks here and there, without success as the Tutsi had no way of protecting themselves. Yet when you listen to the stories of survivors, sometimes their passive attitude is shocking. They all knew that something terrible was about to happen, but many persisted in believing that nothing would happen to them, despite overwhelming evidence to the contrary. Some didn't even try to run away. How do you explain this behaviour?

It is a phenomenon which is difficult to understand. Many Tutsi thought that if there were going to be massacres, they would take place in Kigali or in the big towns, but they did not really feel targeted. What did they have to blame themselves for? During the genocide of the Jews in Europe, many people did not take the last opportunity to flee, simply because they were at peace with their conscience and had nothing to reproach themselves. That is the unbelievable horror of genocide: you are targeted just because you've been born.

At the beginning, some Tutsi sought protection with local authorities. They did not know yet that by placing themselves under the protection of gendarmes and military officials, they were throwing themselves into the arms of their killers. Even at the end of the genocide, some people, who were in a state of psychological ruin and physical exhaustion, continued believing in the 'authorities', in the organs of the state. When the militiamen ran out of 'quarry' to 'flush out', they made the *bourgmestre* announce that the war was over, that people should return home and that the time had come for reconciliation. Those Tutsi who came out of hiding were killed on the spot.

In some cases, this 'passive' attitude is more a sign of a kind of fatalism. People had run out of strength in the face of the barbaric behaviour which had been unleashed. They lost all courage and all hope. Many lost their taste for life when they saw their former friends, those with whom they had shared everything, take up a machete and kill their own people. What was the point of carrying on living? To live with whom? As for dying, some people preferred to die at home, on their own land. Others had somehow swallowed the government propaganda which had sealed their fate: they could not see any future for themselves, anywhere. Others hoped until the very end that they would be saved *in extremis* by the RPF – which did happen in some cases, but the militiamen often got there first.

Survivors have remarkable stories to tell. Some claim to have tried to commit suicide several times but were physically unable to do so because their assailants did not leave them enough time. Many claim to have survived not in order to live, but because they feared a cruel death. It was only this fear of death and of the barbaric acts of the militiamen which helped them survive. But these people who are alive today have not been able to rekindle a desire to live: the earth has opened up under their feet.

Those who have survived often speak of a kind of emptiness inside, into which they keep falling. 'After the killings, there were only a few of us who survived. We couldn't even cry, we couldn't feel sadness any more, we were broken inside', explains one survivor. For days on end, men, women and children kept repeating to themselves, 'If it isn't my turn today, it will be my turn tomorrow.' They are still filled with this sense of existing somewhere between the world of the living and the world of the dead.

There were also acts of resistance among Hutu.

This is a distressing observation. There shouldn't have been 'acts of resistance': resistance should have been the rule and crime the exception. That is not what happened. Having said that, nowadays people try to make you believe that all Hutu were involved in the genocide; this is obviously an aberration. How could Tutsi have survived if Hutu hadn't provided them with a hiding place and food?

What happened in your parish?

There was just one attack, on 12 June, on the presbytery. The militiamen attacked during the religious service. Perhaps they thought they would be left alone. A parish sacristan alerted us. I interrupted mass and we fought off the *interahamwe*. Five people were abducted and thrown alive into a latrine. Six hours later, the same sacristan walked past the latrine and heard the sound of voices. He called out and a young girl called Adelaide Micomyiza replied. Two people were still alive. Thanks to the darkness and with the help of a young priest called François Twagirimana, we hauled them out of the ditch with a rope. Both were injured, one on the head, the other on the back and foot. In their fall, they had hit the sharp bones of other unfortunate victims killed just before them. I looked after these two young people as best as I could. They survived.

Were you able to save Tutsi yourself?

You are asking a very painful question. It was extremely difficult to save Tutsi, to hide them and feed them. In Rwanda, in normal times, everyone sees and knows everything immediately. So in this context, where everyone is spying on each other, you can imagine! For many people, not killing was in itself an act of resistance. Peasants were killed because they refused to beat the dead bodies of their Tutsi neighbours. There are brave people, people of integrity, who could not or did not have the courage to save their neighbours and who are still living with that guilt today.

I cannot take any credit for having saved a few people, because I had the power to do so. My position meant that I could do more than others. Yes, I can mention the name of Oliva Mukanyarwaya, whom I hid throughout the genocide. Yes, I saved the life of Straton Kagenza, whom I dragged away from the killers in return for payment. I saved the life of an old man called Thomas that a young man wanted to kill with a club studded with nails at the entrance of the parish church at Muyunzwe. I could mention other names. I accompanied many refugees right up to the RPF military posts, fooling the vigilance of the militiamen under the cover of moonless nights. What is the point? The people I saved know what I did. Those who accuse you of being a killer when you are innocent, just because they covet your land or your wife, or simply because they want to take their revenge or make you suffer, those people are not trying to find out the truth. During this tragedy, each of us was alone with our conscience.

What struck international public opinion most of all, apart from the speed and the scale of this genocide, was the incredible cruelty of the killers. How do you explain such cruelty?

I don't explain it. You can't explain everything or understand all forms of human behaviour. It's a fact: during the genocide, not only were hundreds of thousands of people killed, but many were victims of cruelty, torture and forms of ill-treatment which defy imagination.

I can't explain this cruelty, but I think it was an integral part of the genocide. Such cruelty isn't the result of individual 'excesses'; it belongs to genocide. The gratuity of the crime, its careful planning, the passionate desire to destroy not only the body but the soul of the victims before ending their life are elements which characterize genocide. The killers took the trouble to invent the worst kinds of cruelty. There were militiamen who travelled long distances to go and kill in person a Tutsi that they knew. I mentioned that some people were forced to kill under threat. But others revelled in it. They inflicted horrific injuries without going as far as killing the victims, simply to intensify the cruelty of death and to prolong the suffering. They did it just like that, without any worries, in complete indifference. They stood around drinking beer calmly, watching their former friends literally dying in agony at their feet.

It all happened as if those who committed the genocide were submerged in a hatred which had been contained for a long time. I myself saw militiamen, not satisfied with having killed people, attacking their dead bodies. Taking life away was not enough: they had to deny the person who had lived. Where did it come from, this hatred of others? I can only explain it by an insurmountable hatred of one's self. Indeed some killers committed suicide after they had killed. There were many, especially among young people from poor districts of the capital, whose lives were completely empty, who had no family, no religion, no work and no hope. They saw no future for themselves in the world. They turned upside down the value system to which they no longer had access: instead of taking advantage of their youth to build themselves a life, they used their energy to destroy the lives of others. These young people denied others not only the right to live, but also the right to die in dignity and to have a proper burial.

Others acted under threat or under the influence of drugs, or else agreed to go along with the killers out of weakness or opportunism. The genocide saw looting on an unbelievable scale. Whole families were killed for a foam mattress, which is worth less than 50 francs in France. Then the looters killed each other. After several days of this horrific bloodbath, the killers went completely mad. Politics, ethnic divisions, the war, none of this even entered their minds. They killed for a crate of beer, for a look which may

have been too insistent, or just because they didn't know what else
to do.

There is no doubt that a very large proportion of the population
was involved in the genocide, whether willingly or not. But it is also
true that the hordes of killers were made up of a few hundred
people, sometimes only a few dozen. It is striking that many of those
who confess to having killed claim to have assassinated dozens of
people. And that's without counting the children ...

The propaganda which had been broadcast for several years, the
careful planning of operations, the fear, the reflex of self-defence
in the face of the RPF advances which the media had portrayed as
the ultimate danger, the incitement to act faster than the enemy –
'kill so as not to be killed' – all this explains the speed and the scale
of the genocide.

*There were some attempts to destroy the evidence of the genocide
immediately.*

There were mainly attempts to destroy the memories of those who
had survived and who – it had been decided – no longer had the
right to live. Houses which belonged to Tutsi who had been killed
were demolished: they were not only looted and set on fire, but
razed to the ground. Banana trees were planted on some of the sites
of houses belonging to Tutsi. The cattle were slaughtered and
every last cow was eaten. Bodies were chopped up into little pieces,
dismembered, thrown into graves, burnt, thrown to stray dogs
and crows.

*The mechanisms of the genocide have been described a thousand times
over by journalists, by survivors and by United Nations experts.
Nevertheless, we are dismayed and unable to understand such barbaric
behaviour. How can such acts be possible?*

Which acts? Killing a human being is a crime. But in the minds of
those who committed the genocide, it was not a question of killing
human beings. They believed that they were eliminating a kind of
vermin. In the countryside, stamping out vermin is a domestic
virtue; it is a necessity even in order to avoid disease and to survive.

Once again, this genocide was planned. Those who organized
it probably did not imagine that it would take on such proportions.
But they had certainly ensured that its terrifying machinery could
be set in motion. There has been a lot of talk about the training of
the militia and the distribution of arms – quite rightly. But I don't

think that such a catastrophe would have been possible without the psychological pressure generated by propaganda. Insidiously, gradually, through obsessive and repetitive means, it changed people's perceptions and prepared them to accept inhuman behaviour.

The extremist propaganda described Tutsi as cockroaches or snakes. For many uneducated peasants, if the official authorities state that Tutsi are snakes, it can't be wrong. If the local official of the commune orders people to kill snakes, it makes sense. When you kill a snake, you smash its head, then you cut it up in different places to make sure it's really dead. These very same forms of torture were inflicted on many Tutsi.

In the countryside, the upkeep of the yard is a hard task: as soon as you have swept away the dirt, it comes back. You should not spare any effort to cleanse the place where you live. The authorities compared Tutsi to dirt which had to be eliminated. So peasants threw Tutsi into latrines, without it troubling their conscience. Why into latrines? Not only because it was 'convenient'. All houses have latrines; it was easy to get rid of a body by throwing it in. There is another explanation: latrines are full of excrement, the most revolting aspect of human life. Throwing Tutsi into latrines was an additional way of denying them that essential quality: belonging to the human species.

Did you personally ever feel abandoned?

Several times, as a priest, I wondered what the Lord expected of me. Why give me that vocation and make me a priest, why give me a parish? To watch my parishioners kill and be killed? Father Gabriel Maindron tells the following story in a book of conversations: among the militiamen who came to attack Tutsi who had sought his protection, he recognized former members of the parish choir, including a young man who had just been awarded the first prize in poetry! One militiaman wore rosary beads around his neck 'to increase his chances of finding Tutsi'. It is difficult to confront failure on this scale. Among the militiamen who attacked the presbytery at Muyunzwe, I recognized the son of my paternal uncle. He himself was manning one of the roadblocks where many Tutsi were killed. It was terrible.

As a journalist and a human rights activist, I felt abandoned, and this sense of abandonment was painful. Before the war, I had worked with many international organizations, particularly the Committee to Protect Journalists in the USA, but also Human

Rights Watch and the International Federation of Human Rights, Amnesty International, Reporters sans frontières ... When the genocide broke out, no one telephoned me, no one tried to reach me or to save me. I had the impression that each person was looking after their own problems and that, in the end, you can't help others.

But these people needed to know where you were. Did you let these organizations know your whereabouts?

No, it was too dangerous. They could have found me. Both sides were looking for me. Towards the month of May, approaches were made to the French authorities, who then ordered soldiers in Operation Turquoise to find me. When this information was broadcast on RFI, an RPF detachment went looking for me at Muyunzwe. They wanted to kill me before the French found me. In the end, I remained in hiding.

How did you renew contact with the outside world?

A journalist working for the French weekly, *L'Express*, Vincent Hugeux, came to see me in Kibuye in July. I was very rude to him and I hope that he has forgiven me since then! It was around 6 o'clock in the morning; I had just fallen asleep after spending the night ferrying food for refugees when this young journalist woke me to ask me for an interview. I don't know how he managed to find me. After the interview, he asked me if I wanted to broadcast a message. A message for whom? What for? For Amnesty International? For yet another report to be drafted and added to the huge pile of reports already written in vain? I felt very removed from all that. I have learnt to keep a sense of proportion about my relations with NGOs. As long as everything is fine, they are happy to use your work. But when things become complicated, they abandon you. The genocide revealed the limitations of NGOs. They ought to think more carefully about their responsibilities and assume them to the full before landing in a country.

In June, France decided to send an expeditionary force to Rwanda to create a 'safe' area in part of the country and to facilitate the transport of humanitarian aid. This part-military, part-humanitarian operation, known as Operation Turquoise, provoked much debate. Some people believed that France was rushing to the rescue of its former allies and preparing an exit route for them to Zaire. For others, despite its dubious

intentions, this operation turned out to be effective in the field and saved
many human lives. What is your opinion?

I don't know what France's intentions were. It is a fact that, until
the bitter end, France supported the Habyarimana regime against
which I was fighting. It supplied arms, military advisers, money,
political support, and all sorts of facilities which made life very
difficult for the democratic opposition.

The first time I heard about Operation Turquoise was on RFI.
The United Nations were due to study a proposal for a French army
intervention within the framework of an international mandate. I
was worried about this approach. Why had there been such a
turnaround in French policy? Having armed the FAR, were the
French now planning to disarm them? Where was the logic in this?

I was living in a state of fear and stress because we were hiding
Tutsi and, at any moment, we could have been arrested by
militiamen. For us, in these circumstances, any gesture towards
us was like a window opening out on to life. Of course, I thought
that France had opened its eyes and, realizing how low the regime
it had supported had sunk, it was preparing to defend itself to international public opinion. But at the time, these political motives
were not important. The French soldiers first landed at Goma, in
eastern Zaire. RFI announced their arrival in Kibuye on 30 June.
It was a relief.

It would be dishonest not to recognize that Operation Turquoise
saved thousands of human lives. I will mention just one example:
15,000 Tutsi who had sought protection in Cyangugu Stadium had
been moved to a camp at Nyarushishi. From one minute to the
next, they could have been killed; their extermination was actually
planned. Had the French soldiers not arrived in time, they would
be dead today. Had the French not created the safe humanitarian
zone, massacres would have continued unhindered. The fact that
Tutsi continued to die in the safe humanitarian zone does not mean
that we should forget to mention those who were saved.

I have a lot of admiration for Colonel Sartre. When he arrived
in Kibuye, he gave clear orders to his soldiers. They were allowed
to open fire on looters. At least that was the rumour which went
around and which looters believed. It produced immediate results:
the looting stopped. What would have happened to the 3,000
Tutsi who had sought protection at Bisesero if French soldiers
hadn't come to their rescue?

If the Turquoise forces hadn't been there, hundreds of thousands
of Rwandans would have thrown themselves into Lake Kivu and

others would have gone to die in Bukavu. Look at what happened in Goma: from 14 July, when the RPF arrived near the region of Cyangugu, almost 1 million people crossed the border. Those who died of cholera, famine and exhaustion during this exodus are estimated at 50,000. More than 5 per cent dead in two weeks! Operation Turquoise came too late. But what did other countries do? What did Belgium, the UK and Germany do? What about South Africa, which had made so much money from selling us arms? What about the countries which armed the RPF and enabled it to massacre civilians?

When the RPF took control of Kabgayi, you fled further south. Why didn't you want to cross into the zone controlled by the RPF or flee to Zaire?

For the RPF, I was – and continue to be – a suspect. As for Zaire, I would have found the militiamen there and all the officials of the old regime that I had spent so much time fighting. I didn't have much choice. I fled with my people towards the south.

When did you go back home?

We had fled to Kibuye because we didn't trust the behaviour of the RPF soldiers. Unfortunately, in that respect, our fears proved to be well founded. On 5 June, three bishops, including the Bishop of Kabgayi, and around ten priests were shot dead by an RPF squad. Why? 'It was a mistake, an accident, an unfortunate incident,' the authorities told us, 'an act of individual disobedience.' There was no further inquiry.

Some eventually admitted that it was a deliberate attack, but claimed that they had made a mistake about the victim. The soldiers wanted to eliminate Vincent Nsengiyumva, the Archbishop of Kigali, and killed his namesake, Thaddée Nsengiyumva, the Bishop of Kabgayi, by mistake. This theory doesn't make sense as the two men were executed side by side.

A French academic, Gérard Prunier, has put forward an explanation which seems more convincing to me: Thaddée Nsengiyumva had launched negotiations between the RPF and the provisional government. These negotiations could have succeeded. If that had been the case, if only a ceasefire had been declared, the RPF would have lost the opportunity to take control of the whole country. Especially as on 5 June we were only a few days away from the arrival of the Turquoise forces, which could have ensured that a ceasefire was enforced. According to this theory, the killing of the bishop was been intended to prevent such an outcome.

In any case, as far as we were concerned, it was clear that it was not safe for us to stay in Kabgayi. But it was not feasible to continue staying in Kibuye either. So on 17 July 1994, I made contact with the forces of Operation Turquoise. I gave them a petition from the people displaced by the war, laying out the conditions for their return. Here is an extract:

> Those displaced by the war who have signed this petition are appealing to the French military and political authorities to:
>
> - Guarantee the security of the displaced population now in the *préfectures* of Kibuye, Gikongoro and Cyangugu, the only zones of protection, in order to prevent a massive population exodus (towards Zaire).
> - Help the Rwandan people set up a government and an army of national unity which would not be entirely under RPF allegiance.
> - Ensure the protection of people who have worked in human rights organizations, who have been and continue to be portrayed as close to the RPF by a sector of public opinion and whose lives could be in danger.
> - Guarantee the security of the signatories of this petition.
> - Guarantee humanitarian aid to those displaced by the war to ensure their survival.

At the same time, I made contact with the RPF and wrote a letter to the Minister of the Interior on 24 July 1994, asking him to guarantee the security of the refugees for whom I was responsible. I also wrote to the UNAMIR representative to inform him of our intention to return to Kabgayi. I asked him for protection for the group of 230 people I was taking with me. The risk was not only that they would kill us all; they could also ensure that our bodies disappeared and that militiamen would then be accused of exterminating us.

So on 5 August, we set out on the road. After walking for three days, we arrived in Muyunzwe. It was a distressing sight: everything had been looted. The following day, I went to Kabgayi. There was a deathly silence – for a good reason – creating a surreal impression in this place which I had always known as bustling and full of life. On the road leading to Mukingi commune, there was a choking smell of pestilence. Revenge had not spared these poor peasants who were at peace with their conscience and had thought the nightmare was over ... The place has kept the date of the massacres.

It is called 'the 19th', because it was on 19 June that RPF soldiers massacred hundreds of peasants there.

These were painful days. On 10 August, I celebrated mass in the cathedral at Kabgayi. When I came out of the basilica, soldiers were waiting for me. They wanted to prevent me from saying mass and to force me to leave. I did not give in. I stayed, and never saw them again.

The following day, the apostolic nuncio officially appointed me apostolic administrator of the diocese at Kabgayi. Then on 3 December 1994, Pope John Paul II confirmed my appointment. I held the post for two years, until a new bishop was officially nominated on 25 March 1996.

Some people strongly opposed my nomination on the grounds that a 'little journalist' would be unable to run such a large diocese. They were right: I would never have managed it alone. But with the help of my parishioners, everything became possible. Together, we started rebuilding from the ruins.

6 Words Fail Us

André Sibomana, this morning [13 August 1996] we were at the Yad VaShem Memorial in Jerusalem. The memorial was built in memory of the genocide of the Jews by the Nazis during the Second World War. You were overwhelmed by what you saw there and you remained silent throughout the visit. However, before leaving, you said, 'They show us how, but they don't explain why.' Now it's my turn to ask you that question: why was there a genocide in Rwanda in 1994?

The reason those who conceived and built the Yad VaShem Memorial have not answered the question 'why?' is not that they forgot to answer it, but that they can't unless they enter the logic of the perpetrators of the genocide. As Rony Brauman said, you can analyse the historic conditions and expose the bases on which the Nazis organized the destruction of European Jews, but you can't explain Auschwitz.[27] Only those who planned the genocide can provide the detailed argumentation to justify the abominable act they committed. I can analyse the historic conditions and expose the bases on which the extremists organized the genocide of Tutsi and Hutu government opponents, but I can't explain why.

Nevertheless, we all ask ourselves this question – to which we know there is no answer – every day, sometimes several times a day, and we need to keep asking it in order to continue living together.

We must reflect on the historical conditions which made this genocide possible and on the motivations of those who exploited this possibility. It is a necessary task, which must be carried out in a scientific way. There's no point in politicizing or dramatizing the debate: the facts are sufficiently overwhelming and speak for themselves. But we mustn't stop there either. We must also ask ourselves if the course of history could have been changed and, if so, who had the power to prevent or stop the genocide and why that wasn't done.

Before going any further, I must apologize in advance for giving such a long explanation, but as you can see, the history of Rwanda is complex, confusing and riven with conflicts. You have to take

[27] Rony Brauman, *Devant le mal. Rwanda, un génocide en direct*, Paris, Arléa, 1994.

77

time to dissect it if you want to highlight the various elements which led us towards the genocide. As Charles Péguy said at the time of the Dreyfus Affair, some truths are long and you have to take a long time to tell them; other truths are boring and you have to tell them in a boring way.

I would also like to recall a fact which is important to understand what follows: Rwandans were subjected to colonization, which brought them both advantages and problems, but they also manipulated it, just as today they are manipulating the international press or the diplomatic community. That's how it is; in Rwanda as in Burundi, we are masters of the art of lying, probably more so than any other people. In fact, traditionally, lying is viewed positively: it is a sign of maturity and clear-sightedness. Why? Because it is often the only means of survival. Traditional arms are not enough; people have had to resort to cunning and lies to have a chance of survival. Perhaps lying, for us, plays the role which secret diplomacy played for a long time in Europe. In any case, we must bear in mind that historical falsification is not the result of an accident but of a strategy: it is part of the conflict. We rebuild the past, like Hitler who invented a past for Germany to justify his ambitions of domination or like Stalin who erased Trotsky's portrait from official photographs.

Where should we start?

With a non-fact. Every history book should open with a sentence like: 'It was in the seventeenth century that Rwanda was not discovered.' Because Rwanda was 'discovered' very late, at the end of the nineteenth century. It wasn't until 1894 that a German explorer, Franz Stuhlmann, succeeded where John Hanning Speke and Sir Henry Morton Stanley had failed in 1861 and 1876 respectively. The *New York Herald* gave Stanley the mission to find Livingstone; he got as far as the shores of Lake Tanganyika but was driven back by the arrows of skilful warriors and had to turn back.

The late colonization of Rwanda bore many consequences. When the first explorers arrived, their minds were already full of stereotypes and prejudices about blacks, or rather about 'Negroes'. After a century of colonizing the continent, they had become used to considering the social organization of traditional societies as an additional proof of black people's inferiority; they saw these societies as archaic and inefficient, as they had not led to the fantastic industrial progress which Europe was experiencing at that time. So when the whites eventually arrived in the Great Lakes region, they had a preconceived idea of what they would find there. In a sense, they did not 'discover' Rwanda: they went there to confirm the conceptions they had formed of the country before ever going there.

The influence of this ideology was particularly strong because, in the eyes of Europeans, the Great Lakes region had a unique status on the black continent. Bonaparte's conquest of Egypt in 1798 had led to a rediscovery of the civilization of the Pharaohs. Throughout the nineteenth century, European archaeologists were fascinated by this civilization born on the banks of the Nile. They demonstrated its extreme political refinement and its technological and artistic sophistication. The source of the Nile is at the foot of the hills – the 'mountains of the moon' as Ptolemy called them – which surround the curves of the Great Lakes. In a sense, discovering the source of the Nile amounted to tracing the roots of one of the most prestigious civilizations in the world. The inaccessibility of this mythical region did not discourage explorers; on the contrary, it increased its attraction for them.

Far from finding 'Negroes' surviving in a semi-vegetative state – which would have confirmed the prejudices of the first explorers about the superiority of the white race – the settlers had to deal with fearsome warriors and a highly organized society. This was not what they had expected to discover. They therefore had to find a rational explanation which would immediately clarify this historic anomaly.

I must exclude straight away a conclusion which some commentators would put forward at this point, motivated by obvious political considerations. It would be wrong to conclude that Rwanda's colonizers were *de facto* responsible for creating all the problems which have befallen our country, just because they arrived there with preconceived ideas and contributed towards shaping the society according to imported stereotypes – not only in the present, but also in its memory of the past. The whites undeniably created problems. They also undeniably brought solutions. I would not try to blame the whites for all our problems, unlike some who have specialized in this approach. As I describe the historical process of the establishment of colonization, I just want to show how at a time when traditional Rwandan society was going through a serious crisis, the whites provided tools of interpretation which had nothing to do with the history of Rwanda, but which were seized upon by Rwandans, initially to their benefit and later to their detriment.

This is how official historiography, or history as it has been taught in schools since Rwanda's independence in 1962, presents our past. Originally, the population of Rwanda was made up of Twa, descendants of the Pygmies, who were hunters and gatherers. Then came the Hutu, a branch of the Bantu people. The Hutu cleared the forests and developed agriculture. They lived with the Twa in perfect harmony. The Tutsi came last; they were cattle-herders who came from the Horn of Africa with their cows. The Tutsi cunningly seized power which until then had been in the hands of the Hutu. They imposed an oppressive, feudal system of monarchy and used the presence of Belgian settlers to consolidate their power. This situation lasted until the Hutu peasants were finally freed from serfdom, first by the social revolution of 1959 and the declaration of a republic, then by independence. Since then, under the regimes of President Kayibanda (1961–73) and President Habyarimana (1973–94), Rwanda has known peace and prosperity.

Obviously, this official history written from 1962 does not stand up to the scrutiny of factual, historical analysis. It is no more satisfactory than the official history which dominated before 1962, which it replaced.

One of its most prestigious advocates was Alexis Kagame. He belonged to the group of elders whose responsibility in the royal court was to know the order of succession to the throne. Unlike most monarchies, the crown was not handed down from father to the eldest son. There was a much more complex process of selection of pretenders and a group of specialists had to inform the court about this process. Alexis Kagame was therefore a very well educated and well informed man. Nevertheless, his account of the history of Rwanda consists of nothing but falsehoods from the first page to the last. All he did was legitimize the royal order. He kept silent about all the problems in the country and did not devote a single page to Hutu culture, to their role in the country's history, their lives or ambitions. He subscribed to the theory that Rwanda was conquered by a people of nomadic cattleherders who brought monarchy and development and did not include a single line on the monarchy which existed before the Tutsi arrived. Because it was not the Tutsi who invented the Rwandan monarchy; it existed before them; all they did was use it to their profit. This is not meant as a value judgement and does not detract at all from what the Tutsi brought to the country. But it is absurd to falsify history in such a grotesque fashion.

In the wake of Kagame, all historians, whatever their ethnic origin or their political opinions, dressed up Rwanda's history and turned it into a tool for political propaganda. It is not a coincidence that one of the main brains behind Hutu extremist ideology,

Ferdinand Nahimana, was a historian. The stories have been muddled to such an extent that today, no one can see straight any more.

I am not a historian and I certainly would not claim to be able to tell the 'true story' of my country in my own words, having challenged the propagandist version of history. But at least I can summarize the points on which most serious historians agree.

When the Germans took over Rwanda at the end of the nineteenth century, Rwandan society was in crisis. It is worth noting first that at least in this country, the borders created by the settlers coincided almost exactly with the country's traditional borders, with the result that the population was linguistically, culturally and religiously homogeneous. A very small proportion of the Kinyarwanda-speaking population found itself outside these borders, in Uganda and in Zaire.[28]

But territorial unity does not mean national unity. There was a sharp division between north and south. The south of the country was subjected to a regime of a centralized, single monarchy dominated by the Tutsi lineage, whereas the north, a region of rebellious mountain people, was under the domination of several Hutu kings. Rwandans from the north – the Bakiga or 'mountain people' – had a different name from those who lived in the south – the Banyanduga or 'people from Nduga'. The royal court was fighting to impose its authority over the south and to take the opportunity to extend it further north. Obviously, when the moment came, the traditional monarchs of the north, the Bakonde or 'land-clearers', stopped fighting among themselves to form a common front against the enemy from the south.

The whites who settled in Rwanda noticed these divisions straight away, but reacted in different ways, according to their own interests. The religious groups, particularly the White Fathers, were by far the best informed and the most sensitive to these subtle differences. They had settled across the country and lived with the people. Their main concern was to spread Christianity throughout the population. The congregation was split by a major conflict on this issue. Some White Fathers wanted to proceed with a gradual Christianization of the Rwandan population, while others preferred to rely on the conversion of the leaders, in accordance with the doctrine of the

---

[28] The Banyamulenge, who organized a rebellion in October 1996 in the Kivu region leading to the collapse of Zaire and the victory of the rebels led by Laurent-Désiré Kabila, are among these Kinyarwanda-speaking people who found themselves outside the borders of Rwanda at the time of colonization.

founder of the White Fathers' society, Cardinal Lavigerie. They believed that this would inevitably lead to the conversion of the masses. Eventually, this was the option which prevailed.

But having made that choice, the problem remained. Who were the leaders of the country? The White Fathers who had settled in the south, where the royal court was based, relied on the man who seemed to be the undisputed master of the country, the *mwami* (the king). But in the north, it was a different story. The *mwami* often had little or no authority outside the Nduga region. Unfortunately, the White Fathers who lived in the north failed to impress this point of view upon their hierarchical superiors. They were unable to convince them of the significance of these differences or to protect the traditional organization of the kingdoms in the north.

As a result, by overestimating the extent and legitimacy of the *mwami*'s real power and by relying entirely on his authority, the Church found itself taking sides, albeit reluctantly, and ending up on the side of the *mwami* and the Tutsi lineage. Of course, this side took this unexpected opportunity not only to strengthen its power over the local population, but also to extend it further north, into a region which it had never really managed to penetrate. A fatal mechanism had just been set in motion.

At this stage I have to go off on what might seem like a long tangent to explain a crucial point to which I have only referred in passing until now. I said that the White Fathers relied on the *mwami* and that the monarchy in the south was dominated by the Tutsi lineage. But what is a Tutsi? What is a Hutu? What is a Twa?

The mere fact of asking these three questions leads you immediately into a political discussion. Some people refuse to even formulate these questions and believe that any question beyond 'what is a Rwandan?' is entering the logic of those who believe that there are different races or ethnic groups in Rwanda.

Conversely, refusing to ask these questions amounts to an *a priori* belief that there are no significant differences between Hutu, Twa and Tutsi, which is completely absurd. It is one thing for a person not to want to state that they are Twa and to assert their national identity instead. It is another thing for people living in the same country to refuse to see that person as anything other than a Twa. Denying these facts is not going to help the situation.

Those who decided to commit genocide in Rwanda and organized and executed it did not go and ask Tutsi how they thought of themselves. They decided unilaterally that Tutsi no longer had the right to live just because they were Tutsi.

Therefore I don't think it's a good idea to refuse to ask the question and to bury our heads in the sand. But there are different ways of asking the question; the main thing is to find a formulation which does not presuppose a particular answer.

What is a Tutsi? What is a Hutu? What is a Twa? A Tutsi is a person whose father is a Tutsi. A Hutu is a person whose father is a Hutu. A Twa is a person whose father is a Twa. That is just about the only point on which everyone agrees. If you go beyond this fact, you enter the debate which ended in genocide.

The history of origins implies that there have always been Hutu, Tutsi and Twa in Rwanda. Aren't children taught that Gatwa, Gahutu and Gatutsi were brothers and that all three were sons of Kigwa?

Yes, but the heart of the debate – to use a euphemism – centres on the nature of the differences between these three 'brothers'. Are the categories of 'Hutu', 'Tutsi' and 'Twa' castes? Are they social classes? races? ethnic groups?

Before describing what separates them, it is better to remember what unites them. Hutu, Tutsi and Twa have lived on the same land since ancient times. I won't enter into the debate which has gone on since Rwanda was discovered to establish whether the Twa came from the forest or whether the Tutsi were Ethiopians who came with their herds five centuries ago. Up to this day, there are no scientific answers which go beyond hypotheses. These three groups speak the same language, Kinyarwanda, a language which is spoken only in Rwanda. In Burundi, Rwanda's 'pseudo-cousin', people speak Kirundi. They understand each other, but Kinyarwanda and Kirundi are two different languages. Hutu, Tutsi and Twa practise the same animist religion and have the same cultural traditions. Therefore, Rwandans have their own strong identity, especially if you compare them to their neighbours. This identity is so strong that a French academic, Dominique Franche, even wrote that the Rwandan people constitute an 'ethnic group' in itself, which I doubt.

Because aside from these similarities, there are also strong differences. I don't know whether we should talk about races, ethnic groups, clans, social, religious, cultural or linguistic groups. What I have noticed is that each of us belongs to an ethnic group and we know it. I have also noticed that the stories which children are told in the evenings differ according to the ethnic group to which the family belongs. For example, in the royal court, there was a particular form of war poetry. A man would gain credit in the eyes of those around him if he spent the evenings praising murders carried out during the war. The historian Alexis Kagame collected these kinds of stories during the 1930s. This form of poetry does not exist in Hutu culture.

Each person is able to locate their identity, from childhood. Most people who claim that they did not know their ethnic origin before the genocide or that it never influenced their life are lying. They are saying this for political reasons.

I want to choose my words carefully. It is not true that, on the one side, there are Tutsi children who have been brought up to be warriors from an early age and indoctrinated to kill, and on the other, Hutu children who have been pacified by a democratic, republican and pluralist culture. It would be idiotic to make such a statement. In the countryside, Hutu peasant children have also been indoctrinated and trained to hate. From an early age, they have been taught to beware of the Tutsi who had been their masters, who had reduced them to a state of slavery and who would use every means to try to wrench power back from them. This discourse took various forms, including the most extremist ones. Sometimes it consisted of just a few remarks which, after being repeated in many circumstances, ended up creating stereotypes such as 'don't eat like a Hutu' or 'don't be arrogant like a Tutsi'.

The three ethnic groups have different attitudes towards sexual modesty. For the Twa, sexuality follows specific rules. The Hutu have a reputation for great sexual modesty. The Tutsi, on the other hand, were notorious for practising incest and adultery. In 1931, the king was even deposed in part because of his sexual escapades which had taken on such proportions that they became a source of embarrassment even to his close advisers. This cultural attitude is very marginal among Tutsi, but it is unthinkable among Hutu. That said, in the vast majority of cases, all Rwandans behave in the same way: shyness and discretion have always been the rule.

It is equally absurd to deny that there are physical stereotypes. Tutsi have finer facial features and are taller than Hutu. There are many exceptions to this stereotype. One of my Tutsi friends is 1.50m tall, has dark skin, a wide nose and a stocky build. There are different explanations for these departures from the stereotypes. In his case, I think he has Twa roots. Some Twa were employed as executioners in the royal court. In particular, they had the responsibility for executing young unwed Tutsi mothers. Sometimes they obeyed, but sometimes they spared their victim and kept her for themselves. Children were born from these unions; some of them have even been very successful in life – I could mention several names which would surprise you. During these last decades, there were also lots of mixed marriages, especially in the towns. The structure of these marriages is uneven. It is not unusual for a successful Hutu businessman to marry a Tutsi woman. Such a union increases his social standing, but it also represents an investment in terms of economic alliance and access to economic networks.

During a round table discussion on tolerance and reconciliation, the Minister for Education, Joseph Nsengimana, thought it would be clever to state that ethnic groups are just political slogans invented by the whites. But it was not the whites who invented the words Hutu, Tutsi and Twa, nor did they invent the traditional stories and tales which articulate different ways of thinking. The whites conceptualized differences which they observed. They imposed on Rwandan society a set of ideologies which were based on real differences. They transformed these differences by making them deeper and cutting off the bridges between ethnic groups, but they did not create them. Steeped in their racial ideology, they froze these differences and organized them into a hierarchy.

If these three categories did not correspond to three different races, why did they talk about races? They could have used different words to describe this reality. They could have talked about castes, for examples. Why didn't they?

This takes us back precisely to the circumstances in which the discovery of Rwanda took place. As a mythical land which had long been inaccessible, as the presumed birthplace of the civilization of the Pharaohs, Rwanda could not have an ordinary history. But as I told you, explorers were surprised to find in Rwanda a population which was very organized, instead of the primitive people they were expecting to colonize. They saw that this population was made up of three groups with very different demographic proportions: the Hutu, who represented the vast majority of the population (around 85 per cent of Rwandans), the Tutsi (14 per cent) and the Twa (1 per cent). They also observed three different physical types, which coincided approximately – but only approximately – with the three categories Hutu, Tutsi and Twa. Finally, as even the least observant among them would have noticed, each of the three groups had an economic specialization – the Twa tended to be hunters or potters, the Hutu were farmers and the Tutsi were cattle-keepers or traders – and there was a hierarchy among them.

All these facts have been established historically and there is no point trying to deny them. What was not established was the explanation of these differences.

The whites dealt with the *mwami* and his court because they wielded political, economic, cultural and religious power over large parts of the country. As the *mwami* was descended from Tutsi lineage, the whites concluded that all Tutsi were masters of the country; they 'forgot' to take into account the existence of the northern monarchies which were controlled by Hutu and they assimilated all Tutsi to the royal lineage – including ordinary Tutsi who had no wealth at all.

There are different explanations for this simplistic vision or caricature of reality: it could have been the result either of an inability to take into account a complex situation, or of a slightly cynical attempt at efficiency which made the colonial authorities deal directly with the strongest to the detriment of the weakest, or of the hold of ideology. The Tutsi began to think of themselves as a superior people whereas the Hutu were internalizing their inferior social and intellectual status. In any case, in the end, Rwandans became the people they had been taught they were.

The Tutsi of the royal court had very distinctive physical characteristics, as you can see in photographs: they were tall, with fine features. Some writers have attributed these physical differences to the conditions of hygiene and nutrition in the court. Others see it as evidence of a specific genetic inheritance. Whatever the truth, for the whites there could be only one explanation: Tutsi belonged to a different race, the superior race. They were descendants of an Indo-European branch who, after migrating through the Horn of Africa, had come to impose its domination on the primitive Negroes of the Great Lakes region, several centuries ago. Suddenly this provided the explanation for the very sophisticated political and social organization which the whites had discovered in Rwanda: it was the work of the local whites, the Tutsi.

As I told you, most historians today believe that the Tutsi just turned to their advantage the political institutions which had been created long ago by the Hutu, or copied institutions which the Hutu had set up in the north of the country, and continued to control them until colonial administration put an end to this. If the settlers had taken into account the realities of the country and if they had refrained from imposing their simplified vision, no doubt Rwanda's history would have been very different. If power had not been given in its entirety to one group (the Tutsi) to the detriment of the other two groups (the Hutu and the Twa) and if, subsequently, it had not been taken away in its entirety from that group and handed over in its entirety to another group (the Hutu), we might have been able to avoid a genocide. If colonization were to be put on trial, that is where the accusations would be levelled. The Belgian settlers implanted racist stereotypes which we were not able to shake off. But the responsibility of these settlers should not obscure the responsibility of Hutu and Tutsi extremists who, one after the other and each in their own way, exploited these stereotypes which served the purposes of their struggle to conquer or to hold on to power.

Anyway, one of the consequences of the colonial administration's attitude was to confine the population within watertight groups. For a long time there had been a certain mobility between these three groups: a cattle-owning Hutu could enter the Tutsi group, while an impoverished Tutsi could become a Hutu. From the colonial period onwards, such changes were no longer possible. In 1931, the administration imposed an identity booklet which specified 'ethnic' identity. During the process of registration, some people were declared to be 'Tutsi' because they owned cattle; others became 'Hutu' because they farmed the land. That also explains why you find people who correspond to the stereotypes of their group side by side with others who do not share any of their characteristics. Those who deny the existence of ethnic groups in Rwanda often use such cases, which appear to contradict the stereotypes, to prove their theory.

So many decisions were quite arbitrary ...

Yes, and these arbitrary decisions cost many lives during the genocide. Militiamen manning the roadblocks searched people who were trying to flee. Woe betide those whose identity cards bore the word 'Tutsi': those five letters amounted to a death sentence, with immediate execution.

Let's come back to the situation just before the First World War. To sum up, Europeans discovered a complex political and social situation in Rwanda which they interpreted in terms of good and evil, either through incompetence or deliberately. They based their power on that of the Tutsi minority, reinforcing the advantageous position it already enjoyed and aggravating tensions between Hutu and Tutsi. These policies were bound to create problems. Didn't they create reticence among some Europeans?

Of course. You could even say that the German administrators held the opposite view to that of the White Fathers, most of whom were Belgian and French. The White Fathers wanted to back the Tutsi elite exclusively because, as I told you, they were relying on the conversion of the leaders for the conversion of the masses. The Germans, on the other hand, had clearly understood that it would not be possible to maintain control over a country where power was so unevenly distributed.

In 1914, the German interim resident drafted an insightful text which showed clearly that he had understood the contradictions already afflicting Rwandan society and which were likely to be aggravated by the colonial system: 'Throughout the country one can sense a deep bitterness on the part of the Hutu against Tutsi domination. Personally I believe that that is where danger lies for us and we certainly cannot prevent it by simply making our guns available to the Tutsi [...] I am not suggesting breaking with the system of Tutsi residence and domination, but gradually reforming the system of authority in ways which take our own interests into account, unlike the current system which makes us unpopular by depriving 97 per cent of the population of all its rights for the benefit of a ruling tribe.'[29]

Perhaps this policy would have been adopted if the Germans had remained in control of the country. But the outcome of the war led to a different fate. In 1916, the Belgians grabbed Rwanda and Burundi. After losing the Great War, the Germans were obliged to give up their colonies. The League of Nations gave Belgium a mandate to run Rwanda and Burundi. The following 45 years of colonial administration had a profound effect on the 'kingdom of Urundi'.

The Belgians briefly considered punishing the Tutsi for having collaborated with the Germans; but they thought better of it and decided to continue relying on the *mwami*. The Belgians' main objective was to rationalize the exploitation of Rwanda. As they built roads and all sorts of infrastructure, they also extended across the whole kingdom the administrative and especially the fiscal rules which prevailed in the south.

---

[29] Quoted by Dominique Franche in *Généalogie du génocide rwandais*, in *Les Temps modernes*, Paris, May–June 1995.

This extension of the *mwami*'s zone of influence was to his advantage, but he also lost much of his autonomy. Conflicts between the court and the colonial authorities became more frequent. Eventually the king was seen as too stubborn; he was deposed in 1931 and replaced by his son, Rudahigwa, who was much more conciliatory.

The Roman Catholic Church was the first to benefit from this change. Under the authority of Archbishop Classe, it became the biggest power in the country; as the biggest employer, the biggest property owner and the biggest provider of education and welfare, the ecclesiastical institution developed in perfect symbiosis with the colonial authorities. The power of the Church in Rwanda was out of proportion with what was happening in other colonies. Indeed, Belgium is a Catholic monarchy. Unlike France, there was no separation of powers between the Church and the State, and at least at that time, the interests of the administrators merged with the interests of priests.

Predictably, the huge majority of the population experienced colonization as a new form of oppression. The living conditions of Hutu and ordinary Tutsi (those who did not descend from royal lineage and did not enjoy any privileges) deteriorated rapidly. Certain duties and taxes which originally had only been collected locally were extended across the whole country. Those who revolted were made to suffer violent reprisals, symbolized by the *chicote* – beatings. The traditional northern Hutu elite lost almost all its power and prerogatives to the Tutsi aristocracy from the south – the Banyanduga – supported by the colonial administration and the Church.

Did the population revolt against the settlers?

Not at all, because the Belgians, quite cynically, relied on the Tutsi to implement their policies, which they knew were unpopular. Only the Tutsi were visible and exposed. But they derived substantial financial and honorary benefits. They attracted growing hatred and resentment, especially as many Tutsi chiefs and deputy chiefs abused their power with complete impunity. Tension continued to increase until the eve of the Second World War.

What was the reaction of the Hutu elite which had been ousted from power?

I don't know what its reaction was; I don't even know if that elite reacted as an oppressed ethnic minority. We must remember that the royal families in the north were constantly fighting each other. You could say that seizing or losing power was just a part of life. What I do know is that several factors strengthened a new wave of public opinion which eventually resulted in the declaration of the 'Manifesto of the Bahutu' in the 1950s, the social revolution and, later, the declaration of the republic and the independence of Rwanda.

The most important of these factors was the emergence of a new Hutu elite. Few Hutu had access to education. The Belgians more or less deliberately restricted access to children of the Tutsi elite because, logically, these were the children who would be called upon to succeed their parents and to lead the country. But within the Church, a new sensitivity had emerged in the aftermath of the Second World War. The White Fathers had become more sensitive to ideas of justice and equality and no longer accepted ethnic discrimination which was systematically unfavourable to the Hutu.

Some people claim that this development was linked to a sociological change within the White Fathers' society: that the fathers who arrived in Rwanda in the 1950s, most of whom were Flemish, transposed the conflict in Belgium between the Flemish and the Walloons. According to this theory, the Flemish identified with the oppressed Hutu and, from then on, decided to fight their cause.

I'm not sure what to think of this kind of theory. Whatever the truth, the White Fathers admitted an increasing number of Hutu to the minor and major seminaries. Some of these novices went on to become priests, strengthening the power of Hutu within the ecclesiastical institution which until then had been made up almost exclusively of Tutsi. But others abandoned their vocation as novices to become involved in politics. This was the case of Grégoire Kayibanda, for example, the future first president of Rwanda.

In September 1957, an event occurred which revealed the full power of this new wave of thinking. The United Nations had planned an official mission to Rwanda to consider the political future of the territory. The Superior Council of the country, a kind of local representative chamber made up of Tutsi aristocracy, addressed a letter to the delegates of this mission entitled 'Statement of clarification'.

In this document, the Council reduced the problems of Rwanda to 'the question of human relations between whites and blacks'; it portrayed itself as a defender of the national cause and a representative of the oppressed black people, two themes which were very much in vogue in the United Nations at the time.

The new political leaders who had emerged from the 1956 elections – and who were viewed as more representative by the Hutu peasantry – met in Gitarama in March 1957. They believed that Rwanda's problems could not be reduced to the question of colonial dependence and that those who claimed to be speaking for the Rwandan people were only speaking for themselves and acting to defend their own interests. Of course, they wanted Rwanda to become independent. But once this freedom was returned to them, they did not want it to be taken away again by those who had already enjoyed and abused a privileged position during the colonial era. In short, they distanced themselves from the traditional Tutsi elite which claimed to be acting on behalf of all Rwandans when in fact it represented only itself.

So they drafted a 'Note on the social aspect of the racial problem in Rwanda', better known as 'the Manifesto of the Bahutu'. This document stressed 'the agonizing reality of the fundamental Hutu–Tutsi problem' and denounced the state of inferiority in which the Hutu were maintained by the Tutsi minority, with the approval of the trustee administration: 'Some people have wondered whether this is a social conflict or a racial conflict. We believe that the question is academic. In reality and in people's thoughts, it is both. But we can be more specific: the problem is above all one of political monopoly held by one race [the Tutsi]; given the overall structures currently in place, this political monopoly has turned into an economic and social monopoly, which has also managed to turn into a cultural monopoly, given the *de facto* selection in education.'

The style of this document led some observers to view it as the main reference for Hutu extremist ideology. It is true that the Parmehutu, the Party of the Movement for Hutu Emancipation, drew most of its arguments from this document. But many commentators recognized beyond certain awkward formulations (the use of the term 'race' was probably inappropriate) the expression of legitimate demands by an oppressed and impoverished people.

In any case, in the eyes of the trustee administration, this document constituted an official declaration of the existence of a substitute Hutu elite; it emerged just at the right time, when relations between the Belgians and their former allies, the Tutsi, were rapidly deteriorating.

Indeed the Tutsi elite was beginning to cause intractable problems for the trustee administration. On the one hand, it was becoming increasingly unpopular, partly because of the negative role which had been imposed upon it by the colonial administration; there was a risk that the hatred which people felt towards the elite would turn against the settlers. On the other hand, some senior Tutsi civil servants, who had studied in Europe, had seized upon the theme of decolonization, as they quickly saw the political benefits which they could derive from it. They hoped that by edging the Belgians out in the name of a just cause – the struggle for freedom of a black people oppressed by whites – they could win on both fronts at once: they could take hold of all the power inside the country and acquire recognition for a new historical legitimacy outside the country.

In other words, the country's political evolution was precipitated by the coincidence of these various phenomena: the emergence of a substitute Hutu elite, the willingness of the Church to back this new elite and the escalation of conflicts between the Tutsi historical elite and the colonial authorities. Over three years, from 1959 to 1962, Rwanda went through several major changes: a 'social revolution', during which the Belgian administration and the Church lined up on the side of the Hutu, who seized power; the declaration of a republic, which prevented the Tutsi from appointing a successor to the dead king and from returning to power; and the declaration of independence, which neither the Belgians nor the United Nations could prevent. But 30 years have gone by since then and it is hard to see how these events necessarily brought on the genocide in 1994.

I don't believe that anything 'necessarily' brought on the genocide in Rwanda. Men are products but not prisoners of their history. They decide themselves what they do. I felt it was necessary to summarize the history in order to situate the various elements which enabled the crime of genocide to take place. Actually, I haven't finished listing these elements. The genocide had been made possible; but that doesn't mean that it was inevitable.

From the day that Rwanda declared itself a republic, it was trapped inside this mechanism. The difficulties experienced by Rwanda or by the state only aggravated the contradictions which were inherent in society. The risk of a genocide gradually increased as the elite in power strengthened its domination by brandishing the ethnic threat, against a backdrop of economic crisis. The differences had always been there. The whites conceptualized and froze them. The extremists turned them into a political programme. This was the fatal mechanism in which our country had embarked.

What were these contradictions?

I will mention five. First of all, there is the conflict between geography and demography. Rwanda is a small country – 27,000 square kilometres, of which only 17,000 square kilometres can be farmed – which has always been overpopulated: Rwanda has the highest population density in the whole of black Africa, with almost 300 inhabitants per square kilometre, compared to 25 on the rest of the continent. It is not so much a question of defining the threshold of overpopulation, but of studying the inter-relation between population growth and increase in wealth production.

Rwanda has one of the highest rates of demographic growth in Africa. On the other hand, economic growth is very slow. The progress of agriculture is painfully slow. There is not enough land and the soil is eaten away by erosion. So, for example, the shortage of land has meant that falling prices of tea and coffee could not be compensated for by an increase in production.

As for industry and services, they play a marginal role in this deeply rural and isolated economy. For many years the MRND's ideology of 'ruralization' was praised: it enabled people to stay in the countryside; Rwanda's food needs could be more or less met through a very intensive and rational exploitation of the land; and Rwanda could avoid the urban explosion which was taking place in every other country in Africa. But today we are suffering all the consequences of this ideology: the countryside is overpopulated and the land has been over-exploited whereas industry and services are underdeveloped and incapable of producing new wealth.

I don't see a solution to this conflict between geography – or Rwanda's natural features and its economic organization – and demography.

Yet it is a simple equation: either you increase wealth production – and you said that a significant increase in wealth is not possible in Rwanda – or you slow down population growth.

But in Rwandan culture this second option cannot be considered.

Is it Rwandan culture or the Church which is hostile to birth control?

The two go hand in hand. Only urban households which have a high level of education have changed their demographic behaviour and limited the number of births. But we're talking about a tiny minority of the population. For the rest, having lots of children is a kind of equivalent of social security in the event of sickness, protection against attacks if the children are boys, or a pension fund for old age. So any demographic plan is bound to fail unless it can resolve the problem of wealth management and guarantee welfare, security, justice and retirement. In Rwanda all these aspects are linked. Furthermore, the Rwandan Church is generally conservative and its attitude towards birth control is no exception.

The second contradiction is the absence of a coherent national history. I won't come back to this point which we have already discussed at length. I just want to stress its importance. A couple cannot live in harmony unless the man and the woman who have had an argument can discuss their behaviour and agree on what happened and on what they need to do to ensure that it doesn't happen again. This discussion has never taken place between Hutu and Tutsi. We don't agree on what has happened, so we are unable to agree on the future or to prevent further conflicts.

At the time of the social revolution, the Hutu portrayal of their own history was based on a model inspired by European history. They compared themselves to the serfs of the Middle Ages and saw the Tutsi as feudal lords. This made them feel that they were struggling for freedom from the domination of a caste of nobles. In other words, Rwanda was experiencing its version of the 1789 Revolution.

But this was not only a social revolution; it was also a national revolution. The Hutu were motivated in their actions by the belief that they represented the original people who had inalienable and eternal rights on Rwandan soil. Suddenly they viewed the Tutsi not only as a race, but as a foreign race, a race of conquerors who had imposed their domination over the Hutu and had to be driven out of the country. It was their turn to adopt the ideology which some Tutsi had used to justify their dominant position and to refuse all notion of power sharing.

By the way, King Rudahigwa himself had begun worrying about the possible consequences of extremist Tutsi ideology when some high dignitaries in the court claimed to be descendants of noble conquerors who were accountable to no one. Rudahigwa soon disowned one of his closest aides, Alexis Kagame, even though he had asked him to write the history of Rwanda. When he read *Inganji Karinga*, the king immediately saw the dangers inherent in this way of presenting the role of Tutsi in history. But the harm had been done. Tutsi extremism encouraged the development of Hutu extremism, with each group disputing its historical legitimacy, placing the Hutu–Tutsi division at the centre of every political debate and unscrupulously exploiting the most dangerous aspects of this rhetoric. Up to this day we are carrying the burden of these ideologies which spawn political violence.

But is political violence a new phenomenon in Rwanda?

It has always existed; it constitutes the third contradiction in the country. For a long time, the official version was that the republic declared by Grégoire Kayibanda was a pluralist democracy which safeguarded national unity. It only ever safeguarded the power of the minority who had appropriated it.

In the eyes of his contemporaries, Grégoire Kayibanda freed the Hutu masses from Tutsi domination. It is true that he played a decisive role in overturning a social order which was despised by the huge majority of the population. Nevertheless, he put in place a political system which would not tolerate the slightest opposition, wherever it came from. Those close to him exploited the opportunity of the political system born out of the social revolution to exclude from power those who did not belong to the same ethnic group, as well as those who did not come from the same region (the south). We must remember that the inter-ethnic disturbances in the years 1959 to 1962 claimed several hundred if not several thousand lives.

And more than 100,000 refugees.

That is the fourth point I wanted to mention. After the riots of 1959, thousands of Tutsi fled to Burundi, Uganda, Tanzania and Zaire. In their minds, this was just a temporary migration. It lasted 30 years.

Here and there along the borders, there were attempts to negotiate the return of the refugees. But extremists on both sides opposed them. Inside Rwanda, people had appropriated property belonging to those who had fled. It was not in their interest to see them return. Conversely, in Uganda, the refugees included most of those who had ruled the country for decades without sharing power and without any scruples. For them, negotiating their return inevitably meant losing a significant share of the power which they claimed in its entirety. Therefore the only way to return was by force. The hardliners won on all fronts: the refugee question was not solved. As a consequence, the few thousand refugees in 1962, who could easily have been reintegrated into society, grew to 600,000 in 1994. As you know, they did not return to Rwanda through negotiations, but by force. Meanwhile, a genocide had taken place.

The fifth and last point is this: as a priest, I wonder about the conditions in which Rwandans were converted to Christianity. The conversion of the king led to the conversion of his subjects. Did it lead to the conversion of their souls? I am baffled by the faith of some Rwandans who were converted. Is it necessary to recall that adherence to Christianity meant exemption from certain duties? There is a fairly substantial difference between the social practices of the rituals of the Church – let's say piety or devotion – and intimate adherence to the evangelical message expressed through the practice of faith. During the genocide, I saw people wearing a medal of the Virgin Mary around their neck and holding a machete. We are forced to ask ourselves questions.

As you can see, the years 1962 to 1990 were a false respite for Rwanda. Society was already bearing all the contradictions which were exacerbated to the extreme during the war of 1990 to 1994 and plunged it into the genocide.

It seems that all these contradictions were leading Rwanda towards chaos. But there is a significant difference between a revolt, a revolution, or even a war, and a genocide. The insane plan of the conception and implementation of a genocide – the methodical destruction of a people on the grounds of their suspected or real ethnic group – remains an enigma. The question 'why?' remains unanswered.

Isn't it to be expected that words fail us in explaining a reality as inhuman as genocide?

I was disturbed by my visit to the Yad VaShem Memorial. The site – the museum, the exhibitions, the monuments – are a success. Yad VaShem sets out very clearly the events which took place in Europe between 1933 and 1945. The museum enables us to understand the mechanisms which made the genocide of the Jews possible. The memorial is very moving.

But we can't help asking certain questions: how is it possible that human beings decide coldly to destroy a people? How is it conceivable that in a civilization as developed as European civilization, logistics on such a scale were put to use for such horrific ends? Did the genocide take place unknown to the world? There is evidence to indicate that the rest of the world was aware of what was happening. But what did they do? The Shoah was implemented according to plan. The international community is faced with the problem of having let this happen. I am aware of the fact that

Western democracies were already involved in a fight to defeat Nazism and that the Soviet empire had also joined in the struggle. But are we sure that all possible measures were taken to stop this genocide as soon as possible or to limit its scale? I doubt it. I don't have a convincing explanation to understand this phenomenon.

I did not find an answer to the question 'why?' What were the causes of this genocide? The memorial doesn't answer this question. Maybe there is no answer.

I am also struck by the similarity of the mechanisms with what happened in Rwanda: the psychological preparation of the elites, the role of the media in conditioning the masses, the dehumanization of victims before their execution, the sophistication and cruelty of the methods of death, the erasure of all traces of the crimes and of the victims' memories, and the denial of facts.

However, there are at least three major differences between these two tragedies. The first relates to the procedure of execution. In Germany, it was possible for citizens not to know what was happening, even though historians have shown that many people knew more than they ever admitted. In Rwanda, this was not possible. The genocide was not executed in secret by a minority. It took place in broad daylight. It proclaimed itself as a political programme and the whole population was at least witness to the crime.

The second difference relates to duration. Nazism lasted twelve years and the Final Solution four years. In Rwanda, it all unfolded within 100 days, three months during which the country was poisoned, hypnotized by violence. A side issue is the attitude of the victims, which was very similar to that of the Jews during the Second World War. In *The Destruction of the European Jews*, the historian Raul Hilberg presents the account of a German, Hermann Friedrich Graebe, who witnessed an execution:

> The father was holding the hand of a boy about ten years old and was speaking to him softly; the boy was fighting his tears. The father pointed to the sky, stroked his head, and seemed to explain something to him ... I remember a girl, slim and with black hair, who passed close to me, pointed to herself and said, 'Twenty three years' ... The people, completely naked, went down some steps which were cut in the clay wall of the pit and clambered over the heads of the people lying there to the place where the SS man directed them. Then they lay down in front of the dead or the injured people; some caressed those who were still alive and spoke to them in a low voice. Then I heard a series of shots.

I was shocked by this attitude of submission on the part of the Jews. Why didn't they all revolt like the Jews in the Warsaw ghetto? In

Rwanda, it was the same phenomenon. Many Tutsi didn't even try to flee. It was as if they had absorbed the fate which had been planned for them by those who organized the genocide. There was a war in Rwanda in 1994 but it had nothing to do with the genocide. The Tutsi did not die bearing arms: they were killed in cold blood, with the same concern to strip them of their dignity and humiliate them even into the hereafter.

The third fundamental difference between the two genocides relates to chronology. One took place 50 years ago, the other in 1994. Between these two dates, genocide was declared unlawful. Treaties were signed, courts were invented, institutions were created. The world was rebuilt around the notion of genocide for the purpose of preserving its humanity. And yet, genocide took place in Rwanda. It took place before your eyes, thanks to the television crews. How is that possible? We have to admit that intervention mechanisms are still not adequate. Everyone knew from the beginning that a genocide was under way. There is an obligation to assist a people whose survival is at risk. What was done?

It is as if we learn nothing from history. Sometimes I wonder if it is still worth investigating human rights violations. We publish reports which require a huge amount of work, for which we take enormous risks. So what? Who reads them? And what happens afterwards? What is the point of building monuments to the memory of victims? Go to Nyamata and you will see the grave of Antonella Locatelli, the Italian woman killed in 1992 whom we talked about earlier. She died in order to save 300 Tutsi. What was the use of her sacrifice? Her grave rests against the wall of a church in which several thousand Tutsi were killed two years later: today their remains lie in a large mass grave nearby. And straight opposite the church, a huge orphanage has been built in haste.

PART III

TIME IS AGAINST US

7 The Duty of Justice and the Duty of Memory

It took less than a hundred days to carry out the genocide. It seems as if it will take more than a hundred years to bring the perpetrators to justice. Before discussing the problem of justice, could you tell us who you think is guilty?

I am not in position to state who is guilty and who is innocent. I am not a judge or a magistrate. Worse still: I am a priest; my duty towards believers is not to try them or sentence them, but to help them find their way. But as a citizen, I do have opinions. In his book *L'Etat criminel* [The Criminal State], Yves Ternon distinguishes different levels of responsibility among perpetrators of genocide. At the top of the pyramid, there are those who plan it. Their decisions are implemented by technicians, who are supported by those who carry out orders. But the chain doesn't stop there. Yves Ternon also describes the role of the spectators. Their guilt does not depend on action: their presence at the scene of the crime and their tacit agreement, their indifference or their failure to revolt are elements which determine the 'success' of the enterprise.

The genocide was planned by those who were running the country so that they wouldn't have to share power. I don't know whether the head of state, his wife and the presidential entourage initiated the plan to carry out a genocide or whether they 'only' manipulated the plan and ensured its 'success' in order to hold on to power; but they bear total responsibility. The majority of MRND officials, at the national as well as the local levels, were also involved. We should not generalize and I want to insist on the principle of individual responsibility first. No doubt there are MRND officials here and there whose only crime is to have protected their career by supporting or relying on a party whose doctrine is well known.

Other parties or fragments of parties were also heavily involved – for example the *Coalition pour la défense de la République* (CDR), the most extremist of Rwandan parties. There were also the 'Power' factions which broke away from various political parties as of 1993: MDR Power, *Parti libéral* Power, *Parti social démocrate* Power. All these parties which were competing in the democratic debate included people – Hutu extremists, to be precise – who put ethnic divisions above any other kind of division. Together they made up the 'Power' faction.

Intellectuals bear an overwhelming share of responsibility. The ideologues of the genocide were not unemployed young men from Nyamirambo [a poor district of Kigali] but highly intelligent people who had studied at the best universities in Europe or the United States.

The Tutsi were demonized and systematically considered as enemies. One of the consequences of this demonization was that those Tutsi who did not want to support the RPF soon had no other choice but to do so, thus justifying with hindsight the accusations levelled against them by the MRND, but also strengthening the power of the RPF. The circle was complete.

Those in power demonized the opposition and identified it as the enemy in order to justify in advance their refusal to share power – which they had no intention of sharing anyway. The opposition could not win: within a short time the state was portraying the multi-party system as a divisive instrument implanted by the enemy. For many people, this simplistic explanation was obviously much easier to understand than long reflections on democracy and the role of elections.

I don't know whether the timing was a coincidence or whether it was a deliberate strategy, but the fact that the RPF launched a guerrilla war in the north of Rwanda from October 1990, at a time when it was obviously not in a position to go beyond harassment at the borders, was enormously useful to the MRND and especially to the CDR. The CDR used the RPF aggression as a good reason for blocking negotiations and preventing the peaceful return of the refugees. The RPF too benefited from negotiations being blocked: public opinion viewed the internal democratic opposition as incapable of unblocking the situation, so the armed rebellion became the spearhead for the fight against dictatorship. At least that was how the foreign press viewed the RPF in its early days; this earned it international support which turned out to be very useful in not having to answer for its crimes.

The Church, or rather its members, also have a share of responsibility. I'll come back to that point later.

Many intellectuals failed in their duty. Lawyers, university professors and politicians could all have done more. They tolerated the system. We published articles and reports on the Bugesera massacres. We had predicted the disaster and anyone who wanted to know could have had access to evidence. When I say 'we', I am not only thinking of the *Kinyamateka* team or the members of ADL. There were many newspapers and organizations doing this work. International organizations also intervened. The International Federation of Human Rights, Human Rights Watch and Amnesty International published many reports. An international commission of inquiry went to Rwanda in January 1993; it published an alarming report one month later. A particular newspaper or organization could be accused of bias, but not the press as a whole nor organizations as a whole. But these intellectuals closed their eyes, while others simply supported the cause of the killers.

Businessmen and wealthy traders took advantage of the situation: Félicien Kabuga is just one of many examples. Every war drags in its wake its share of unscrupulous opportunists and greedy vultures. Fortunes were amassed at the refugees' expense. Looting soon became a means of subsistence.

Some women are guilty. Unfortunately the cruelty which some of them displayed was equal to that of the men. I remember a woman in my home commune of Masango who told the militiamen when they arrived to look inside the jugs in case there were children hiding there. I also remember a woman who spent a whole day on the river bank killing other women who were handed over to her with a hammer. She was neither drunk nor under the effect of drugs. She was acting of her own free will, without any difficulty or remorse, without feelings; on the contrary, she was motivated by a great sense of morality. She was fulfilling a duty: kill so as not to be killed, eliminate the women who would otherwise give birth tomorrow to the oppressors of her own children.

Some children are also guilty. Unfortunately respect for paternal authority, which is a dogma in Rwanda, turned into a tragedy. Children idealize their father and want to imitate him at any cost. Some felt a sense of pride at seeing their father killing 'enemies of the country'. Once I was told about a child whose father had refused to take him to the roadblocks and who cried out: 'But I want to work too!'[30] His father told him that he was too young and would not be able to do anything. The child replied calmly and coldly, 'But at least I can kill a child of my own age!' We should not be surprised at such reactions in a family environment where killing had become an ordinary act and not killing an act of betrayal.

The spectators are also guilty. I am aware that it was very difficult, not to say impossible, for people to escape the pressure of their sur-

[30] The term 'to work' took on the meaning 'to kill' during the genocide.

roundings. Rwanda is a small and overpopulated country. Everyone knows everyone else. No one can escape attention; absences are noticed immediately and explanations are demanded. Some people died simply because they were not present at the roadblocks. But it was possible to behave in a more appropriate way. There is a difference, which may seem very subtle, between a silent spectator and one who shouts and encourages acts by chanting or other war-like behaviour. If the spectators had remained silent, the killers would have behaved differently.

As you can see, when you talk about responsibility and guilt, you have to be careful and think properly before making a judgement. If there is to be justice in this country, it must be impartial and conclude its investigations. The peasants who had hardly any education and who killed Tutsi because they were obeying orders or because they wanted to steal a mattress or a goat are guilty and must be tried. But those who issued the orders or created the historical conditions which enabled such crimes to take place must also be tried. All of them, whatever their ethnic group, whatever their social rank, whatever the prestige or the secret protection they enjoy today, they too must be tried.

Justice is a basic right. Every human being has the right to justice. In the case of Rwanda, this right has taken on a fundamental importance since the genocide: delivering justice has become a necessity, not only for the dead, not only for the survivors, but for the killers themselves and for all those who witnessed the massacres. How could we carry on living together without justice?

I would like to relate a testimony quoted by Françoise Bouchet-Saulnier, the legal adviser of Médecins sans frontières, in *Maudits soient les yeux fermés*. It's the story of a Hutu peasant who hid a Tutsi family. 'At the market they would check our purchases to see if there was enough to eat for one person, two people or ten people.' He managed to feed the family secretly for several weeks. Until the day militiamen came to search his house. 'Now prove that you are a good Hutu', ordered one of the militiamen, handing him a machete. 'If you don't kill these cockroaches[31] yourself, we will kill your wife and children. Make your choice!' So he killed with his own hands the family he had hidden and fed for several weeks. But that was not enough for the *interahamwe*. Before they left, in order to punish this bad Hutu who had been an 'accomplice' of the Tutsi, they killed his wife and children. Today, this peasant is asking: 'Who

---

[31] Cockroaches [*inyenzi* in Kinyarwanda] was the nickname given to Tutsi.

am I? If those militiamen are not punished, then who am I? If they are still free, then what about me, where do I belong?'

Rwandans want justice. Crimes were committed. People were killed. Survivors, victims of mutilations, widows and orphans are waiting for a judgement which will acknowledge their history and bring meaning back into their life. There are also innocent people in prison who, along with their families, are waiting to be cleared of all suspicion. Finally, there are all sorts of guilty people, killers and opportunists, who are in Rwanda or abroad. It is immoral that they have not been arrested yet. Whether dead or alive, the victims must be recognized as victims and must know that we consider them as victims. Whether dead or alive, the guilty must be declared guilty and recognize themselves as guilty. Whether dead or alive, the innocent must also be declared innocent. Justice does not have several faces; it has only one, and it must be the same for everybody.

Since the end of the genocide, the international press has regularly announced that trials for 'crimes against humanity' are about to begin, but it is as if nothing is happening. The need for justice is overwhelming, but the courts are not working.[32] How do you explain this situation?

The press often refers to our 'culture of impunity', a polite way of saying that the strongest always wins. Under Habyarimana, and even at the time of Kayibanda, political crimes were never brought to light. The best outcome was for a widow to receive a state pension. Her silence was bought and she would have no choice but to accept, if only to spare the lives of her children. In practice this culture of impunity is continuing today. Has anything been done to identify and punish those who brought down the presidential plane on 6 April 1994? There are guilty people who are free and innocent people in prison. There are victims that nobody wants to listen to and killers who are still occupying positions of responsibility.

Of course, there are material obstacles which explain why justice has not been able to resume normally after the war – the partial or total destruction of the Ministry of Justice and the courts, the absence of means and of qualified personnel (there were fewer than 250 magistrates left in the country out of 719 registered before the war), the need to adopt a law on genocide (which was eventually adopted on 6 August 1996), etc. At the beginning, these material

---

[32] Translator's note: trials for genocide-related crimes began in Rwanda in December 1996 (see Postscript).

problems were very real, but gradually they began to be used as an alibi for not delivering justice.

Do you mean that there is a deliberate intention not to restart the judicial system?

Obstacles have been deliberately put in the way of the justice system, straight after the genocide and still today. Some people do not want trials to take place. More than 3,000 case files are ready in Gitarama. Why hasn't a single one been processed for three years? A Belgian human rights organization, Citizens' Network, trained more than 200 judicial police inspectors in a few months. People were hand-picked; after their training, their task was to carry out field investigations into crimes committed during the genocide. What has happened to them? According to information I have received, a third of them have been killed or imprisoned. Why? By whom? Their crime was to have done their work properly and to have refused to tolerate the rule of revenge and arbitrary decisions. They were simply applying the law. Citizens' Network eventually began questioning the meaning of its initiative.

What is the meaning of the word 'justice' when magistrates are killed with complete impunity? Who killed Judge Gratien Ruhorahoza on 2 October 1994, just after he had ordered the release of around forty detainees who had been unlawfully arrested? Who ordered the arrest of Daniel Shumbusho, the first assistant prosecutor? Who is responsible for the detention of Innocent Mbanzamierera, the president of the high court in Byumba, in early 1995? Who killed the judge of the court of Tare, his wife and son and their two servants, on 10 March 1996?

Here is another example: why have the screening committees not worked? The task of these committees was to study the case files of prisoners where all available evidence indicated that they were innocent. These committees included representatives of various ministries; as soon as they were set up, it was apparent that dozens of detainees should be released. Hardly had they been released than all of them were re-arrested. When I say 'all', that is not strictly correct: a few had been killed in the meantime. Who gave the order to kill the *sous-préfet* Placide Koloni on 27 July 1995, along with his wife Immaculée Nyirambibi, their daughters Marie-Claire (15 years old) and Carine (9 years old), and their housekeeper Séraphine Murekatete? The magistrates sitting on these committees no longer dared put forward any case files for fear of sending these people to their death, but also for fear of their own security. We shouldn't hide from reality. This is not the reign of justice, but the reign of terror. Who killed the *préfet* Pierre-Claver Rwangabo on 5 March 1995? His mistake was to have opposed the arrest of an innocent priest.

The screening committees stopped functioning almost as soon as they had been created. Yet some people had been declared innocent. Antoinette Mukaragagi, the wife of one of my journalists, Ladislas Niyongira, was arrested in July 1994. She was declared innocent of the crime she had been accused of – a crime which was proved never to have taken place; by the way, the person who accused her is now in prison himself. The prosecutor of Kigali ordered her release on 9 January 1995. In vain. A representative of a human rights organization who was outraged after visiting her several times in prison finally raised her case in a very detailed way with the president of Rwanda himself. Pasteur Bizimungu agreed to intervene personally in her favour. This was on 18 May 1996. She is still in prison. Why?[33]

Why would the state want to obstruct the justice system?

It's convenient for those in power. No justice means justice delivered quickly and summarily by those in a position of strength. Settling scores becomes legitimate. People say to themselves, 'The justice system is not working, so I will deliver my own justice.' And they take revenge. Others who are more cynical take advantage of the situation. For a house, for a field or a tool, people are denounced without evidence, and awkward neighbours are arrested. There are no investigations, no case files, no risk that the deceit might be discovered.

Impunity is always in the interest of the state, and the current state in Rwanda is no exception. It claims to be installing order based on justice and controlling its own excesses of power. In Rilima Prison, in the Bugesera region, between 500 and 1,500 Tutsi military officials are detained for having committed various crimes. Some senior officers are detained there, including those who committed the massacres of Kibeho and Gisenyi, such as Colonel Dodo. But those who know Rwanda will not be deceived by these few cases.

I would add that the absence of justice does not only benefit those who are running the country. Inside Rwanda there are still

---

[33] Translator's note: Antoinette Mukaragagi was eventually released in December 1998 after spending almost four and a half years in prison.

notorious killers living in complete impunity. In some villages, Tutsi survivors who are completely destitute, humiliated and weakened are forced to live side by side with those who massacred their families and stole all their belongings. They cannot rely on any assistance. It's a terrible scandal.

Trials have not started, yet the prisons are continuing to fill up: in the last three years, around 100 people have been arrested every day, and the number of detainees will soon rise above the 100,000 mark.[34] *The Rwandan government believes that this figure is much lower than the number of people who took part in the genocide.*

I won't play the numbers game; I find it sinister. I just want to point out two things. On the one hand, hundreds of thousands of people were killed, but not all of them were Tutsi and not all of them were victims. The RPF killed a lot of people when it took over the country; no one can deny that. Innocent people died in revenge killings. But so did guilty people. On the other hand, an estimated 2 million people fled Rwanda in 1994 and it is obvious that the majority of the killers were among those who fled. Therefore I find it completely cynical to rely on such statistics to justify the incredibly high level of arrests.

All the more so because instead of using the polite term 'prison', it would be more appropriate to call them 'places of detention'. People in Europe imagine that detainees are sitting peacefully in their rooms, between meetings with their lawyer, waiting for their trial to begin. What an illusion! The reality is that our prisons are inhuman death-traps in which death sentences are executed without trial. The living conditions are such that if you let enough time go by, the suspected killers or accomplices of the genocide will just die one by one. Whether innocent or guilty, these prisoners are gradually rotting away.

When I say 'rotting away', I mean it literally. At least one UNAMIR officer can testify to that. When he visited Gitarama Prison and gave a nice speech to the detainees, one of them ripped his toe off and threw it in his face. After weeks of standing upright, day and night, in the mud, the prisoners' feet had started decomposing. When I visited Gitarama Prison for the first time, in early 1995, what I saw defied imagination. There were three layers of prisoners: at the bottom, lying on the ground, there were

---

[34] Translator's note: by the end of 1998, an estimated 125,000 people were detained in Rwanda.

the dead, rotting on the muddy floor of the prison. Just above them, crouched down, there were the sick, the wounded, those whose strength had drained away. They were waiting to die. Their bodies had begun to rot and their hope of survival was reduced to a matter of days or even hours. Finally at the top, standing up, there were those who were still healthy. They were standing straight and moving from one foot to the other, half asleep. Why? Simply because that's where they happened to be living. Whenever a man fell over, it was a gift to the survivors: a few extra centimetres of space. I remember a man who was standing on his shins: his feet had rotted away.

I am not the only person to have witnessed this. In June 1995, Médecins sans frontières estimated that an average of 6.6 prisoners were dying every day out of a total of 10,000. By way of comparison, two deaths for every 10,000 people (including natural deaths and childhood mortality) is universally considered as the critical alert threshold in a refugee camp. Within nine months, almost 1,000 detainees – 13 per cent of prisoners – died in this way as a result of deliberate ill-treatment.

Some people, including in the international press, tried to justify this unjustifiable situation and to find excuses for the government: lack of space, shortage of means, scarcity of food in the aftermath of the war ... All lies! As soon as the bishopric of Kabgayi was allowed to intervene in the prison, mortality dropped from 168 deaths in April 1995 to 85 in June, 15 in August and 2 in October. Do you know why? We used old tyres to cut out thousands of makeshift sandals made of rubber and we distributed them to the prisoners. Their limbs started drying out.

We created a larger space for the detainees – a decision which earned us harsh criticisms. We installed showers and toilets. We turned the buildings of the bishopric into podiatry rooms, which enabled us to treat many sick prisoners. We appointed a permanent medical team to Gitarama Prison. All these measures led to an end to amputations and cases of dropsy and gangrene. Thanks to these measures, prisoners who had been sentenced to death by slowly rotting away are still alive.

Article 12, paragraph 4, of the Constitution of the Republic of Rwanda states that 'every person is presumed innocent of the offences of which he is accused until a final sentence has been issued'. The presumption of innocence is also recognized in the Universal Declaration of Human Rights to which Rwanda adhered at the time of its independence in 1962; in the International Covenant on Civil and Political Rights, signed on 12 February

1975; and in the African Charter for Human and Peoples' Rights, ratified on 17 May 1983. Furthermore, as a member of the United Nations, Rwanda should make every effort to apply the Standard Minimum Rules for the Treatment of Prisoners and the Body of Principles for the effective implementation of these rules (United Nations 1955, 1977 and 1988). As a human rights defender and as administrator of the diocese of Kabgayi, it was my duty to think of actions which would ensure that prisons did not turn into death-traps.

The prison guards accused me of wanting to help the *interahamwe*. In their minds, even before they had been tried or simply heard, these people had ceased to be human beings. Every apostle of Jesus Christ is sent to preach the good news to the poor, the oppressed, the prisoners and the sick. He must search for justice and preach love and forgiveness. For a priest, caring for the oppressed is simply his mission. Whether Hutu or Tutsi or Twa, all the oppressed have the right to be freed from oppression – which does not relieve them of their responsibility or of account-ability to human justice for their actions. Only the oppressor believes that working for the freedom of the oppressed is a serious offence.

You are calling into question the Rwandan justice system, but it is not alone. There is also an international system of justice, under the respon-sibility of the International Criminal Tribunal for Rwanda (ICTR). But it doesn't appear to have produced significant results yet.

Until now, the main effect of the ICTR has been to enable the inter-national community, or rather the countries within it, to save face and give the impression to the public that the crime which they watched without intervening would not go unpunished. Honour can be lost more than once.

I have met some of the ICTR officials; I am amazed by their incompetence. They are very intelligent people, but completely incapable of carrying out research. They don't speak Kinyarwanda – which is understandable – but nor do they know how to employ competent interpreters. I agreed to talk to the ICTR investigators. I spent a lot of time with them. When they presented me with an account of our meetings translated from Kinyarwanda into English and transcribed in French, there was only a remote link between the text and the subject matter of our discussions in French. I was angry with them for this flippant attitude and I refused to sign what was intended to be my deposition. Do you think the investigators tried to rectify the mistakes? They simply put me in the category of those who refused to cooperate with the ICTR. That was the last straw. They are incapable of approaching those who lived through the genocide. They don't ask the right questions. People are offended by their attitudes and their discourse. Rwandans had invested great hope in the ICTR. They are very disappointed.

Rwandans are not the only ones who are unhappy. The ICTR has been criticized by insiders for its slow procedures and its meagre budget (30 million US dollars for 1997). It was supposed to recruit 140 investigators; only 80 have been recruited, and in practice only about 50 are in the field. 'Yet we need to speed up investigations,' says the deputy prosecutor of the ICTR, Honoré Rakotomanana,[35] 'because the longer they take, the more evidence is disappearing and testimonies are becoming vague.'

In early 1997, the ICTR had only indicted 21 people, 13 of whom were in detention around the world. Only 4 were detained at Arusha Prison, where 55 cells have been especially prepared. Cameroon arrested one of the masterminds of the genocide, Colonel Théoneste Bagosora, but for a long time refused to extradite him.[36] A new prosecutor has succeeded the South African judge Richard Goldstone. She is a Canadian, Louise Arbour. She has been given a special additional budget of 600,000 dollars to investigate mass rape and other sexual crimes. Fine. With these resources, can we reasonably expect the ICTR to get through the case files of 100,000 detainees within one or two centuries? Who are they fooling?

There is much talk of the victims – Tutsi and 'moderate' Hutu – and the killers – interahamwe *militia and soldiers of the government forces. What about the Hutu who saved Tutsi?*

Those who are alive today are deeply unhappy. First of all, many of them were killed. Not participating in massacres, refraining from reporting the presence of a Tutsi, worse still, hiding a family of fugitives were all sufficient reasons for being killed. We will never find out the stories of these unknown heroes.

Among those who survived, some preferred to flee before the RPF arrived and sought protection in Zaire or Tanzania. Others

---

[35] On 26 February 1997, the Secretary-General of the United Nations, Kofi Annan, accepted the 'resignation' of Honoré Rakotomanana and Andronico Adede, the ICTR registrar, for serious mismanagement.

[36] The extradition finally took place at the end of 1996.
Translator's note: in March 1999 Théoneste Bagosora was still awaiting trial in Arusha.

stayed in Rwanda, with a clear conscience, and were killed by the RPF when it took over the country. Then there are those who are in prison, who were denounced by unscrupulous neighbours who wanted to steal their property. For a while they hoped that those they had helped would come to their rescue. Then hope was replaced by hatred. I don't know how they would behave today in a similar situation. Finally, there are those who protected Tutsi and who haven't fled, haven't been killed and are not in prison; they just keep quiet.

Who could they talk to and what would they gain from talking? They would be putting themselves at risk and putting those they saved in an awkward situation. If the militia returned tomorrow, they would kill them for having helped the RPF. If they named the Tutsi they saved, those people would be accused of collaborating with Hutu and could end up in prison themselves. This is not just an academic hypothesis: there are several hundred Tutsi in prison in Rwanda.

These men and women who risked everything to save their neighbours are denied all rights of recognition. Yet they exist, and there are many of them. How else could Tutsi have survived? Where did they hide? Who fed them, who cared for them, who transported them from place to place to save them from death?

The Tutsi extremist press will take any opportunity to state that all Hutu are bad and useless and that only the RPF – or possibly God – saved the Tutsi. The survivors know who saved them but they don't say anything. They are ungrateful and irresponsible. Some have become involved in human rights organizations. In practice they only defend the rights of Tutsi and draw up lists of Hutu whom they believe were responsible for crimes, some of which never even took place. Many Hutu took risks to defend Tutsi between 1990 and 1994. Why don't the Tutsi take on their share of responsibility? Now that they are in a position of strength, why don't they come to the assistance of the weak? This abdication will have dramatic consequences for the future of our country.

In any case, for me, these 'righteous people' who saved the lives of others while risking their own have preserved the most precious part of their being: their soul and their conscience.

Sometimes there is talk of plans for a general amnesty for detainees.

I am completely against it. The intention is to make us believe that behind this gesture, there is a desire for reconciliation and appeasement. But it's quite the contrary. Who do you think would be appeased by random releases, without people being declared innocent or guilty? The guilty would not have paid their dues. The innocent would not have been washed of their shame. The Hutu as a whole would have to bear responsibility for crimes committed by a minority. And those who ensured that innocent people were imprisoned would not be made to answer for their lies. It would all be too easy.

For Rwandans there is the duty of justice, but there is also the duty of memory. They must preserve the memory of what happened. It is a moral duty as well as a political necessity: it is said that those who forget their past are condemned to relive it. Do you feel that Rwandans are taking on this duty of memory?

I am not able to make an overall judgement. What I know is that those who are in the best position to build and maintain the memory of this dark page of our history are not doing it. One example is the behaviour of some representatives of human rights organizations who have set themselves the task of gathering facts, writing them up in reports and publishing them. This applies to Rwandan as well as international organizations.

Before the war, there were five main organizations in Rwanda: ARDHO, the oldest; ADL, of which I was the president; Kanyarwanda; AVP and LIPRODHOR. To simplify, let's say that their members had different political opinions and, in one case, an ethnic slant. Nevertheless, these organizations had managed to bring their work together within an umbrella organization, CLADHO. All of them had terrible experiences during the genocide: ADL lost half its members. These organizations formed again after the war. They enjoyed a certain prestige because of their early denunciation of the Habyarimana regime.

CLADHO undertook to draft an exhaustive report on human rights violations committed during the genocide. It was a huge task which required considerable resources, but it was absolutely necessary. It is not enough to claim that 500,000 or 1 million people were killed. We have to identify them, place them, describe exactly where, when and how it happened, because of whom and in the presence of whom. That is where the duty of memory begins. We needed – and we still need – a work on the scale of Raul Hilberg's, the author of *The Destruction of the European Jews.* CLADHO received money from a Canadian organization, CECI, to carry out this investigation.

The report was published on 10 December 1994, on the anniversary of the Universal Declaration of Human Rights. ADL immediately disowned it and CECI suspended its cooperation. Why? I will refer you back to *Maudits soient les yeux fermés*, which I have already quoted. In this book, Françoise Bouchet-Saulnier quotes the former president of CLADHO, François-Xavier Nsanzuwera, and one of its main investigators, Joseph Matata – both of whom are now refugees in Belgium where they had to flee for their security. What do they say? 'Some people are deceiving us. Some people are propagating rumours or describing events which they have not witnessed. Some are also taking advantage of our investigation to settle old scores with neighbours or creditors', states Joseph Matata. Just before the document was published, names were added behind his back; others were withdrawn. By whom? Why? In a letter dated 4 November 1995, Francois-Xavier Nsanzuwera wrote: 'Jean-Bosco Iyakaremye [who chaired the commission of inquiry] ensured that the report was published without consulting the team of investigators and especially without consulting the board of CLADHO [...] I demanded that [he] give the executive secretary a confidential list of witnesses who had been interviewed by the commission members [as the report contained serious accusations attributed to unknown witnesses]: the list was never handed in.'

A second example is the place of memory. I was very moved by the sobriety of the Yad VaShem site. The monuments, the forest of trees, the lists of names of disappeared victims, the flame of memory, all this contributes to forming a memory which is entirely focused on the victims. Unfortunately in Rwanda, it is not at all in this spirit that memorials have been built. The first one was inaugurated on 7 April 1995 at Rebero, near Kigali, on the first anniversary of the start of the genocide. I won't describe the morbid way in which the 200 coffins were displayed, covered with a purple cloth and giving off a putrid smell: Rwanda has been drenched in so much blood that we have lost our points of reference. I especially remember the speeches on this occasion. Instead of remembering the dead, they were calling for revenge. And what about Ntarama, Gikongoro and scores of other sites where bodies have been denied burial and are rotting in the open air, supposedly to mark their memory?

Let's leave the dead in peace! Have you displayed burnt corpses in the church of Oradour-sur-Glane? Are there ashes in the crematoria at Auschwitz? The dead have the right to be buried and to rest in peace. All these performances are unnecessary and I don't believe that the real motive of those who organize these displays has much to do with respect for the memory of the victims.

A third example: what is being done to help the survivors? They are living in poverty and isolation. People say that Tutsi are occupying houses belonging to Hutu. But I must tell you that those Tutsi are rarely survivors of the genocide. They are those who came back from Burundi or Uganda after the war. They have legitimate rights which must be respected. But not to the detriment of others. And least of all to the detriment of survivors, most of whom are living in plastic tents.

The plight of survivors has become a taboo subject. We can't say anything about them. I have tried to publish articles describing their distress. As a journalist, I have discovered that apart from a few Tutsi peasant families who have managed to get their place back in rural society, most survivors are still wandering from refugee camps to transit camps. Many of them are living, or rather surviving, in a state of complete dejection and loss. Most of them are the only ones to have survived after a thousand coincidences and strokes of luck; they have no families. They have settled together and, three years after the genocide, they are still in the same place where the RPF found them when it took over the country. You can go there and ask them: they live together in warehouses or schools, sometimes just a few kilometres away from their own houses. But they are afraid of going home and don't have the psychological strength to rebuild their lives. They have been destroyed, abandoned by life and by those who claim to speak on their behalf.

I have published a few articles on this subject. But I was immediately accused of trying to set the survivors against the government and wanting to create social divisions. Those who have a monopoly on speech today can't tolerate it when this kind of truth is brought to their attention. The saddest thing is that the survivors themselves put forward the principle of ethnic solidarity above their own interests. They fail to see that the government is not doing what it could for them.

Another example is the denial of justice. Does the failure to try the guilty help us fulfil the duty of memory? Thousands of detainees are waiting for their fate to be decided. Are they guilty? Are they innocent? The truth is that the absence of judgement serves the interests of crime. Innocent prisoners, who are victims of injustice and are subjected to sub-human living conditions, end up subscribing to the views of the guilty: some regret having protected Tutsi who are responsible for their imprisonment today. What a fine victory for those who committed the genocide! The denial of justice is preparing the graves of the future.

The Rwandan government and civil society are not the only ones responsible. We will come back to the role of the Church. But first I want to underline the responsibility of the international community. It allowed the preparation of the genocide to proceed despite all our appeals for intervention. It abstained from coming to our rescue while we were dying by the thousands. And what is it doing today? It is encouraging a propaganda of denial to grow.

I will just mention one or two examples. As soon as they arrived in Goma, the extremists reorganized their propaganda system. Gaspard Gahigi, the former head of RTLM, created an Association of Rwandan Journalists in Exile (AJRE) and a newspaper, *Amizero*. Hassan Ngeze, the director of *Kangura*, quietly resumed the publication of his weekly newspaper of hatred, without any regrets, without a trace of remorse, and without anybody expressing any concern. Reporters sans frontières denounced this scandal; they filed a criminal complaint for incitement to racial hatred and appealed to the United Nations Human Rights Commission, UNESCO and the embassy of Zaire: none of these actions had any result. Full of the confidence inspired by the certainty that crimes are not punished, Hassan Ngeze settled in Kenya, where he not only continued publishing *Kangura*, but even launched an international edition in English, to suit the market![37]

And what about all those officials who have been granted asylum in Belgium, Cameroon, France, Kenya, Switzerland and Zaire? It took an international press campaign for Cameroon to finally arrest four senior figures responsible for the genocide, including Ferdinand Nahimana.[38] Félicien Kabuga would probably still be in Switzerland if the press and human rights organizations had not denounced his presence there. And I could well believe that President Habyarimana's widow might still be living comfortably in her apartment on Avenue Mozart, in the 16th *arrondissement* in Paris, if the media hadn't denounced this scandal. Isn't it an insult to the memory of the dead?

[37] Translator's note: on 18 July 1997, Hassan Ngeze was arrested in Kenya on the orders of the International Criminal Tribunal for Rwanda, along with several other individuals believed to have played a leading role in the genocide. He was transferred to the prison in Arusha and indicted in October 1997. In March 1999, he was still detained there awaiting trial.
[38] Ferdinand Nahimana was arrested in Cameroon on 27 March 1996 on the orders of the International Criminal Tribunal for Rwanda. On 27 January 1997, he was transferred to Arusha where he is still detained awaiting trial.

Finally, alongside this gross denial, there is another, which is more furtive but equally dangerous. There is no doubt that the RPF committed and is continuing to commit a large number of crimes. I won't speculate about the numbers. Several politicians in exile in Europe have made this their speciality. The former Prime Minister, Faustin Twagiramungu, announced publicly that according to very precise information in his possession, the RPA had allegedly killed more than 300,000 Hutu since July 1994. Others have made similar statements. They are trying to outbid each other; they want the number of people killed by the RPF to be on a level with the people killed during the genocide, to restore a kind of equality. Equality in numbers, therefore equality in responsibility. It's totally absurd. Deaths don't compensate for each other; they don't cancel each other out; they simply add up. Furthermore, even though every death is a death, there is a still an essential difference between the RPF's war crimes, however many there were, and the crime of genocide, which is the product of methodically elaborated schemes which are a denial of humanity.

I am very pessimistic for the future of our memory.

Maybe you are too impatient. It took years for Europe to be able to look at itself in the mirror and write down the history of its wars and its attitude towards Jews. It wasn't until 1995 that France recognized the Vichy regime's responsibility in the Holocaust, after Jacques Chirac succeeded François Mitterrand.

I am impatient, but do we have any choice? After the Second World War, Europe experienced the triumph of democracy against a backdrop of extraordinary economic growth. These two factors were critical; the wounds had time to heal. Rwanda is still very far from democracy. As for the economy, if everyone could eat one meal a day, we would be happy. The tragedy of our country is that we do not even have time to nurse our wounds before new ones are inflicted.

Yesterday we spent the day with an Israeli historian and journalist, Tom Segev, the author of a book, The Seventh Million, *which has provoked a lively debate in Israel and in the Jewish world. In this book, he describes the pain of Jews who survived the genocide and have not been able to tell their story or achieve recognition for what they experienced. He shows how various actors on the political scene have turned the political and moral 'gain' of the genocide to their advantage or to the*

advantage of the cause they are defending, in particular the national
cause. What is your response to this analysis?

There is a striking similarity between this story and the story of Tutsi
survivors today. The Jews of Palestine did not worry too much
about the fate of those who were dying in Europe. For them, the
political issues at stake were not a priority at the time. It was only
after the declaration of the state of Israel that the survivors became
an essential political argument: anything was allowed in the name
of the genocide, and no one had the right to criticize Israel. Israeli
politicians were speaking in the name of the survivors. But at the
same time they were only paying superficial attention to their
concerns. Worse still: some people blamed them for having survived
the Holocaust. Many survivors were ashamed of having survived.
So there was a tacit agreement to maintain a silence which suited
everybody: the politicians who had abandoned the European Jews
and the survivors who were suffering from still being alive. But
reality has eroded the reign of silence. The genocide in Cambodia,
the tragedy in Ethiopia and now Rwanda have constantly forced
similar problems into the headlines.

Genocide has been very useful for justifying criminal actions.
Didn't Begin write a letter to Reagan in 1982 in which he claimed
to have gone to Lebanon to capture Hitler, meaning Arafat? We
are the victims, therefore we can't be wrong: this was the dominant
argument. The world has no right to judge us because, at best, it
abandoned us and, at worst, it planned our destruction. This
strategy also aimed to prevent any real political debate within
Israeli society, particularly on the question of negotiations with the
PLO. In addition, supporters of Zionist ideology appropriated the
Holocaust: the genocide was made to prove with hindsight that the
only possible salvation for the Jewish people was to gather in Israel.

The political exploitation of the Holocaust does not only relate
to manipulation. There was a cynical attempt to take advantage of
a unique situation in the history of humanity and to reach specific
political goals on the basis of a catastrophe. But there was also
political exploitation 'in good faith', which led Israelis to behave
in an insane way, but in which they found their own identity. Why
did the state of Israel acquire the atomic bomb in the 1950s? It was
a ridiculous plan, which cost exorbitant amounts for no purpose
at all. There wasn't even any strategic motive. Has the atomic bomb
been of any use in defending the state of Israel since 1948? It was
purely psychological: 'never again'.

According to Tom Segev, the history of the Holocaust is only just beginning to take shape. Some excellent academic works have been published but they are not yet part of the collective memory. Among many other accounts, films such as *Shoah* by Claude Lanzmann or books such as *The Destruction of the European Jews* by Raul Hilberg have increased the popular appeal and the urgency of the debate on the scientific history of the Holocaust – a history which lends itself to historical comparisons and the interpretation of documents. A history without complacency.

How can we fail to see the parallels between the history of the Jews and the history of Rwanda? Of course, I'm not going to fall into the trap of comparing the Tutsi to the Jews and the Hutu to the Nazis. Some Tutsi extremist circles, in Rwanda or in the diaspora, have become self-styled specialists in this kind of falsification of history. The history of the Jews and the history of the Tutsi obviously have a lot in common: you could write a book on the subject. But we must refrain from making abusive historical comparisons. What impressed me in Tom Segev's analysis was the way he highlighted certain psychological or political mechanisms which are neither Jewish nor Tutsi but human; as such, they are relevant to all human beings and all societies.

Can Rwanda base itself on the experience of the Jews? Historians have remarked that people who have been victims of genocide always refuse to allow their tragedy to be compared to those of other peoples – often vehemently. They fear that the gravity of their own suffering might be reduced by a similar suffering experienced by another people. Jews, for example, insist on preserving the absolutely unique character of the genocide to which they were subjected. Yet today there is a general agreement that the Armenians were also victims of an authentic genocide. It is possible that in the future, Rwandans, or rather the Tutsi, may reject any comparison with other tragedies.

But this is not the case at the moment. On the contrary, many educated survivors base their arguments on a comparison with the genocide of the Jews and want to establish parallels. Some do it in bad faith, for the sake of political gains. Others – the majority – do it with the despair of those who try to grab on to anything which will enable them to understand what happened to them. I have absolute respect for their pain and for their desire to understand.

The experience of the Jewish people can help us. But it is very difficult to transfer cultural practices from one country to another, or from one civilization to another. The Jewish civilization is closely linked to the written word and even to the Scriptures, whereas

Rwandan tradition is an oral tradition. What would be the meaning of a memorial monument in a country which does not have a culture of monuments? I have greater belief in the construction of educational museums, which recall facts and exclude propaganda. But we can't hope to succeed in writing a common history of victims and killers within 50 years. Will history 'in the making' leave us enough time?

8 The Role of the Church: Guilty or an Incriminating Witness?

Despite its late conversion, Rwanda soon emerged as one of the most Catholic countries in Africa, at least judging by the number of church officials and the political, economic and cultural power of the Church. It was a real pillar of strength in Rwandan society, so it could not have failed to have been shaken by the genocide. Some people accuse the Church of having actively participated in the ideological preparation of the genocide; others have called into question the behaviour of several priests during the killings. Whatever we may think of these accusations, we can't help wondering about the role of the Church over the last few years.

There is no doubt that the Roman Catholic Church did not live up to its moral responsibility in the years which preceded the genocide. It's a reality which no one can deny. Actually priests were among the first to denounce this weakness, long before the genocide. When the Pope visited Kigali in 1990, *Kinyamateka* made sure it expressed its concerns on this subject to its readers. We felt that the statements made by the Pope and by the Rwandan Roman Catholic hierarchy were not sufficiently explicit about the serious problems which Rwanda was already facing. In July 1991, Father Gabriel Maindron published an article entitled 'I accuse' in the journal *Dialogue,* in which he openly criticized the Church for its lack of insight, its passive attitude and its complicity. He was attacking the Church's overall hypocrisy and position of compromise. But on the day that the article was published, he was called by the Archbishop of Kigali, who asked him, 'Are you accusing me, Gabriel?'

In December 1991, priests from the diocese of Kabgayi published a 40-page document entitled *Let us convert to live together in peace.* In this document, they attacked the passive attitude of the Church in the face of 'mismanagement of public funds, corruption, social injustice, individual freedoms, the war and AIDS'. In early 1992, a pastoral letter took up the same arguments and called for a meeting of a National Conference. When I received Cardinal Etchegaray in May 1993, this is what I said in my speech:

> Your Eminence, let me be frank with you: in this context of human rights violations, the main moral authority in the country, namely the Roman Catholic Church, should have made every effort to rectify the situation and revive people's consciences. Instead, it has distinguished itself by its complicit silence and its absence in the most stricken places. The cry of distress of the people of God has not always been heard in time; and with a few exceptions, Roman Catholic officials have lost their credibility because of their complacent attitude towards the state.

As you can see, there was deep unease within the Church. A few of us were aware of this and wanted to find a way forward. In my capacity as director of *Kinyamateka*, the Church's organ of social communication, I had several clashes with the Archbishop of Kigali, Vincent Nsengiyumva, who, as I told you, had been a member of the MRND central committee and remained a close friend of Juvénal Habyarimana.

The Church did nothing to prevent tragedies which it could have prevented. When the bishops were informed that a genocide was about to happen, when they saw the increase in killings in the period leading up to the genocide – on average five every night – their attitude didn't change. The heads of the Church stood by the government, particularly the Bishops of Kigali and Byumba. They failed to react in an appropriate way towards the role of the government in the preparation of the genocide. They should have broken away.

But the Church is not just made up of the ecclesiastic hierarchy. President Habyarimana, most of the army, most of the judges, ministers and *préfets* were Roman Catholics. The fact that society was unable to prevent the catastrophe shows that there was a fundamental breakdown. Christians shouldn't just suffer a situation; they have a responsibility to take control.

Did the Church take part in the ideological preparation of the genocide? No, certainly not. The basis for such an accusation is purely political. Rwanda was converted to Roman Catholicism from the top down: the first missionaries started by converting the chiefs – mostly Tutsi – in order to accelerate the conversion of the masses. Until the 1950s, the Church relied primarily on the Tutsi elite which provided most of the clergy. Then things changed. For various reasons which we have already discussed, Hutu started achieving recognition or took on a more important place in society. The Church played an active role in this process which culminated in the social revolution of 1959. Since then, some Tutsi circles, who are descendants of those who were ousted at that time, have viewed the Roman Catholic Church as a traitor and an enemy and have accused it of supporting what they call 'Hutu ideology' – the intellectual trend which campaigned for the liberation of the oppressed Hutu people.

The Church did not plan the genocide on an ideological level, but there is no doubt that, just like the politicians, the military or the United Nations, the weakness of the Church's reactions to daily violence prepared people psychologically to accept violence as something normal. It is not a collective or diffuse form of responsibility; each person must examine their own conscience. But there's no point in demonizing an institution which gets in the way; it does not help move the debate forward.

What was the role of the Church during the war and during the massacres?

The Church was hit hard by the war, by the genocide, then by the massacres which followed the victory of the RPF. One of the very first killings of the genocide took place at the Christus Centre at Remera on 7 April. Seventeen people were killed, including priests, religious officials and nuns. Among the victims was the Jesuit father who used to hear Juvénal Habyarimana's confessions; perhaps this explains the massacre. I also see it as a symbol of the collapse of our country into a barbaric state. Other religious officials were also killed later. In total, 3 bishops, 103 priests, 40 religious brothers, 60 nuns and countless believers and members of congregations were killed in various circumstances.

As I said, part of the Church did not live up to its moral, spiritual, political or economic responsibility. But another part of the Church managed to confront the hardships; it emerged strengthened, and if there hadn't been such a trail of bloodshed and pain, I would say that it could be proud of its behaviour on many occasions, as well as that of its officials and congregations.

I don't accept the language of generalization which states that the Roman Catholic Church participated in the genocide. Because this Church – and I say so with the eyes of a believer – is above all a divine institution, a reality which transcends, a place of salvation. It is not the Church as such which is called into question, but its members. The Church is composed of a hierarchy, which starts from the level of the lay believer and goes right up to the Pope. And what did the Pope do? Some claim he couldn't do anything.

I don't know. The fact is that when Cardinal Etchegaray came to Rwanda, the massacres stopped wherever he went.

Regarding the Roman Catholic clergy, I don't know of any priest who took up a machete to kill. Priests were seen carrying arms. Were they intending to use them to kill or to protect? I don't have the answer. I know one priest who organized training sessions for young people in his parish. Was it sports training or paramilitary preparation? Was he preparing militia or a self-defence guard? What I know is that the same priest protected Tutsi in the major seminary.

The White Fathers were present in large numbers in Rwanda. All or most of them left. Did they leave out of cowardice or obligation? Was it better to risk death or to save what could still be saved by thinking ahead to the time when, sooner or later, the country would have to be rebuilt? Among those who chose to stay, several priests were killed. Father Kesenne was killed by the *interahamwe*. A Spanish father called Vallmajo was killed by the RPF. I don't have a reaction to the choice made by most of the White Fathers; I leave each of them to his own conscience. Before you make a judgement – if you think you have the right to make one -you must remember that at that time people were not counting in days, but in hours. No one is obliged to be a hero or to remain a hero for long.

Some believers were weak, irresponsible and did not weigh the consequences of their actions. I asked one of my parishioners who carried a grenade, 'What are you doing?' He replied, 'Don't you understand the situation we're in? We'll think about religion later.' The killers included believers and non-believers, lucid people and people under the effect of drugs; some were acting of their own free will, others because they were forced or terrorized. Among the killers, there were Christians; among the victims too. Many victims felt completely abandoned and probably lost their faith at the fateful moment. But others discovered faith through this tragic experience. Many people died as they sought protection in religious buildings; many more survived by turning towards the people of God. People risked their life – and often lost it – trying to save their neighbour. They too represent the Church.

It makes me indignant when the Church is criticized on the basis of the weakness of a few, whereas many others died trying to protect people who were being pursued, or even just staying at their side until the end to testify to their love for Christ.

It also makes me indignant to hear the Minister for Social Affairs, Pie Mugabo, claim that the Church did nothing during the genocide, whereas he was fed by Father Blanchard during the two months that he had to hide at Gisimba orphanage in Nyamirambo (Kigali). Who fed 35,000 refugees in Kabgayi and 40,000 refugees in Kamonyi, every day, throughout the war? If Caritas hadn't been there, who would have cared for these unfortunate people who were trying to escape the killers? We weren't always able to save them from being taken away by militiamen. But priests were injured as they covered huge distances to find enough food for all these people. If you want to accuse the Church in an honest way, you have to base your accusations on specific facts.

Those who accuse 'the Church' of having done nothing during the genocide or of having been an accomplice are right to denounce acts of cowardice. But their determination not to see the Church's role in relieving suffering makes me suspicious of their real motives. The Rwandan Church is portrayed in a ridiculous way, for political reasons. It is described only through its clergy; and in the ranks of the clergy, the behaviour of particular individuals is singled out. It is logical and predictable that in a poor country like Rwanda, some people decide on a religious vocation just to have access to education or to have enough money to buy clothes or food. The ecclesiastical institution strives to discourage those whose faith or whose vocation is weak; but like any institution, it can make mistakes. In the ranks of the clergy, there are remarkable individuals and there are weaker individuals. Some may discover real faith along the way, while others may start to doubt. All this is true, and it would be wrong to deny it. But does this justify political accusations?

I have the feeling – which is supported by certain facts – that people attack part of the clergy because it constitutes a counter-power which could be awkward. Some priests were eliminated – I mean physically eliminated – because they had seen too much or because they knew too much. Will there ever be an outcome to the investigation into the killing in September 1994 of Father Simard, a Canadian priest who had witnessed a massacre of Hutu by the RPF? I doubt it. Will the investigation into the killing of Father Pie Ntahobali, the parish priest of Kamonyi (diocese of Kabgayi), on 1 August 1995 ever reveal the identity of the soldiers who dragged him into a banana plantation, two kilometres away from the parish, before killing him? I doubt it. He was a friend, a man of faith. Why was he killed? Are there too many men like him in this country after the bloodbath we have suffered? Why was Father Guy Pinard, a Canadian, killed in the middle of a service on 2 February 1997?

Those who attack the Church in this way have short-term objectives motivated only by political concerns. But those who like to portray themselves as judges are not delivering justice if they ignore the greatness and the sacrifice of those who saved Tutsi from certain death. In fact, by behaving in this way, they are likely to fuel feelings of bitterness which could turn into resentment.

Since the genocide, has the Church – the clergy and the believers – set about examining its own conscience?

I'm not in a position to make a statement about the Church overall. But I can describe what happened in my own diocese. Some believers handed me back their christening certificate. A number of Tutsi seminarians who survived the genocide gave up their vocation. They still believe in God but have lost confidence in the religious institution. Many of them now devote their time to relieving the suffering of other survivors. Others still believe, but have stopped coming to church. In a sense they have become deists. But there are others whose faith has deepened. They organized a day of prayer in memory of survivors saved by Christians who put their religion above any other kind of identity. Five thousand people took part in a memorial service on 2 June 1995 in Kabgayi.

We didn't organize public exorcism sessions. All those who had been christened were considered to be outside the Church, but we didn't want to organize systematic new christenings. Those who volunteered were asked to register at the parish again for a new and deep conversion and to exchange ideas and information with the priests about the massacres. In those parishes where priests appealed to the Christian people by inviting them to register again with officials in the community, many Christians responded. There were very positive results in terms of consciousness of evil and of the sins which were committed, the ways in which people's attitudes had strayed from the Gospel and the decision to make a commitment to a new life which would be closer to the Gospel.

During the period of mourning, which lasted until Christmas 1994, we suspended the administration of sacraments – christenings, communions and weddings – with the exception of the Eucharist, as some people had behaved in a truly Christian way. Every parishioner 'who knew he had killed' was asked not to receive communion any more and to come to the confessional to give a full and sincere explanation as to how the sin was committed as well as any mitigating or aggravating circumstances. We have to show an interest in human beings individually and stop treating them as a mass.

In the diocese of Kabgayi we set up a special procedure. We created a specific pastoral policy, the 'policy of dialogue'. Those who wanted to remain in the Roman Catholic Church were accepted on condition that each of them stated what they were expecting from religion and expressed, each in their own words, their regrets and the improvements they hoped for. I wrote a synthesis of these 'statements' in a pastoral letter which was circulated from November 1994 under the title *Convert and believe in the good news*. What was the content of this letter?

The first element was an appeal to all Christians to express their desire to be Christian, to live the Gospel to the full and to make a commitment to do all they could to ensure that what happened in Rwanda would never happen again.

The second element was an exhortation to priests to live in unity and brotherly harmony. Priests should be authentic men of God and not allow themselves to be manipulated by men. They should devote themselves to their mission and ensure respect for human rights. They should pay particular attention to people who are suffering, orphans, widows, people whose houses have been destroyed and all those who are victims of injustice; there are so many of them.

I also stressed the need for better training for lay officials, whether catechists, heads of centres or grassroots community leaders. They must be properly trained to be able to testify to Christ's faith and provide direction for others.

I also touched on other problems, including the need to rebuild what had been destroyed as soon as possible, to completely renew the spirit of parish life, and especially to remember the importance and value of the sacraments.

As you can see, we were quite far from the intention expressed by some White Fathers, who had come back after the massacres, to rebuild in an identical way, without learning from our failures. That would have been absurd. Of course, we had to bury the dead and build from the ruins. But this couldn't be done as if we were dealing with an earthquake or a hurricane. The hurricane had been inflicted by human hands, and it was human beings, their relatives, their families and their neighbours who had to be re-integrated into society. Of course, there must be trials and lawful justice. But the law is not enough and will never be enough to rebuild the social fabric. I have been accused of rejecting the justice of the courts by preaching the justice of hearts. But the two are not

exclusive. The law must be respected, but it will not conquer the root of evil. We must search for what has failed and find the fibre which is waiting to be revived at the bottom of our souls.

The Church as an institution, with its individual members, its history, its properties and its moral responsibility must certainly examine its own conscience. It has started to do so and it would be naive to believe that it will take anything less than several years to complete the task.

The process of believers examining their own conscience is the opposite: it can only be an intimate and individual process. As a priest, I sometimes have access to people's hearts through confessions. I can't betray the secret of confession. But who knows what lies at the bottom of our hearts, even among those who have crimes on their conscience? Some Rwandans have sunk into deep spiritual distress. Through their pain, they put faith back at the centre of their lives and examine their conscience in an authentic way, without any fuss or publicity.

From a more personal point of view, did these events ever shake your conscience as a priest or your faith as a believer?

On several occasions I have wondered: 'Lord, what am I doing here?' How could I not have had these thoughts?

Were you afraid?

That's not what I meant. One thing is certain about life on earth: no one will come out alive. Everything else is just a question of timing. I know that I am at risk. But I don't have the right to leave. I could have gone into exile ten or twenty times. I often travel to Europe. But I belong here, among my people. Some people believe that their life depends on mine and, in some cases, I know that they're right. My duty is here.

This situation had never occurred to me until I experienced it. When I became a priest, I never thought that I would become a campaigner speaking on behalf of innocent people who don't have a voice. In 1982 I went to Rome for a priests' retreat. I won't comment on my reaction to the institutionalization of the Church and the accumulation of material wealth over the centuries. But what I learnt from that stay is that every human being is called upon to act in godliness, without exception. We must never allow ourselves to be discouraged by our own weaknesses or the weaknesses of others. It is God who gives us strength. We must be ready to receive that gift and to bear our cross better each day.

I went to Rome for the second time in January 1996. Cardinal Etchegaray, who chairs the papal Justice and Peace Commission, encouraged me to pursue the pacification work which we had begun in the diocese of Kabgayi, as had Bishop Berthelo, the Vatican's representative to the United Nations in Geneva, a short while before. But I was surprised by the words of Bishop Joseph Tomko. He urged me to be careful, discreet and silent; he asked me to limit my work to pastoral activities and to stop writing editorial columns in *Kinyamateka* which he thought were too 'political'. When I came back from Rome, I felt very wary. Is it an excess of pastoral duty to defend the dignity of innocent people which has been violated?

For me, the bishop is the guardian of the people. Rwandans today are like a flock of sheep without a shepherd, standing on the edge of a cliff. The bishop must go towards his sheep and guide them. It is his duty to forge the way and lead those who are in his care. He must make a commitment to them. I have noticed that few bishops share this opinion. I wonder: is it normal that neither the Bishop of Kibeho nor the bishops' conference saw fit to denounce the massacre of refugees at Kibeho by the Rwandan Patriotic Army in April 1995 (see Chapter 9)?

I have never questioned my faith and I have never doubted. But through bloodshed and tears I have discovered that the path of truth is not necessarily a path of happiness. It is not God who makes me question, it is man. God created us as free beings; He is not responsible for what we do with this freedom. He shows us the way; it is not He who makes us stray from it. Some people raise doubts and think that God has abandoned them because they have suffered grave injustices or cruel situations. Many Jews had the same feeling and the same reflections during the Shoah.

Has God abandoned us? I can't answer this question. It is a metaphysical and individual question. As far as I am concerned, as a human being, as a believer and as a priest, I try to find the right path, to follow it and to lead others along it.

In November 1994 you were appointed administrator of the diocese of Kabgayi; you held this post until May 1996. What did your work consist of during those two years?

The situation was catastrophic when I started running the diocese. Everything had to be rebuilt, all at the same time, without any resources. Eighteen out of eighty-seven priests had been killed, including the bishop, the vicar-general, the head bursar, the rector and the director of studies; many were in exile. We had to rebuild everything including minds and bodies, public buildings, houses, families... The diocese of Kabgayi is not only the biggest in Rwanda, it also has the largest number of inhabitants. An investigation in December 1994 estimated that it had 680,000 inhabitants – around 10 per cent of the population of Rwanda.

The most urgent task was to stop the mortality which was devastating the country, whether in the form of massacres, individual acts of revenge, disease or famine. Thanks to donations from various benefactors and international organizations, like the Catholic Relief Services, we managed to halt the famine which was affecting 70,000 people and ensure a regular supply of food to tens of thousands of displaced people. In terms of health care, from September onwards the hospital of Kabgayi resumed its activities. Before it closed in June 1994, it had 400 beds; we installed 800. We also set up health centres in outlying areas. The needs were overwhelming: apart from caring for the injured, most of whom were victims of machete wounds, we were dealing with a population which had no access to hygiene, which was physically weak and vulnerable to disease. In order to deal with the abuses and arrests carried out by the military, we negotiated to secure the presence of a detachment of UNAMIR and UN human rights observers, which helped reduce the number of abuses.

Our second objective was to ensure the survival of 20,000 orphans who were wandering around without a home. Through a large-scale pastoral initiative, we succeeded in integrating 17,589 children who were orphans of the genocide into 9,019 Christian families who agreed to take care of them completely. Imagine what a sacrifice that represents in a country which was in ruins and where, even before the war, people did not have enough to eat every day.

Then we initiated actions for the detainees in Gitarama Prison. I have already mentioned the sandals we distributed, which contributed significantly to reducing the mortality rate. We also enlarged the prison compound by adding 4,000 square metres – 80 per cent under cover – 50 toilets and 40 showers. All these measures helped reduce the population density – more than four people per square metre – and improve the conditions of hygiene.

In terms of health care, in addition to caring for ordinary patients, the hospital of Kabgayi took care of sick prisoners – a task for which the Minister of Justice eventually thanked us. This is what Marthe Mukamurenzi wrote to me soon after she was appointed [Minister of Justice]: 'I was pleased to learn through my technical services about the medical assistance project at Gitarama Prison by the hospital of Kabgayi. I take this opportunity to express my sincere gratitude for your continual kind assistance to the detainees of Gitarama Prison. I strongly support your noble interventions for the reconstruction of Rwanda and your commitment to improving conditions of detention in Gitarama Prison.'

Then I organized the 'rebuilding of hearts'. The priests of the diocese appealed to Christians who had stolen to return what they had looted and to receive penance. Converting hearts is a long task and it is impossible to measure the results. I also initiated the 'policy of dialogue' which we have already talked about.

The actions we initiated to help the youth were particularly important. The chaplaincy for youth in the diocese carried out its own evaluation of the life and activities of the youth who used to go there before, during and after the genocide. Their first observation was that 5,500 of the 30,000 young people registered before the war had died (almost one in five) and 4,200 were in exile. The young people who survived, two-thirds of whom were girls, were asked to evaluate themselves and understand their own behaviour. What did they say?

The girls commented on a great increase in moral depravity, characterized by debauchery, a taste for luxury and easy money, a lack of modesty, idleness, laziness and lack of concern; an absence of honesty and self-serving friendships; a lack of respect towards the elderly and their parents; and finally, the reign of jealousy in the race for a husband, as boys had become scarce.

The boys were equally self-critical. They complained of a strong tendency towards idleness, theft, looting, delinquency, sexual debauchery, use of drugs and drunkenness. They want to live beyond their means and possibilities and can never get enough leisure. Religious indifference was dominant. They believe that many of those who were involved in the genocide, especially street children, were driven by poverty, ignorance, a lack of human conscience, unemployment and misery.

We need to rebuild our spirits and our hopes. The Christian Workers' Youth and the Xaveri Movement have been relaunched; with difficulty they are helping young people to regain confidence, to speak to each other again and to think about the future. Whenever possible we try to provide professional training, but we have few resources.

At the same time, I organized the reconstruction of schools and public places, as well as 14,357 houses which had been destroyed during the genocide. The houses were intended for survivors who had lost everything. The workmen were Hutu or Tutsi. At the beginning, the Tutsi and the Hutu did not speak to each other. But this communal work helped rebuild bridges. At the inauguration of the first 200 houses on 21 August 1995, Hutu and Tutsi drank banana beer from the same jug – a symbol of harmony in Rwanda. I am not fooling myself nor am I being lulled by symbolic actions. The road is still long and it will take years, maybe generations, for people to be truly united again. But I am very hopeful.

In the region of Kabgayi, I wouldn't say that there was no inter-ethnic tension but people did not hate each other. They were manipulated by the media. Some had been paid to kill. I am convinced that for many, the genocide was a 'lapse' along the way. This does not diminish their responsibility in any way, nor does it mitigate the cruelty of what happened. But it's important for the children of those who killed to know that they are not damned and that their future has not been set in stone. If they are careful and if they learn to beware of manipulators, they will not fall into the same traps. Those who are constantly reiterating on the radio or in newspapers that all Hutu are bad and are killers are seriously endangering the future and are pushing the most fragile to become what they are accused of being.

Since the spring of 1995, there have regularly been hostile campaigns against you in the press, not only in Rwanda but also in Europe. For example, in France, the magazine Golias *has published very serious accusations against you on several occasions, including 16 pages about you in a 'special Rwanda edition' in August 1996. These accusations appear to be based on lots of testimonies. What is this about and what is your response to these attacks?*

Indeed I have been the object of several slanderous campaigns. I have been accused of being an ideological accomplice of Hutu extremism. I have been criticized for various statements, friendships and unworthy attitudes. I have been accused of persecuting Tutsi before the genocide and refusing to protect fugitives during the killings, thus leading them to their death. Some claim to have seen me carrying arms. Others believe that I collaborated with the militia. Since the end of the war, I allegedly sabotaged the process of national reconciliation systematically and obstructed recon-struction. Apparently, the only people I care about are Hutu, prisoners, killers and their families. I am allegedly responsible for a network to smuggle out priests who were involved in the genocide.

I am hiding killers. I am using the standing that I enjoy in Rwanda and in some diplomatic circles to criticize and discredit the current regime by spreading lies. I am allegedly using the alibi of human rights and my public standing to defend the Hutu in the south. I am a regionalist, etc. I'll stop there, although the list is far from exhaustive.

What can I say in response to this web of stupid, ridiculous and criminal lies? I was lucky in my misfortune that an organization which campaigns for freedom of the press, for whom I am a correspondent in Rwanda and which awarded me its Freedom of the Press prize in December 1994, took the trouble to investigate the bases for these accusations. Reporters sans frontières pulled apart the mechanisms of this crude plot, point by point. You can read the substantial report which was published in December 1995 entitled *La Désinformation au Rwanda: Enquête sur le cas Sibomana* [Disinformation in Rwanda: Investigation into the Sibomana case]. I will limit myself to one or two observations.

First of all, as you can see, I have not been arrested, despite these very serious accusations, some of which accuse me of active participation in the genocide. No complaint has been filed against me. Yet I have no shortage of enemies. If there was even a trace of evidence for these accusations, you can be sure that they would have seized the opportunity to imprison me.

Secondly, who is accusing me and since when? Under the Habyarimana regime, I was accused of being an RPF agent because I was defending persecuted Tutsi. I was not defending them because they were Tutsi but because they were human beings and because human rights are universal and inalienable. After the war, I resumed my activities as the head of *Kinyamateka* and ADL. I didn't change the political stand of the newspaper or of ADL: to tell the facts as they are, to hide nothing and to have a single objective: the search for truth. This led me to say and to write publicly what everybody knows but does not dare admit: human rights are no more respected today than they were under the previous dictatorship. From that moment onwards, I started becoming an awkward hero. My behaviour became a real problem when it became apparent that I was turning my words into action in the diocese of Kabgayi, for which I was responsible. I was accused of being an agent of the *interahamwe* because I was defending persecuted Hutu. I was not defending them because they were Hutu, or Hutu from the south, but because they were human beings and, as I said, because human rights are universal and inalienable. Finally, I want to point out that many episcopal posts are vacant in Rwanda. Some see me as 'bishop material', a kind of awkward rival. It's quite pathetic, but sadly that's the reality. People decided that it was time to get rid of Sibomana. So they started off by tarnishing my reputation in order to sow doubts in the minds of those who know me and to prepare the ground for 'the individual act of an uncontrolled element', which they would immediately deplore. Those who plan these kinds of operations are intelligent people; those who execute them, much less so. One of them is Gaspard Gasasira. He runs a newspaper, *Umusemburo*; almost every edition includes an unsigned article about me which tarnishes me a little bit more. For me, it is painful, but for the author of these articles, it's a very worthwhile activity. He is now *sous-préfet* of Butare and holds a senior post within the RPF. This is just one example – there are many others.

The purpose of all this business is to settle scores. I escaped several assassination attempts under the previous government. Killers on both sides failed to reach me during the genocide. But the threat is still there. In 1995, I survived several ambushes, one of which, on 16 September, almost succeeded.[39]

As for the people in Europe who echo these accusations, their behaviour is bewildering. I prefer not to reopen the debate with the magazine *Golias* and its director, Christian Terras. I don't know what his real motives are. I have noticed that the dramatic – not to say sensationalist – features which he publishes on Rwanda excite public curiosity and generate commercial profits, as well as a certain reputation. Such commercialization of the horror which we experienced is awful. I don't know whether he is being manipulated or whether he is acting in good faith, but I feel sorry for him. At least I hope that he thinks about the consequences of his articles, the risks he is creating for those he singles out for public revenge in Rwanda – I am not the only one whose actions are called into question – and that he is prepared to accept responsibility in relation to his own conscience. Nor will I respond to the attacks of Rakiya Omaar, the co-director of the British organization African Rights. Those who know Rwanda know how easy it is to be blinded by one's own passions.

---

[39] Translator's note: on the evening of 16 September 1995, two men came looking for André Sibomana in Kabgayi; they lay in hiding, waiting for him to return home. He escaped the ambush because he did not return at the expected time.

More recently, André Sibomana was taken in for questioning on the morning of 26 February 1997, after being accused of participating in the publication and distribution of a document described as subversive. This incident provoked a strong reaction in the diplomatic community. He was released the same day.

These campaigns are painful and difficult to bear. But I have derived great comfort from the very many statements of trust and friendship I have received from all over the world – from priests, diplomats, representatives of human rights organizations, journalists and known specialists on Rwanda. I express my sincere gratitude to those who spoke out.

How do you see the future of the Church and of Roman Catholicism in Rwanda?

Rwanda has just been through a particularly dark page of its history. It's not the first; we must make sure it's the last.

The attitude of some believers and Church officials has been unworthy and quite rightly creates confusion in people's minds. There are many problems for us to overcome, some of them new problems. We have to confront fear, ignorance and the distrust which has driven people apart. Society has been devastated by poverty, injustice and a spirit of accusation – not to mention the culture of violence, hatred and revenge. Disbelief and lies have become widespread. The increase in sects is also a challenge.

But we must not lose hope. I will repeat this again: men and women have sacrificed their lives to save strangers. They acted in the name of faith, in the name of the message of the Gospel which they not only learned but lived through, and for which they paid the highest price. These sacrifices are a sign and a hope. We have initiated a new catechesis which aims at deep conversion, revives the heart, preaches repentance, forgiveness, divine mercy, justice, peace, brotherly love, unity, respect for human life and the practice of the holy commandments. It's a long-term task. It is easier to turn a man into a killer than to educate him in the faith of God. We need time, but the will is there.

However, I am more pessimistic with regard to the ecclesiastical institution. First of all, as we are talking about reconstruction, I think we need to review completely the training for seminarians. Their training is much too theoretical and dogmatic and cut off from the reality of most Rwandans. Secondly, the clergy, unfortunately, is very divided. Members of the clergy are politicized and adopt partisan attitudes. This is very unfortunate.

Last but not least in terms of worries, I have noticed with a certain bitterness a strong continuity in the history of the Church. Yesterday, its senior officials colluded with the state. The same thing is happening today. Power has changed hands, the ideology is different, but the attitude of the heads of the Church is the same: instead of looking after the most destitute, those who are suffering and can't see the light at the end of the tunnel, their eyes are fixed on those who run the country and from whom they expect rewards. Just as before, some Church officials are closing their eyes to what is happening in the country. I don't want to go into the details or speculate about their motives. I just know that serious human rights violations are being committed today. The facts are known to all, and the Church, as an institution, is not reacting. Officials know what is happening, but they can't agree on what attitude to adopt. It is as if they have learnt nothing from what we have just lived through.

9 Rwanda Caught in an Impasse

We have talked about the need to deliver justice to the victims of the war, of the genocide and of the massacres. You have highlighted the deliberately slow pace of justice in Rwanda as well as international justice. When we talked about attempts to conserve the memory of past events, you expressed pessimism in the face of political manipulations of history. When we talked about the Church, you commented on the persistence of 'bad habits' and sharp divisions, alongside a deep desire for renewal. You don't seem very optimistic.

How could we be? After all we had been through, we had the right to hope for a different life. Many of us spent years struggling against the Habyarimana regime and its system of corruption. We were fighting for the right to freedom and dignity. We had started achieving significant results through peaceful means. Things were gradually changing, and changing for the better, for everyone. Yet the dictatorship ended in an unimaginable bloodbath. That was not necessary. It could have been avoided. If the October 1990 war had not upset the political chessboard, if certain foreign powers had not provided such strong support to the Habyarimana regime, if the international community had exerted stronger and more sustained pressure on the government, and particularly if Rwandans had been more responsible, especially the Rwandan elite – politicians, religious officials, intellectuals, journalists, military officials – many people would still be alive today.

But there was war, genocide and massacres. For four years, from 1990 to 1994, hundreds of thousands of civilians were shunted around from one end of the country to the other, dragged from displaced people's camps to transit camps, suffering from hunger and cold, completely destitute and humiliated. Not to mention those who were killed, tortured, mutilated, imprisoned just because they were Tutsi, political opponents, or poor and defenceless. Every society bears its own divisions; we have talked about the divisions which consume Rwandan society. These divisions exist; there is no point in denying it. But it was not necessary to revive them and turn them into political arguments. Divisions were deliberately exacerbated by unscrupulous politicians, simply to satisfy

137

their basest designs, their hunger for power and money, their pride and their desire for revenge. Pushed to the extreme, cynicism and hatred led to genocide and massacres. We really paid a high price for freedom.

And what have we achieved? What have we received in return for these killings? What has replaced the dictatorship of Juvénal Habyarimana? Is it the pluralist democracy for which so many of us struggled to raise awareness in people's hearts and in the public arena?

For years the RPF was the only hope for some Tutsi who were victims of oppression; they thought it would defend them and restore their rights. Very well. But when the RPF added armed struggle to its political battle in October 1990, it overturned the geopolitical order. Whether accidentally or deliberately, it accelerated the process of social disintegration; it facilitated the work of Hutu extremists who wanted nothing better. The RPF bears a share of responsibility for what followed. But we should also give it credit for its achievements: who put an end to the genocide? Not the United Nations peacekeepers, who were on the spot and fled at the first sound of gunfire. Not the international community, which took its time before deciding to do nothing. Not the Hutu masses who, at best, could delay the death of Tutsi by hiding them but who had no way of protecting them. If the RPF army hadn't been there, I don't know how many Tutsi would have survived.

Does this justify the policies of the RPF since the end of the war? Some people have said that sooner or later, the pendulum would swing the other way. I don't agree. The struggle for democracy was not necessarily lost. When the RPF took control of Kigali in July 1994, everything was still possible. The country had been crushed; it was in a state of shock. One million dead, two million displaced and as many refugees, a state of moral, psychological and material ruin, and, for once, strong mobilization of the international community in our favour: all this created the conditions for a new start, albeit at a heavy price. The vast majority of the population distrusted the RPF, because of the propaganda of Hutu extremists or because of the crimes it had committed. But it could prove itself: by taking power, it could stop being a minority armed rebellion movement and commit itself to promoting a new Rwandan state.

Wasn't this its policy? The government which was formed on 19 July 1994 more or less respected the peace accords negotiated in Arusha the previous year: the Prime Minister, Faustin Twagiramungu, was the one who was supposed to be appointed before the war; the Minister of the Interior, Seth Sendashonga, enjoyed a certain prestige among Hutu; his presence in the government was reassuring, as was that of Alphonse-Marie Nkubito in the Ministry of Justice. The government has spent three years preaching national reconciliation and the renewal of the Rwandan state. Its official policies mark a complete break with the past and its political plans consist in laying the foundations for a new Rwanda.

Official declarations are one thing; reality is another. First of all, the government of national unity which was formed in July 1994 only lasted one year. Three of its four Hutu ministers are now living in exile; the fourth died in suspicious circumstances.[40] We have to ask ourselves why.

Secondly, national reconciliation does not mean forcing people to subscribe to an ideology or to obey a new form of authority unquestioningly. As for reconciliation, it is as if Rwandans have been handed over from one administration to another without ever acquiring the right to think for themselves. That is extremely dangerous. The country had already seen the results of a cult of authority and blind obedience to orders. The Rwandan state or Rwandan society will never recover without prior recognition of fundamental public liberties, which is far from being the case.

The problem is not only that Rwanda missed the opportunity of a new start. Everyone can make mistakes. The problem is that, since 1994, the mistakes have not stopped and internal tensions have continually increased. You can kill people, but you can't kill their ideas. Whether good or bad, they will always survive. I can see that today, apart from official statements and gestures, the country is not moving towards reconciliation at all. Each month wasted is a month against us: if we don't learn to live together now, we will never manage to do so when demographic pressure makes our economic situation even more difficult. Time is against us.

That said, to be fair, we should stress that the RPF is not the only culprit. We can criticize the way in which the official policy of reconciliation is conducted, but we must remember that it takes two to achieve reconciliation, and many people on the other side are not playing by the rules either. I am not only referring to Hutu extremists in exile who are proud of their crimes. I am thinking of those inside the country who have not always succeeded in shaking off the terrible propaganda which led them to murder. The methods

---

[40] Translator's note: Alphonse-Marie Nkubito died in Kigali on 13 February 1997; Seth Sendashonga was killed in Nairobi, Kenya, on 16 May 1998 (see Postscript).

used by the RPF to close the camp of Kibeho, massacring several thousand refugees, were scandalous and unacceptable. However, we should not forget that extremists who had been involved in the genocide were maintaining their propaganda activities inside the camp and blocking all attempts at reconciliation.

What do you see as the main problems affecting Rwanda today?

I won't come back to the problems of justice and the prisons, or the challenges facing the Church, all of which we have already talked about. I am not in a position to talk about the economic or administrative problems of rebuilding a country which has been devastated by years of neglect, followed by a long and costly war, a genocide, systematic and organized looting, then equally systematic and organized counter-looting. I will limit myself to talking about the problems that everyone can see and understand. These are also problems which each of us can contribute to resolving by changing our behaviour.

The first, without a shadow of a doubt, is fear. Our country is living in a state of terror. It would be simplistic to reduce this phenomenon to fear of Hutu for Tutsi and fear of Tutsi for Hutu. It's a much broader, deeper phenomenon. Peasants distrust each other. They live in fear of authority in general, whether it is the authority of the *bourgmestre*, the *préfet*, the gendarme or the military. Peasants live in fear of the urban population. Tradesmen live in fear of civil servants. Soldiers live in fear of their commanders. Ministers live in fear of their citizens. The army lives in fear of infiltrations. Rwanda lives in fear of its own shadow.

Where does this fear come from? We don't need to look very far. It is based on past events, but it feeds on daily life. Human rights are not respected in this country. Stating this reality is not a matter of opinion but a duty. Shall I read you ADL's interim report, published in July 1996? Until this day, no one has challenged its contents. In ten dense pages, we registered the most blatant cases of unpunished murder, commune by commune. It's always the same scenario: men, women, children, priests and magistrates are killed, in the daytime or at night, with knives or with firearms. Witnesses accuse armed men wearing military uniforms who, strangely, move about freely without fear of being arrested. How can we fail to conclude that they are soldiers of the Rwandan Patriotic Army?

Unfortunately they are not the only ones. Former FAR soldiers and militiamen are still hiding in our villages. They have their weapons and they know how to use them. They kill survivors of the genocide to eliminate witnesses of their crimes. They attack RPF soldiers and spread terror.

I will give you a few examples. On 7 April 1996, these extremists marked the second anniversary of the genocide in their own way by attacking the cement works at Mashyuza, in Bugarama commune. Soldiers who were guarding the factory repelled the attack and defused explosives which had been attached to pylons. A few days later, on 19 April, another armed group attacked the local detention centre to release the detainees. The outcome: 46 of the 49 prisoners were killed on the spot and two were taken to hospital. The assailants accuse the soldiers who were guarding the prison of taking the opportunity to eliminate the detainees. The military, on the other hand, claim that the assailants were responsible for the killings. Meanwhile, 46 people were killed.

Here is another example which we describe in our statement on the resurgence of insecurity published on 13 February 1997. On 9 February 1997, an armed group set up a roadblock on the Kigali–Ruhengeri–Gisenyi road. They stopped all the passengers and stripped them of their possessions. Then the members of the armed group separated their hostages according to their ethnic group and systematically killed all the Tutsi.

We have recorded all these crimes in our reports, alongside those committed by RPA soldiers. We don't describe them from the point of view of the killers, counting their respective scores, but from the point of view of the victims, who are targeted from all sides. FAR soldiers who have infiltrated our villages or are hiding there benefit from a certain complicity among the rural population: some peasants who have been victims of RPF abuses are gradually siding with those who committed the genocide or who are perpetuating this struggle. This is a terrible and very dangerous development.

Much has been written about these continuous human rights violations. The Office of the United Nations High Commissioner for Human Rights, which has deployed dozens of observers in the country since 1994, has published reports on these abuses. Personally I find their reports infrequent and very cautious, but they are overwhelming. Some observers were threatened following the publication of these reports. These threats have to be taken seriously: on 4 February 1997, two observers, a Briton and a Cambodian, were killed, along with three Rwandan interpreters and assistants who were with them at the time.

Do we need to come back to the massacre at Kibeho in April 1995? The RPF had decided to use force to close a camp of displaced Hutu. The peasants opposed it; they were terrorized and manipulated by extremists who controlled the camp. On 20 April, the RPF cut off the water supply and prevented humanitarian organizations from providing food to the refugees, with the aim of forcing them to leave the camp. UNAMIR – whose mandate was to prevent abuses – was there, on the spot, at the entrance to the camp. As tension increased and it became clear that the situation was getting out of control, it failed to intervene. Then the situation exploded. There was an incident between some refugees and the soldiers who were guarding the camp: the soldiers opened fire. The official estimate was 338 dead. The estimate of Médecins sans frontières: 7,000 dead. The estimate of the United Nations: 2,000 to 4,000 dead, according to successive and different versions in internal reports. The camp was emptied with bursts of mortar and machine-gun fire ...

Do we need to recall the circumstances of the massacre of Kanama on 12 September 1995? An RPF officer was killed in unexplained circumstances in the region of Kanama, near Gisenyi, in the west of the country. Without having carried out an investigation, the regional military commander decided that the officer had been killed by elements of the former Rwandan armed forces who had infiltrated the region. He launched a reprisal operation. The counter-attack was horrifying: 110 Hutu peasants were massacred, one by one. At first the RPF claimed that the people killed were soldiers who had infiltrated the area. When United Nations observers went to the scene, they saw that most of the dead were women and children.[41]

I mentioned the ADL interim report of August 1996. This is what I had written in an ADL statement one year earlier, on 28 August 1995. You will see that there is a sinister stability about the human rights situation:

> The Rwandan Association for the Defence of Human Rights and Public Liberties deplores once again the killings which constitute the climax of a campaign of intimidation and harassment of public and religious officials who are usually recognized among the population for their human qualities and their moral integrity. The repetition of these barbaric acts of savagery, the similarity of certain circumstances and the

---

[41] On 12 September 1997, a military court in Kigali sentenced four RPA officers to 28 months' imprisonment for non-assistance to persons in danger in Kanama. The charges of murder and complicity to murder were dropped.

commissions of inquiry which are set up but never publish their results all lead us to believe that these acts are not the work of criminals acting in isolation. There is no excuse which can be used indefinitely as an alibi to legitimize such a shameful situation and one which shows so little respect for human dignity.

The RPF started killing as soon as it arrived in the country. In my own commune, in Masango, in the space of two months, between July and August 1994 – one month after the RPF took control of the area and after the end of the war – I personally counted 216 dead and more than 2,000 disappeared. Where are these people? Do you want to come and dig up the mass graves in Mukingi, Mushubati and Tambwe? These massacres are continuing today.

The second problem is information. As you know, a lack of transparency in information often feeds fear and fuels the wildest rumours. Freedom of the press is an excellent barometer for democracy. The democratization movement which began in Rwanda in 1989 started with the emergence of private, independent newspapers. The persecution of journalists was also one of the first signs of the government hardening in 1990. Then, as it couldn't defeat the private media, the government began to flood the market with extremist publications which it secretly supported, with their notorious, terrible capacity for indoctrination.

What have we seen since 1994? At first the government allowed the press to resume its activities freely; then it continually restricted its freedom. It was quite understandable and desirable to limit the scope of the extremist press. The media should participate in public debates by contributing opinions and points of view. But a call to murder is not a point of view; it is a criminal offence. Yet behind the official objective of raising the moral standards of the press, a real censorship has gradually settled in. It started at the grassroots, within the editorial teams of public and private newspapers, and rose to the top: even the Minister of Information ended up fleeing the country. He is now living in exile in Belgium.

Persecution of journalists started again in the autumn of 1994. Arrests, disappearances, attacks and various forms of intimidation increased in early 1995. One event marked the turning point: the attack on Edouard Mutsinzi, the director of the independent weekly *Le Messager* [The Messenger]. Towards the end of the day, in a café in the centre of Kigali, a group of Tutsi extremists beat him for a long time without anyone intervening. He was left for dead; he managed to survive and is living in Belgium; he is seriously disabled. But the message got through: from then on, anyone criticizing the government knew what to expect. Other attacks followed, as well as disappearances, such as that of Manasse Mugabo. Where is he? He was an intelligent and refined journalist, who always gave a qualified account of the situation – it was not a coincidence that he was director of the Kinyarwanda service of the United Nations radio station, Radio UNAMIR. Then one day, he disappeared without a trace. Two years later, his wife is still without news. Apparently RPA officers had warned him that he was going too far.

Today, apart from *Kinyamateka*, there is virtually no opposition press. Rwandans realize perfectly well that there is a significant discrepancy between what they see with their own eyes every day and what they hear through the official media or private newspapers which support the government line. They can see that they are not being told the truth. Once again, we have fallen into an era of suspicion and speculation, which is so favourable to the dissemination of the worst kind of propaganda. It's a serious situation.

The third problem is poverty – the ordinary poverty of peasants who can't feed their families or buy tools; the poverty of orphans abandoned to their fate by the war or gathered in large orphanages; the poverty of survivors who dare not return to their land or reclaim their property or who don't have the strength to rebuild their lives; the poverty of those whose hearts and bodies have been mutilated, those who have lost their minds, and the hundreds who have been left with stumps or extensive scars. Rwanda was a poor country before the war; now it is considered one of the poorest countries in the world.

I would also mention despair as one of the most serious problems we are facing. As I said, survivors have lost the will to live. They are deeply unhappy. Many believed that the government would treat them as a priority and would take care of their future. Their illusions have been shattered. Not only is the government not caring for them, but it blames them for having survived. Beyond the solemn speeches and gestures, nothing is being done to resettle them.

The future of women has become a problem. Our country is suffering from a situation similar to that of France in the 1920s or Germany in the 1950s: there are too many women and not enough men. The first problem is the widows. Many lost their husbands during the genocide or during the war. How will they earn a living? Then there is the problem of women whose husbands are in exile, or, worse still, in prison. The exile of the head of the family means the loss of moral and material support. But the imprisonment of a spouse is an additional responsibility: they have to visit him and take food and clothing to him. Finally, young women can't find a husband because young men have gone into hiding or have fled the country. On top of all these calamities, there is AIDS: it is still impossible to evaluate the impact of this disaster.

The widows and victims of the war are generally inactive. They have been stunned by what happened to them. There are widows' organizations, of course, but these organizations are very politicized. They cultivate hatred, instead of looking for ways of surviving. They represent only themselves.

There is one category of women who deserve special attention: those who have been victims of rape and who find themselves mothers of unwanted children. FAR soldiers and *interahamwe* militia carried out rape on a large scale. For some, it was part of a political strategy: rape was one more step in the process of humiliating a Tutsi family. Many women were raped in front of their family, then killed with them. But for most of the perpetrators, I think it was just another form of delinquency, like theft or looting. Because it was not only Tutsi women who were victims of rape; many young Hutu women were also subjected to this violence. Indeed, that is why we have to look after so many single mothers today. Who will see to their future? Which men will agree to set up a home with these young women and their children? They are even more in need of help because they have been rejected on all sides and have sunk into a profound misery.

Many mixed families are also in a desperate situation. The families who have survived tend to stay together. But many couples live separately. These families are in an impossible situation. Many Hutu spouses are living in exile, while the rest of their family is in Rwanda.

The problem is different according to the ethnic group. In most mixed couples, the husband is Hutu and the wife Tutsi. The children are therefore Hutu. In many cases, the wife has been killed – sometimes by her own husband or in his presence – and the family is in exile. If the husband was able to save his wife and the family had time to flee ... When the wife is Hutu and the husband Tutsi, the children are Tutsi. If the husband has been killed, the widow has to justify her situation: why didn't she protect her husband? Why has she survived? The Tutsi from her region bear a grudge against her. Her own children may also reject her.

These are impossible situations. Maybe this is one of the reasons why mixed marriages have virtually disappeared. The influence of extremist Tutsi newspapers, like *Umusemburo* or *Imboni*, which incite Tutsi not to marry Hutu, is very weak. But the opportuni-

ties for Hutu and Tutsi to meet are increasingly rare and there are
strong family and social pressures.

Finally, there is the despair of the youth. I was struck by the
results of research we carried out in Kabgayi to understand their
state of mind. What do they say and how do they see themselves?
Many are completely helpless or disillusioned. The girls don't see
any future for themselves. The war disrupted their schooling. Lack
of money prevents them from resuming their studies. Men have
become scarce; they have difficulty finding a husband and setting
up a home. They can't find work either. Many have family responsibilities and have to help their mother or their brothers and sisters,
and replace a father who is absent, or dead, or in prison, or in flight.
Some have been victims of violence; many are traumatized and dis-
orientated; they are unable to enjoy life and have closed in on
themselves.

Young girls have explained how they had to confront their own
family which was hostile to national reconciliation. I read the
testimony of a young woman who had given birth after being
raped. Having suffered this terrible aggression and the difficulties
of pregnancy, she then had to fight the shame within her own circle:
'Everyone was telling me that he would become an *interahamwe*
too and that he would end up killing me.' She had the courage to
resist and to keep the child, who is her only family. But how many
others won't have had the courage to exercise their freedom of
choice? Young girls are suffering from a terrible loneliness and
human misery which is even greater than their economic misery,
let alone the problems of health and AIDS.

Young men are not much more optimistic. They lack education,
they suffer from insecurity and are afraid of being imprisoned. Many
complain of a lack of training; they feel that they are wasting their
time and can't find work. These are the young people who will build
the future of our country. We must urgently find ways of looking
after them properly.

The fourth problem is the refugees. First the Tutsi refugees, who
fled Rwanda between 1959 and 1994. There are approximately
600,000 of them and although there are no reliable statistics, it
seems that almost all of them have now come back to Rwanda. But
these refugees are not all the same and have not all lived the same
life in exile. Some were wealthy and prosperous; they were
successful in exile and have come back to Rwanda with an entre-
preneurial mentality. They can make a big contribution to the
country. They can also behave like conquerors. Some are devoting
considerable energy to reviving the national economy. They will

benefit from it themselves one day but, in the meantime, everyone is benefiting from their efforts. Others adopt the attitude of the former masters and the pride they derive from returning by force makes them arrogant and aggressive. They provoke hostile and dangerous reactions.

Some refugees are disappointed. They believe that they have a right to the country and expect the government to reward them for returning. Some provided financial support to the RPF in the same way that one makes an investment in providing education for a brilliant child. Now they want to claim their dividend. Among those who are disappointed there are soldiers who took risks during the war, who are badly paid and deprived of schooling (many soldiers are under 18) and deprived of a future. They live in the same poverty as those over whom they are keeping watch and often share their fear. Their fate cannot be compared with that of the refugees who returned from Bujumbura after the war, who sometimes behave like bandits.

The second category of refugees is the 2 million Hutu who fled in 1994. Some were displaced within Rwanda; for example, some sought temporary protection in the safe humanitarian zone created by the Turquoise Force. Others went into exile in Uganda (very few), in Tanzania (where the famous Benaco camp was), in Burundi (along the northern border) and in Zaire (in the Lake Kivu region, between Bukavu and Goma). What has happened to them? Very few have returned to their homes. The refugees from Tanzania who did not return to Rwanda in December 1996[42] are rebuilding their life, or what is left of it, in camps controlled by their former leaders who were heavily involved in the genocide. In Burundi, the camps were closed by force throughout 1996. The Burundian army expelled these refugees towards Rwanda or Zaire without taking their fears or wishes into account. Indeed in Zaire, where there is the largest concentration of refugees in the world, the population was taken hostage by those who committed the genocide. The United Nations High Commissioner for Refugees and the International Committee of the Red Cross deployed huge resources to enable them to return: only a few thousand returned between July 1994 and October 1996. The extremists who were controlling the camps would kill those who gave any indication of wanting to return.

---

[42] Translator's note: in December 1996, the majority of the 500,000 Rwandan refugees who had been living in Tanzania since 1994 were forced back to Rwanda by the Tanzanian security forces.

Then the situation suddenly changed in October 1996. The Banyamulenge – Kinyarwanda-speaking Tutsi who have lived in eastern Zaire for hundreds of years – revolted following persecution at the hands of the local Zairian population and Hutu extremists among refugees in the region. In just a few weeks, fewer than 3,000 Banyamulenge managed to drive a million refugees out of the Kivu region ... Against all expectations, many of these refugees (an estimated 500,000 people) returned to Rwanda, free from the grip of the Hutu extremists who had been controlling them. Many others (estimates vary from 200,000 to 700,000) fled deep into the interior of Zaire, into very hostile regions.

What has happened to them? Laurent-Désiré Kabila's rebels pursued them until they withdrew into totally uninhabitable areas. France defended plans for an intervention force, but the Americans blocked it until the situation on the ground made it impossible to implement. Thousands of Rwandans were left to die of thirst, hunger and exhaustion because they had the misfortune of being in the wrong camp. Nobody wanted to get involved with 'the Goma people', because it was well known that they included many criminals who had been involved in the genocide. Does this justify the horrific death of tens of thousands of children?

According to information published in the Western press,[43] many refugees who had been 'liberated' by the rebels of Laurent-Désiré Kabila and their allies from Rwanda and Uganda were massacred on the spot, the very day that they were captured. Those who didn't have time to flee were killed, one by one or in groups of several hundred. Between October 1996 and May 1997, tens of thousands of people disappeared in eastern Zaire. Who cares about the fate of these people? I am profoundly indignant at the attitude of the international community which didn't lift a finger and abandoned these completely vulnerable and destitute people to their fate.

I will mention one last problem: the sharing of power, that is the sharing of wealth. Each ethnic group, and within each ethnic group each clan, wants to seize power in its entirety. That's what happened at the end of the Kayibanda regime, when a group of politicians

---

[43] Following overwhelming testimonies of massive and systematic massacres of refugees in eastern Zaire, particularly in the Goma region (*Libération*, 10 March 1997) and south of Kisangani (*Libération*, 30 April 1997), the United Nations Human Rights Commission despatched an investigative team led by Roberto Garreton [the United Nations Special Rapporteur on Zaire]. The team was forced to leave Zaire on 12 May 1997 after Laurent-Désiré Kabila's forces prevented it from visiting alleged massacre sites.

from Gitarama, in the south of the country, drove from power all those whose origin was different. To fulfil their goal, these politicians physically eliminated opponents. The same phenomenon occurred at the end of the Habyarimana regime: the Hutu from the north, particularly the clan of the wife of the head of state (the *akazu*) excluded from senior posts not only Tutsi, but also Hutu from the south. It started with changes in postings within the civil service. Then an increasing number were dismissed from their posts. Finally – this was the last phase – the awkward ones were killed. Habyarimana not only ordered the killing of his opponents, but also of their families and loved ones.

What is the RPF doing today? It is monopolizing all spheres of power for the Tutsi. We are also witnessing a ruthless struggle within the Tutsi community: between the Tutsi inside Rwanda – the survivors of the genocide – and those outside Rwanda – the diaspora. Finally, even the diaspora which has returned to the country is fighting over the loot.

The RPF was not created to fight a war, but to encourage the return of refugees who had been in exile since Rwanda's independence. It did not need to fight a war: there were other ways of reaching the same goal, as proved by archives relating to the Arusha negotiations. What is the RPF's real vision of society? It's difficult to know.

What about Burundi?

It's a wound which we have to live with, just as Rwanda is a wound for Burundi. The history of both countries is a series of misunderstandings and cross-purposes. It would be wrong to say that they are similar. The mutual influence of the two countries only seems to come into play to aggravate the situation. Rwanda's independence, the *coup d'état* in 1973 and the war in 1990 shaped Tutsi radicalism in Bujumbura. Conversely, the genocide of the Hutu elite in 1972, the massacres in 1988 and the assassination of Ndadaye in 1993[44] convinced the Hutu in Rwanda that they had to get rid of the Tutsi once and for all. It is not a coincidence that

[44] Translator's note: Melchior Ndadaye was Burundi's first Hutu president. He came to power in July 1993 in the country's first presidential elections. He was assassinated on 21 October 1993 following an attempted military coup. In the weeks that followed, Hutu armed groups killed thousands of Tutsi; these massacres were followed by reprisal killings of Hutu by the Burundian army and Tutsi militia. A total of at least 50,000 people are thought to have been killed between October and December 1993.

RTLM became more radical after the assassination of Ndadaye. Many believed that, even if the Arusha accords were concluded, they would not be implemented as each side suspected the other of not playing fair.

You have listed a number of problems which confront Rwanda today. In the face of these social dilemmas, it is as if it is always the extremists on one side or the other who end up winning. Why?

You have to ask the people who support them.

When foreign powers such as Belgium, France or the United States intervene, they are always suspected of having ulterior political motives; it seems that they can no longer help Rwanda. What about the United Nations?

Only the Office of the High Commissioner for Human Rights is still here.[45] Obviously they don't see everything, but they see enough to know what is happening in the country. I find them surprisingly silent. But what does it matter? Even when they publish reports or statements, nothing changes. In Rwanda the UN is using traditional means of action which are completely unsuitable. Five thousand four hundred UN peacekeepers were sent to Kigali for peacekeeping and for the security of the population; at the first incident, in other words when their presence became necessary, they left the country. I'll leave out the details of the individual behaviour of some soldiers and officers, which ranged from trafficking to prostitution and all sorts of irresponsible actions, and hardly contributed to improving the image of UNAMIR and the UN.

It would seem that no one has learned the lessons of the past ...

The Americans have chosen to support Paul Kagame. Their support for him is all the more vigorous because they did absolutely nothing to help the Tutsi during the genocide. They are acting with a perfectly clear conscience; they don't ask themselves questions about how all the arms they are providing will be used. Doesn't this remind you of France's behaviour under the previous regime?

---

[45] Translator's note: the UN Human Rights Field Operation left Rwanda in July 1998 (see Postscript).

*In a refugee camp on the outskirts of Jerusalem, you met a Palestinian
who, like you, is a journalist and a human rights activist. What are your
thoughts about Bassem Eid's fight for his fellow citizens?*

I was struck by his speech about the sad fate of Palestinians today.
Our histories seem to reflect each other like mirrors. The rights of
the Palestinian people were not recognized for a long time, like the
Hutu under the monarchy or the Tutsi under the Habyarimana
regime. Many were forced to flee into exile after violent wars; this
led to the creation of a large diaspora, united and militant, like the
Tutsi diaspora. The Palestinians created a political organization,
the PLO, and an armed wing, the Fatah. It is like the RPF and the
RPA. They waged a war of national liberation which eventually
brought to power a charismatic leader, Yasser Arafat; it is like the
story of Paul Kagame. I could continue the list of similarities: the
role of the international community and campaigning support
groups, the sympathy of the media, the existence of extremist
movements which sabotage the peace process, the arbitrary and
ideological character of the leadership ...

Many of those who gave what they had to support the PLO – a
child, money, shelter – seem to regret it bitterly. In Gaza I met
Palestinians who today would like to cut off their arm which threw
stones at the Israelis yesterday. They supported an armed rebellion
which was supposed to bring them if not prosperity, then at least
peace, freedom, democracy and dignity. Instead, the Palestinian
authorities are carrying out barbaric acts; they are monopolizing
power and imprisoning and torturing people. Parallels can be
drawn between the PLO movement and the RPF movement.

According to Bassem Eid, one of the explanations for the current
conflict between the majority of Palestinians and the Palestinian
Authority is that their leaders have lost all contact with the real
country after years of exile and more or less clandestine struggle.
When they returned to Palestine, they expected to find it as they
had left it several decades ago. I was staggered by what one
Palestinian told me, 'We need a president who was born here and
has lived here. The Palestinians of the diaspora have lost contact
with people's aspirations.'

The Palestinian Authority constitutes a minority which
monopolizes power and claims to impose its truth on the whole
population. Palestinians have won autonomy but they have lost their
rights to their country. Bassem Eid said, 'We have become strangers
in our own land.' He told me this anecdote: 'When I criticize
Arafat, I am accused of being anti-patriotic. Uri Avneri, a well-

known independent Israeli journalist with a "pro-PLO" reputation, blamed me for publishing a report in July 1996 which "upsets the peace process". Just because I was reporting true facts, which everyone knows and which anyone can check.'

I am not an expert in Palestinian history and specialists will find it easy to pick me up on certain quick comparisons. The fact remains that the similarities are disturbing. They make me think that the Hutu–Tutsi question is not the heart of the problem: it is only one part of the picture, a pretext manipulated by politicians, an ingredient in the fight for power. We shouldn't deny the existence of the Hutu–Tutsi conflict; it has always existed and unfortunately today, more than ever, it is in all our hearts. Everyone agrees that what we need to do is attack the root of evil, that is man's unrestrained taste for power in all its forms and at any price, a price society has paid for with misery.

Conclusion
We Must Not Give Up Hope

There is often a paradox which emerges from our conversations with you – whether as a priest, a journalist or a human rights activist. You are always very critical towards your contemporaries and you tirelessly denounce the failings of the society in which you live. At the same time you refuse to resign yourself or to give in to pessimism. It would appear that the duty of hope has become your guiding principle.

We don't have the right to give up hope. Life has been given to us; it is a gift from God. As a believer, and especially as priest who must help other believers find the way, I don't have the right not to hope. We have to accept the gift of life and rise towards God, if possible along the path of happiness, and if not, by searching for the paths of truth through unhappiness. Unfortunately in Rwanda the paths of unhappiness are the most common. But this does not entitle us to abdicate from our human condition. We must work towards creating a better life for everyone; the Gospel shows us the way.

Our country has just lived through one of the most tragic pages of its history. This ordeal was not necessary. We could have made other choices and human lives could have been spared. Large numbers of people were killed. Justice must search for those who are guilty and try them. Survivors must preserve the memory of this tragedy and learn lessons for the future. The failure to take on the consequences of our past would amount to killing for a second time those whose life has already been stolen.

Nothing is inevitable. Our future has not been predetermined. It will be what we decide to make of it. We build our future every day; it is the fruit of each person's labour. We should not delude ourselves or believe that statements of good intentions are sufficient to build the future. Human beings are judged by their actions.

We have to overcome great hardships. Before the war, we were poor and life was not easy. Now we are even poorer and, in addition, we have to assume a collective memory which has been flayed alive. When we met Tom Segev in Jerusalem, he mentioned that the traumatism of the genocide is far from having disappeared in Israel.

On the contrary, it seems to have become part of the 'genes' of Israelis. Even those whose families were never directly affected by the genocide identify with this tragedy and consider themselves as survivors. It is a sinister victory for Nazism after the event: today Jews define themselves through the condition of those who were humiliated yesterday. How will we Rwandans live with this 'dark stain' on our collective memory? I don't know. I don't have the solution.

I am very harsh towards the current government, as you rightly pointed out. Is this an injustice towards survivors? I don't think so. In fact I believe the opposite is true. The victims of massacres in 1994 died under the blows of a government which had put respect for human rights low down on its list of priorities. The tyrants who ruled us yesterday did not attach a high priority to respect for human beings, whoever they were, whatever their opinions or their ethnic, religious or social origins. We must ensure that this happens today.

Governments always have good reasons for not respecting human rights. They always claim mitigating circumstances or historical, political or economic justifications. They always postpone their commitments towards human conscience. This is not honest and it is not good enough. Human rights are not negotiable and there are never mitigating circumstances. Those who accept small concessions today, whatever the motive, will close their eyes on more important concessions tomorrow; they will only wake up when it is too late. That is what happened in Rwanda. Once is enough; we must not allow the seeds of a new genocide to grow.

We must be uncompromising in the sphere of human rights, but we must be more flexible in the political sphere. I am not among those who want to wipe away the past. It happened, it is there, and we have to take it into account. But it should not blind us either or prevent us from moving forward. There will never be peace in Rwanda or in the Great Lakes region if we each turn towards our own past and simply insist on our historical rights. History has evolved in such a way that legitimate and contradictory histories are intertwined. It is the responsibility of politicians, at least those who have the stature of statesmen, to take on these contradictions and to convince the people that there is no possible future without conciliation. Negotiating does not mean forgetting or denying the past. It means striving for a future where divisions are not perpetuated and ensuring that the tears of the past do not run down our cheeks for ever.

In that respect, I wholeheartedly wish for the emergence of politicians of stature from Rwandan society, people who are capable of putting the destiny of our country above the interests of their ethnic group, their clan, their family or themselves. Many men and women who could have played that role in Rwanda – at all levels of the social hierarchy, in all fields – have been killed. These Rwandans who have disappeared are a huge and irreparable loss for our country. We must prepare to take over from them.

I have high expectations of intellectuals, sociologists and historians. They must get to work and try to understand, to explain, to write. They must help us make sense of our past. We need our memory and we have to understand what led us to the edge of the cliff. That is the only way not to return there.

We must learn to live together again. Some diplomats who presumably thought that we would never be able to live together again have suggested creating a 'Hutuland' and a 'Tutsiland'. This idea is not only stupid, but very harmful. Apart from the fact that a division of Rwandans along these lines would be a magnificent victory for advocates of racism, I don't think that problems are solved by shifting them or pushing them to one side; quite the contrary.

The militia were not sent by the Hutu people. They didn't represent them any more than the RPF represented the Tutsi as a group. Not all militiamen were Hutu and not all Hutu were militiamen. The presence of a few Tutsi among the *interahamwe* strengthened some people's belief that the movement had a national legitimacy and was fighting the enemy, just as the presence of a few Hutu within the RPF led some to believe that the RPF could legitimately represent the struggle for national liberation. We must stop falling into these traps and clichés. Let us form judgements on the basis of facts. Let us shake off these stereotypes in which propaganda has drowned us.

The authority of the state must be strengthened and its power diminished. The state should represent public good; it should act beyond individual interests or the personal interests of those who run it. It must have a vision of the future and prepare the ground for new generations. We need to train professional executives who hold positions of power because of their competence, and no longer because of their origin or political links. At the same time, we must take away the sacred aura of the state and of the government in general; instead we must encourage a sense of criticism and public spirit. Instead of hammering out new dogmas, the current government would do better to reflect on what would constitute the best guarantee against peasants taking up machetes again in the future just because they are ordered to. One set of dogmas is easily replaced by another. It is more difficult to change mentalities and to sharpen critical faculties. Yet that is the most pressing need.

The Rwandan state exists; it has proved so on many an occasion. If our country had not been so well organized, the genocide might not have been carried out on such a scale. But for better or for worse, we are a strictly governed people. I would like this characteristic not to be corrupted any more. In this respect, I deplore the fact that the census organized between April and May 1996 was abused to carry out arbitrary arrests. People lose trust in the authorities and feel that the state which is governing them is not their own, that it is not at their service but that it is trying to entrap them. This is not a healthy situation. There are more urgent things to do than spend public funds on spying on the population. Almost 30 per cent of the urban population is HIV-positive; 80 per cent of prostitutes have AIDS. The threat of AIDS has been considerably accentuated by the intermingling of populations during each successive exodus, not to mention rape. Urgent action is needed in this field.

Rwanda suffers from being hemmed in and from endless self-analysis. It is suffocating and it has been stunned by what happened to it. We must open up the country. The international community can help us. It can help rectify the errors of the past. Once again, nothing is inevitable.

The diplomatic community and the non-governmental organizations present in Rwanda can make an important contribution. I am not only talking about the considerable material assistance they give us. I am thinking of the people who participate in these operations and from whose reflections and criticisms we can learn. Of course, we can criticise the NGOs for many things; not all of them behave in an exemplary way and there is a lot of waste. It's true that some of the 40 or so NGOs who were expelled from Rwanda in 1996 were not very competent. However, others were driven out because they were too good at their work. Organizations like Médecins sans frontières did not limit themselves to supplying aid: they testified to what they saw. We don't need doctors who turn a blind eye to the origin of the wounds they are treating. The two go hand in hand: relieve suffering and testify to the origin of the suffering.

The international press also has a role to play. Three years after the genocide, there are no more 'strong' images to show, so journalists are losing interest in Rwanda. Yet the press can play an educational and preventive role. It must continue to come here and report what is happening. It can play the role of an intermediary and defuse the debate. It must denounce the slow ethnic purge which is taking place. Part of the population is being eliminated through a long, slow process; the press must come and provide an account, with supporting facts. It must also follow the situation of the survivors and denounce the threats against them: the killings, the indifference, the oblivion. The press should pay attention to what the government is saying, but also to the daily experiences of the population.

My stay in Israel has enabled me to see things from a distance. I have reflected on the meaning of my work. We have to be patient. We should not expect immediate results. The fruits may only come a long time after the seeds are sown. Here I have discovered a little corner of land which seems to have to taken on all the problems which have befallen humanity over the last 2,000 years. We are not the only ones living in the eye of the storm. I did not find answers in Israel to the questions I was asking myself before leaving Rwanda, but I have understood that these questions are not my questions: they belong to all who suffer the violence of history and are seeking the path of freedom.

Just before leaving Kigali, one of my journalists asked me this question, 'So when will Rwandans ever be able to hope to die of old age?' That is my wish now. Let us give Rwandans time to live and let us give children time to bury their parents. Of old age.

Jerusalem, 15 August 1996
Kigali, 15 May 1997

Postscript
What Future for the Defence of Human Rights in Rwanda?

THE DEATH OF ANDRÉ SIBOMANA

The publication of *Hope for Rwanda* (*Gardons espoir pour le Rwanda*) in France in October 1997 attracted much interest, not only from those who had known André Sibomana, but from a broader constituency of people with an interest in Rwanda. It provided a rare, thought-provoking insight into the tragic events which the world is still struggling to understand.

For André Sibomana himself, the book was also to take on great significance. It represented the synthesis of the positions and principles he had defended for years and provided him with a unique opportunity to communicate those views to an international audience, speaking from the heart and without any form of censorship.

Below, Laure Guilbert and Hervé Deguine, who initiated and recorded the conversations in this book, describe André Sibomana's reaction to the publication and the circumstances of his sudden death in March 1998:

> As soon the book was published in October 1997, the publisher sent us a few copies in Paris. Without delay, we sent them on to André Sibomana in Rwanda; it had taken a long time for the book to be published and we knew that he was getting impatient.
>
> He received our parcel in Gitarama in early November. In an uncharacteristic gesture, he immediately wrote to us to express his joy and emotion. His letter was both tender and serious:
>
> '[This evening] I touched [our book] for the first time. It was very moving, in the faint candlelight (since 31 October we have been living in a town deprived of electricity and water) [...] Only you know the deep reasons which drove you to devote yourselves unreservedly to this task which has enabled me to regain courage, to live and to make my own small contribution to the rehabilitation of this little country called Rwanda [...] As for the book itself, I could not put it down. My first impression is that it is easy to read and contains serious statements. It

might provoke anger and wrath among several categories of people, including the Roman curia. I hope that beyond such feelings, it will enable many Rwandans and friends of Rwanda to reflect and to make every effort to finally build social harmony in Rwanda. I am very grateful to all those who have contributed to the realization of this work. You have helped Rwandans think of things other than hating each other and killing each other. I wish you all success in forging ahead and enjoyment in producing such good work.

We will be in touch again soon, maybe.

A. Sibomana.'

Not without pride, he distributed the few copies he had among his friends. Rwanda being a country of oral tradition, the publication of a book, especially in French and in Europe, is like a consecration. For this journalist-priest, this book, which summed up his struggle as a campaigner for faith and human rights, represented a landmark. But it soon turned into a testament.

Exhausted by the tough living conditions to which he was subjected, or to which he had been subjecting himself, psychologically devastated by the assassination of his former right-hand man, Father Vjeko Curic, in Kigali on 31 January 1998 [described below], André Sibomana fell ill in early February 1998. What was first presumed to be a simple indigestion soon turned into an attack of hyper-allergy known as Lyell's syndrome; it turned out to be fatal.

The news of his death on 9 March 1998 was shocking. Within a short time, doubt was added to the pain. Did Sibomana really die of illness, as announced by the bishopric of Kabgayi? Was this illness natural? Did he receive the correct treatment? Did those who could have intervened for him do everything in their power to try to save his life?

In order to dispel the doubts and put an end to the rumours which were beginning to circulate in Rwanda and abroad, we decided to carry out an independent and thorough investigation on the spot, without delay. Thanks to many testimonies – from members of his family, friends, academics, religious officials, government representatives and members of the diplomatic community – we were able to piece together, day by day, the events which led to the death of André Sibomana. This investigation led to the publication of a small book entitled *Enquête sur la mort d'André Sibomana* (Investigation into the death of André Sibomana), published in Paris by Reporters sans frontières in 1998. The conclusions of that investigation are summarized below.

The first conclusion is that André Sibomana's death was indeed the result of a natural illness. He was struck down by a particularly violent strain of Lyell's syndrome, which may have been triggered by a form of indigestion or by a strong reaction to anti-malarial treatment. He had already suffered an attack of the same illness in his youth [see Chapter 2] and he had only survived then thanks to his exceptionally strong physical resistance. But by 1998, he was physically exhausted and extremely demoralized. He was no longer able to mobilize the same resources to fight off the attack.

The situation was aggravated by the fact that the medical treatment he received was inadequate – this is the second conclusion. Initially, the illness was not correctly diagnosed. Then, it was not treated properly. And – perhaps most critically – the request for an emergency evacuation to a European hospital which had been prescribed by his doctor was turned down by the Rwandan authorities.

This is the third important point: since returning from Israel, where we had recorded the conversations related in this book, André Sibomana had been denied a passport. The Rwandan authorities had taken his passport away from him almost as soon as he landed in Kigali and had refused to give it back. In the following months, none of the official or unofficial negotiations which were undertaken achieved any result. The situation worsened after the publication of the book: more than ever, André Sibomana had become a dangerous opponent. Even when he was on death's door and his evacuation had become an emergency – a matter of hours – the Ministry of the Interior used a thousand devices to delay the delivery of the precious document and to ensure that all the last minute interventions were doomed to failure. In the end, under pressure from the diplomatic community, the authorities resigned themselves to producing a passport in haste. But André Sibomana died just before it was ready.

The Rwandan government bears a large share of responsibility for the death of André Sibomana because it prevented him from receiving appropriate medical treatment in Europe. But it is not the only institution responsible – and this is the fourth and final conclusion. The Church, or rather the ecclesiastical hierarchy – a distinction upon which André Sibomana had always insisted – displayed an astonishingly passive attitude. It abstained from intervening in his favour when he was trying hard to obtain a passport. It refrained from giving him any new, meaningful responsibilities after he was replaced at the head of *Kinyamateka* in September 1997. It did not intervene to ensure that he received appropriate medical care at the onset of his illness. Nor did it make any effort to find out more after his death – neither in Kigali, nor particularly in Rome, where the Vatican seems unconcerned about the sad fate of Rwandan or foreign priests who stand up to the military government in Kigali. Today, like yesterday, it seems as if the top layers of the ecclesiastical hierarchy prefer to close their eyes and wait for better days.

It was this attitude of waiting which André Sibomana could not accept. For him, the precepts of Christianity were only valid if they were all practised at once and immediately. His faith would not make allowances for strategies or calculations. This is what led him to write this last text, just a few days before his death. When he found out that his friends and Western diplomats were trying to force the government to agree to his evacuation, his reaction was one of determined rejection:

'Here are my wishes relating to my illness and the possibility of a transfer.

1. As a human rights defender, I submitted an application for a passport a long time ago, but the Rwandan state did not want to respect my rights. Agreeing to give me a passport at the peak of this illness which has struck me down is also a way of relieving themselves of responsibility for several other situations of injustice, some of which remain cloaked in silence.

   I refuse to accept this passport [and] I also refuse to be complicit in the violation of the rights of citizens. The refusal to accept this passport which has been rushed through should be seen as a forceful demand for situations of injustice to be resolved in the fairest ways.

2. As for the illness itself: I am familiar with it, because it is the same illness I caught in 1976. Rwandan doctors treated me then. This time, the illness has returned with renewed arrogance in my old age. If it can be cured, so much the better. If it kills me, they who denied me my fundamental rights should be among those held accountable.

Gitarama, 4 March 1998
André Sibomana'

When André Sibomana visited the site of Massada on the shores of the Dead Sea in August 1996, he was literally fascinated. As the sun rose above the ruins of the ancient fortress at dawn, he stood there in silence; he was impressed in a deep, religious way. It was on that hill at Massada, around the year AD 73, that one thousand Jews sought protection from persecution by Roman soldiers. After a siege which lasted several months, the men, women and children chose to commit suicide together. When the Romans eventually reached the site, they discovered a large quantity of untouched supplies, next to the bodies which lay intertwined. The Jews had left them this message: 'We could have continued resisting, we could have given up and lived in submission, but we chose to die free so that our faith and our values would live on eternally.'

Laure Guilbert
Hervé Deguine
Paris, 9 March 1999

This English translation of André Sibomana's book was completed exactly one year after his death. As soon as I read the book in 1997, it struck me that it needed to be made available in English, to enable André Sibomana to reach a large and influential audience with whom he had less direct contact and to improve the understanding of the situation in Rwanda in the Anglophone world. André Sibomana's book would provide a unique and precious insight to English-speaking readers.

I last saw André Sibomana in February 1998, less than a month before he died. It was an informal visit to his new office in Kigali; three months earlier, in November 1997, he had been appointed to a new post in charge of social communications for the Roman

Catholic Church. The office was in a new, empty building in a quiet location in the suburb of Kacyiru, off the beaten track. Despite having been put in charge of communications, André Sibomana's office had not even been equipped with a telephone. He felt isolated and deliberately marginalized by the Church authorities who had relegated him there. His new post was ill-defined and his initial hopes of using it to develop a dynamic policy of public information were quickly dashed. It had become clear to him that his new responsibilities were not intended to enable him to work in a meaningful way – quite the contrary. Attempts to silence him were beginning to pay off. In August 1997, André Sibomana's term as editor of *Kinyamateka* had ended; his successor, Father Dominique Karekezi, had been given clear instructions by the Church about the future direction of the newspaper.[46] Under its new leadership, *Kinyamateka* had adopted a conciliatory tone and, in stark contrast with the previous years, was carefully avoiding controversial topics. Several of its staff, as well as readers, have been deeply disappointed by the loss of the independent spirit and courage to criticize which had forged its reputation.

I spoke with André Sibomana in the echoing corridor outside his office. When I proposed to him that we translate his book into English, his eyes lit up; he said that many of his Anglophone friends wanted to read it and were frustrated that it was only available in French. In characteristic fashion, he quickly checked his own excitement and insisted that the translation be undertaken with great care and remain faithful to the original. Our conversation lasted only about 20 minutes because of prior commitments. We agreed to meet again the following week for a fuller discussion.

When I returned to his office on 25 February, his distinctive red car was nowhere to be seen and the office was deserted. A young girl informed me that André Sibomana was ill and would not be able to see me. Throughout the rest of my stay in Rwanda, I continued enquiring after his health, presuming that he would recover in a matter of days. At that stage, none of his friends or colleagues seemed aware of the gravity of the illness. But his health did not improve. I left Rwanda without being able to see him again. One week later, he died.

André Sibomana has left an immeasurable and lasting legacy in Rwanda. His death was followed by a flurry of tributes, none of which will ever convey fully the impact of his work and actions. Some of his achievements emerge directly or indirectly through this

---

[46] See *Enquête sur la mort d'André Sibomana*, Paris, Reporters sans frontières, 1998.

book. Others may only become apparent in more subtle ways, or in years to come.

THE DEFENCE OF HUMAN RIGHTS AND FREEDOM OF EXPRESSION IN RWANDA TODAY[47]

The state of the human rights movement in Rwanda over the last two years can only be understood within the broader context of developments which have taken place in the region since 1997, in particular the dramatic resurgence of violence in Rwanda and in the neighbouring Democratic Republic of Congo (former Zaire).

THE CONFLICT IN THE NORTHWEST AND MASSACRES OF CIVILIANS

The mass return of hundreds of thousands of refugees from the former Zaire and Tanzania in late 1996 was followed by a sharp escalation of violence in Rwanda. Among the returning refugees were an unknown number of militiamen and others who had been responsible for massacres during the genocide in 1994. The sheer scale of the mass return – mirroring, at least superficially, the mass exodus of 1994 – made it impossible to separate the militiamen from the refugee population.

During 1997 and 1998, massacres in the northwest of Rwanda reached the highest level since 1994. Insurgent groups commonly known as 'infiltrators', made up of ex-FAR, *interahamwe* and other elements, stepped up their attacks in President Habyarimana's region of origin, Ruhengeri, and in neighbouring Gisenyi. But the infiltrators were not alone in terrorizing the population. RPA troops were deployed in vast counter-insurgency operations, during which entire families were killed by soldiers. Both sides actively fuelled

---

[47] This section outlines some of the main developments in the situation in Rwanda since the conversations between André Sibomana and Laure Guilbert and Hervé Deguine were completed in 1997. It does not claim to analyse the political or social situation, but provides a brief update on some of the main themes covered by André Sibomana in this book, in particular freedom of expression, the role of human rights organizations and the process of justice. Originally, the intention had been to include in the English version an additional chapter of interviews with André Sibomana on these more recent events. Sadly, André Sibomana died before this work could be undertaken.

the conflict by deliberately targeting the most vulnerable people. Thousands of civilians died, including many elderly men and women and young children, some of them Hutu refugees who had been forced to return in 1996, others Tutsi survivors of the genocide.

As the conflict escalated, positions became increasingly entrenched and uncompromising, reflecting the determination and ruthlessness of those who have become immune to horror or who are blinded by the desire for power. Killings of several hundred people in a single attack became increasingly common. In 1995, the massacres of Kibeho and Kanama had attracted widespread international condemnation; by mid-1997, massacres on that scale had become a regular occurrence and were not even reported any more.

By early 1999, massacres have become rarer. Hundreds of thousands of people in the northwest – the predominantly Hutu population of the region – have been moved into large camps by the authorities, in a controversial policy officially intended to separate them from the insurgents. Large swathes of the countryside in Gisenyi and Ruhengeri lie empty; crops and villages have had to be abandoned. Many families, exhausted by the violence, were willingly led into the camps, or were too afraid to resist. Others were deeply suspicious of the motives of the authorities or simply did not want to leave their homes. Nevertheless, all of them were forced to move, sometimes by violent means. The camps are tightly controlled by the military and the region remains tense. For months, Rwandan human rights investigators have found it difficult to venture into the region, let alone gather information from its inhabitants. Gradually, in the context of a national policy of villagization, the internally displaced are being moved from the camps into new 'villages', where, they are told, they will benefit from greater protection and improved facilities. They do not know if and when they will ever see their homes again.

Despite the recent lull in the violence inside Rwanda, most Rwandans still live in a state of fear. The legacy of terror cannot be shrugged off so quickly, not least because of the fighting which broke out again in August 1998 in the Democratic Republic of Congo, just across the Rwandan border. The alliance which had brought Laurent-Désiré Kabila to power in 1997 – which had included Rwanda – fragmented and a new alliance composed of Congolese Tutsi, RPA soldiers and Ugandan soldiers, took up arms against their former leader. Within a short time, Congo was in a state of war, with several foreign countries sending troops to back either President Kabila's army or the rebellion,[48] and the remnants of the ex-FAR fighting alongside President Kabila's forces. In early 1999, prospects of an early end to the war seem remote, despite attempts by several regional leaders to negotiate a ceasefire and mediate between the parties.

In Congo as in Rwanda, civilians have been among the first victims and thousands have been massacred at the hands of the various parties involved in the conflict. The border between the two countries is ridiculed by Rwandans: 'There is no border', they say, and the nature of the violence which spills over proves them right. The same actors are using the same brutal tactics. Meanwhile, the greed of arms dealers around the world ensures that weapons continue to flow in, unchecked, and innocent civilians continue to pay with their lives for a war the objectives of which appear remote and obscure to the majority of the population who only long to live in peace.

The Assassination of Vjeko Curic

In addition to the massacres in the northwest of Rwanda, killings of individuals became increasingly common in Kigali in 1997 and 1998. One case had a particularly devastating effect on André Sibomana: on 31 January 1998, his long-time friend and collaborator, Vjeko Curic, a Croatian Franciscan priest who had been living and working in Rwanda for 17 years, was assassinated in Kigali. Vjeko Curic had worked closely with both Tutsi and Hutu communities. His efforts, combined with those of André Sibomana, had contributed significantly to reviving the diocese of Kabgayi after the genocide and had encouraged the population on the path of reconciliation. Like André Sibomana, Vjeko Curic had escaped several previous assassination attempts.

The real motives for the assassination of Vjeko Curic in January 1998 have never been established. An RPA soldier is thought to have carried out the act, but there has been much speculation as to where the orders came from. There are conflicting theories about whether this was a 'political' or an 'economic' crime; some people, including André Sibomana himself, believed that elements within the Roman Catholic institution may also have been

---

[48] Countries which have sent troops to support President Kabila include Angola, Zimbabwe, Namibia and Chad. The rebellion is supported primarily by troops from Rwanda and Uganda and, to a lesser extent, Burindi.

implicated.[49] The results of a government investigation into the killing have never been announced. Vjeko Curic is not the only foreigner – nor the only foreign priest – to have been killed in Rwanda. But his death affected André Sibomana in a more profound way, accentuating his depression and the sense of abandonment which emerges from the text he wrote days before his own death. After the death of Vjeko Curic, he confided to his friends that he thought he would be the next to die.

Justice or Revenge?

Since 1997, there has been progress – albeit slow and painful – in attempting to deliver justice for some of the atrocities committed in Rwanda during the genocide. The International Criminal Tribunal for Rwanda (ICTR), set up by the UN in Arusha, Tanzania, has more than 30 suspects in custody, including several figures who played a leading role in planning and implementing the genocide. In 1998, the ICTR issued its first, long-awaited judgements: Jean-Paul Akayesu, *bourgmestre* of Taba commune in Gitarama, and Jean Kambanda, Prime Minister in the interim government at the time of the genocide in 1994, who pleaded guilty at his trial, were both sentenced to life imprisonment. Further trials are under way. However, the ICTR will only ever be able to prosecute a handful of people, whereas massacres were committed by thousands in 1994.

Meanwhile, several hundred people have been tried by the national courts in Rwanda since December 1996, by specialized chambers which deal exclusively with genocide cases. Trials are continuing, but tens of thousands of suspects remain crammed into detention centres, with little prospect of being tried in their lifetime and every prospect of dying in prison, without their guilt or innocence having been established. A few thousand have been released for lack of evidence, but the number of detainees awaiting trial remains overwhelming. Of those tried, scores have been sentenced to death; many others have been sentenced to various terms of imprisonment and some have been acquitted. With a few exceptions,[50] most of those tried so far are not thought to have been

---

[49] The various theories surrounding the motives for the death of Vjeko Curic are described in *Enquête sur la mort d'André Sibomana* (Investigation into the death of André Sibomana) published by Reporters sans frontières in France in 1998.

[50] For example, Froduald Karamira, a leading figure of the MDR Power faction, was tried in Kigali in January 1997 and sentenced to death. He was among the 22 people executed on 24 April 1998.

high-level leaders or decision-makers in the genocide. Yet many more are likely to be sentenced to death and possibly executed.

On 24 April 1998, Rwanda witnessed the first executions of people found guilty of participation in the genocide. Public executions were staged in five different locations. The government had reversed an earlier decree which stated that executions would not take place in public; crowds of several thousand, including families with young children, attended this brutal spectacle. At the international level, the executions attracted widespread condemnation. Within Rwanda, they provoked a mixture of horror at the public display of state-sanctioned violence and bitter satisfaction at a semblance of retribution for the genocide. The fact that, in some cases, the guilt of those executed had not been established beyond doubt and that several had been convicted after unfair proceedings was generally overlooked.

Among local human rights organizations, reactions were typically polarized. ADL was among the first to issue a public statement, on the eve of the executions, describing them as a 'new form of trivialization of violence in Rwanda'. The statement appealed to the Rwandan government to refrain from carrying out the executions: 'There is a risk that these public executions, which appear to be motivated by a desire to appease certain minds, will produce the contrary effect to that intended.'[51] On 29 April, the human rights organization LIPRODHOR also issued a statement condemning the executions. It stated: 'Rwandans have seen enough atrocities. To force them to witness further killings, however legal these may be, is increasing tenfold the trauma they are still suffering.' In contrast, a statement by the organization Kanyarwanda, dated 28 April, expressed its satisfaction at the implementation of the sentences, which it described as 'a therapeutic and educational action which could lead to true reconciliation'.

In a country where violent death has become part of daily life and where impunity, rather than justice, has been the rule, it is difficult to evaluate the longer-term impact of these executions on ordinary Rwandans. There is a broad assumption – questioned only in private – that most of the population is in favour of executing those responsible for the genocide. André Sibomana was one of the few people who saw the value of an open debate on this

---

[51] A similar point was made in an appeal to the President of Rwanda by Thaddée Ntihinyurwa, Archbishop of Kigali and President of the Episcopal Conference, on 23 April: '[...] I strongly fear that this kind of sentence might be an obstacle to the process of reconciliation and contribute to a hardening of hearts in the contempt of human life [...]'

question. He used his privileged position to raise awareness of the death penalty as a moral and human rights issue and to encourage people to voice their true beliefs; he solicited the opinions of religious officials and others in the columns of *Kinyamateka*. It was a long-term challenge. He would not live to see the results.

Swimming Against the Tide: Campaigning for Human Rights in Rwanda

The death of André Sibomana has left a huge void in Rwanda. The void is more than the loss of one remarkable man. It is part of a greater tragedy which has increased in scope as, one by one, many of Rwanda's most committed human rights activists have either been killed, arrested, forced to flee the country or have died of natural causes.

Violent repression under successive regimes has meant that the number of individuals in Rwanda prepared to fight for human rights has always been small. Under the Habyarimana regime, the dangers for human rights campaigners and critics of the government were well known. In the aftermath of the genocide, with the advent of a new government, there was a sense of future and potential renewal, despite the suffering. The human rights movement could have been revived and become a dynamic, positive influence; there was a desperate desire for hope. But these illusions were quickly shattered. The new government wasted no time in imposing tight control, particularly over the activities of human rights defenders, the press, political opponents and any other real or suspected critics. The polarization and disarray within the human rights movement were exploited to the full.

Journalists were among the first to be targeted. After the near fatal attack on Edouard Mutsinzi and the disappearance of Manasse Mugabo in 1995 (see Chapter 9), other journalists suffered a range of abuses and harassment. Several were arrested; among those still in prison in Kigali in early 1999 is Amiel Nkuliza, director of the newspaper *Intego* and editor of *Le Partisan*, who has been detained since May 1997. In April 1997, his colleague Appollos Hakizimana was shot dead in the street in the Nyamirambo district of Kigali.

The government claims that there is no censorship of the press in Rwanda. But government censorship is no longer needed when journalists censor themselves just in order to stay alive. André Sibomana was virtually alone in refusing to submit to this self-censorship. His own fame and prominence may have afforded him a degree of protection. Others have had no choice but to remain silent.

Peaceful political opponents have also been dealt with ruthlessly. Many open political opponents of the government are now in exile. Several have been killed, among them former collaborators of the RPF and of the government it set up in July 1994. One of the most shocking cases was the assassination of Seth Sendashonga, a former member of the RPF and Minister of Interior in Rwanda from July 1994 to August 1995, who was shot dead in Nairobi, Kenya, on 16 May 1998. During his period in government, Seth Sendashonga had repeatedly denounced abuses by the RPF and the new security forces and had tried to exert pressure from within the government to prevent further atrocities. His appeals fell on deaf ears. Once in exile, he formed an opposition party, the Resistance Forces for Democracy, and continued publishing statements on killings and other abuses in Rwanda. In February 1996, he narrowly escaped a first assassination attempt. There is little doubt that both the first attack and the second one which cost him his life in May 1998 were directly linked to his activities as an opponent and critic of the government.

By early 1999, a combination of state repression and internal divisions has ensured that there is still no credible, peaceful political opposition in Rwanda. Peaceful opponents are also faced with the enormous task of dispelling the myth which prevails inside and outside Rwanda that all Hutu, especially Hutu politicians, are supporters of the perpetrators of the genocide. Persistent propaganda – added to the tactics used by those who planned the genocide to implicate as many people as possible – has ensured that the word 'Hutu', to many ears, has become synonymous with '*interahamwe*'.

What is the state of human rights organizations in Rwanda today? In this book, André Sibomana has described some of the divisions which hampered the work of these organizations as they tried to pick themselves up after the genocide. Sadly, these divisions appear to have increased since 1997.

In 1997 and 1998, the human rights situation in Rwanda became so grave and fears were so acute that human rights organizations had all but ceased to issue public statements. ADL remained one of the few to have continually tried to document abuses committed by all sides, including by government forces. They were one of the last organizations to continue publishing such information. The credit is due in large part to the leadership of André Sibomana, but also to the constant courage and dedication of ADL staff and members. However, even ADL's public statements had become rare by late 1997.

By early 1999, most human rights organizations are displaying the same kind of self-censorship as the press. Several of them continue to investigate cases of human rights violations, when and where security allows, but rarely issue public statements on controversial or sensitive issues. Priority is often given to 'softer' projects, such as human rights education and training, monitoring the progress of justice or the situation in the prisons. Some of these projects are extremely valuable and a new generation of younger activists are committed to producing positive results in these areas.

Other organizations, despite using the label of human rights and claiming to be independent, have rarely investigated abuses attributed to the government since July 1994. Several organizations which claim to represent survivors of the genocide are highly politicized and use their status to further government propaganda or vice versa.

Within this climate, the success of human rights organizations hinges upon the dedication of a small number of individuals. André Sibomana's death in March 1998 dealt a severe blow to ADL. Even though he was no longer president of the organization at the time of his death, he had continued to exert a strong influence on their activities. The effect of his death on ADL's members will be long-lasting. However, remarkably, within a short time, they have resumed their activities, undoubtedly spurred on by the memory of André Sibomana, as illustrated by their statement below.

André Sibomana's death came only one year after the death of Alphonse-Marie Nkubito, another leading activist who had campaigned for respect for fundamental rights under the Habyarimana regime, as well as under the current regime. He had been appointed Minister of Justice in the government formed by the RPF but was forced to leave, along with several other ministers, in 1995. He then returned to human rights activism and resumed the leadership of the organization ARDHO, a role in which he dedicated himself to the pursuit of justice and human rights. His death in February 1997 was sudden and gave rise to a number of suspicions. It was attributed to natural causes, although a post-mortem was never carried out. Since his death, the leadership of ARDHO has fallen into the hands of individuals who are close to the authorities and who have muzzled the organization to ensure that it remains silent on abuses by agents of the state.

The silence surrounding human rights violations by the security forces has been accentuated by the withdrawal of the UN Human

Rights Field Operation for Rwanda (UNHRFOR) in July 1998. Tensions between UNHRFOR and the government had been simmering for months; they came to a head over a review of UNHRFOR's mandate. The government requested that UNHRFOR's work in Rwanda be limited to technical assistance and that it stop its monitoring work. Attempted negotiations reached an impasse as the UN High Commissioner for Human Rights, Mary Robinson, insisted on retaining the crucial function of monitoring the human rights situation. A critical statement by UNHRFOR following the public executions in April 1998 was used by the government as an excuse to expel UNHRFOR's spokesperson. The government also suspended the activities of UNHRFOR until a review of the mandate had been completed. Attempts to reach agreement on the review failed and UNHRFOR had to leave the country in July 1998.

Several Rwandan human rights activists, including André Sibomana, had been critical of the work of UNHRFOR: they perceived it as too willing to compromise and found its reports too lenient towards the government. However, its departure was regretted by many of these same critics; it symbolized a further closing down of the country, a new level of intransigence from the government towards international scrutiny of its human rights record, another way of tightening control over information provided to the outside world. Rwanda was retreating into further isolation and silence.

In the face of relentless bloodshed and misery, continuing absence of justice for the vast majority of these crimes and persistent harassment and repression, it has been extremely difficult for human rights activists in Rwanda to pursue their work in an effective manner and to retain their motivation. Yet against all the odds, there are a few who have carried on the struggle. André Sibomana was foremost among them. Although in the months preceding his death, he had become increasingly embittered, his faith – an astonishing faith in humanity, beyond his religious faith – never left him. Those he has left behind feel a duty to keep it alive. But a sense of duty alone would not be enough. Above all it is the memory of the man himself – his fire, his compassion and his unwavering commitment – which inspires those who still care about human rights in Rwanda and forces us not to abandon hope for Rwanda.

The statement below was issued by ADL on the first anniversary of his death:

Bishop André Sibomana, priest, journalist and human rights activist, died in Gitarama on 9 March 1998. He was 42 years old. He was killed by a rare illness known as Lyell's syndrome.

André Sibomana distinguished himself through his unconditional commitment to defending human rights, especially the rights of the weak. He was one of the founding members of the Rwandan Association for the Defence of Human Rights and Public Liberties (ADL) and was vice-president of the organization from 1991 to 1993 and president from 1993 to October 1997. He was also vice-president of the Collective of Human Rights Leagues and Associations (CLADHO) from 1993 to 1995.

His death took us all by surprise, even those who were closest to him and who suddenly found themselves orphaned, deprived of his wise advice and his brave stands. His frankness earned him enemies as well as friends, but his intellectual honesty and his love of the truth commanded respect, even in the eyes of his critics.

On the occasion of the first anniversary of André Sibomana's death, ADL is appealing to all its members and to all people of goodwill to carry forward the values which were the leitmotiv of this great man's life.

André Sibomana would not have kept silent while people were disappearing or dying. He would not have been at rest while people were being stripped of their possessions or arbitrarily thrown into prison.

He always stood up against corruption, nepotism, clientelism and all the other evils which prey upon our society – and risked his life for it.

Instead of dragging us down into a state of apathy, the death of André Sibomana should breathe new life into us to carry on his struggle.

Carina Tertsakian
London, March 1999

Select Bibliography

Many books, articles and reports have been written on Rwanda over the last few years; below is just a small selection. Most of the authoritative books on Rwanda have been written in French and few of them have been translated into English. Several of these are included in the selection below because of their importance and relevance to the subject matter in this book.

Article 19
> *Broadcasting genocide: censorship, propaganda and state-sponsored violence in Rwanda, 1990–1994*
> London, Article 19, 1996.

An overview of the role of the media in the period leading up to the genocide in Rwanda, by this non-governmental organization which campaigns against censorship.

Bouchet-Saulnier, Françoise; Laffont, Frédéric
> *Maudits soient les yeux fermés*
> Paris, J-C. Lattès, Arte, 1995.

Françoise Bouchet-Saulnier, legal adviser at Médecins sans frontières, has followed the Rwandan crisis closely and presents her testimony. Frédéric Laffont produced a documentary broadcast in 1996 with the same title.

Braeckman, Colette
> *Histoire d'un génocide*
> Paris, Fayard, 1994.

Colette Braeckman, a journalist from the Belgian daily *Le Soir*, is a recognized specialist on Central Africa. Her encyclopaedic knowledge of the region makes her perspective particularly relevant, although somewhat partisan. Having devoted pages of praise to André Sibomana (*André Sibomana, plus qu'un simple prêtre*, in *Dix portraits pour la liberté de la presse*, Paris, Le Monde

Edition, 1995, pages 105–22), she revised her opinion and changed her position (see *Terreur africaine. Burundi, Rwanda, Zaïre: les racines de la violence*, Paris, Fayard, pages 83–5).

Brauman, Rony
Devant le mal. Rwanda: un génocide en direct
Paris, Arléa, 1994.

A reflection on the attitude of the international community towards the genocide in Rwanda by the former president of Médecins sans frontières.

Destexhe, Alain
Rwanda and genocide in the twentieth century
London, Pluto Press, 1995.

Alain Destexhe, a member of the Belgian Senate, traces the events which led to the genocide and denounces the complicit and passive attitude of the international community.

Erny, Pierre
Rwanda 1994
Paris, L'Harmattan, 1995.

A polemical book which defends some aspects of the Habyarimana regime and is very critical of the RPF.

Franche, Dominique
Généalogie du génocide rwandais. Hutus et Tutsis: Gaulois et Francs?
published in the review *Les Temps modernes*, no. 582
Paris, May–June 1995.

In this stimulating article, Dominique Franche analyses the ideological premises of the genocide.

French National Assembly (Assemblée Nationale)
Enquête sur la tragédie rwandaise (1990–1994)
Paris, 1998.

The official report of the French parliamentary investigation into events in Rwanda since 1990, in four volumes.

Godding, Jean-Pierre (ed.)
Réfugiés rwandais au Zaïre: sommes-nous encore des hommes? documents des groupes de réflexion dans les camps.
Paris, L'Harmattan, 1997.

A book which seeks to overcome the blanket 'demonization' of the Rwandan refugee population in Zaire by presenting refugees' own writings, including their reflexions on life in the refugee camps, the perception of the situation in Rwanda, violence, dialogue, peace and forgiveness.

Gourevitch, Philip
We wish to inform you that tomorrow we will be killed with our families: stories from Rwanda
New York, Farrar, Straus and Giroux, 1998; Picador, London, 1999.

Philip Gourevitch, an American journalist, presents an account of the genocide in Rwanda through a combination of testimonies of survivors and his own personal impressions of the country in the aftermath of the massacres. A compelling book, but one-sided particularly in its treatment of the refugee problem.

Guichaoua, André (ed.)
Les crises politiques au Burundi et au Rwanda (1993–1994)
Lille, Université des Sciences et Technologies de Lille, 2nd edition, 1995.

This dense and substantial book provides an excellent analysis of the problems experienced by the countries in the Great Lakes region on the eve of the genocide in Rwanda. It is still topical and relevant.

Hilberg, Raul
The destruction of the European Jews
New York, Holmes and Meir, 1985.

Human Rights Watch
Leave none to tell the story: genocide in Rwanda
New York, Human Rights Watch/Paris, FIDH, 1999.

A substantial and detailed account of the genocide with a particular focus on events in the south of the country, written by Alison Des Forges. Includes an analysis of the role of foreign powers and also covers human rights abuses by the RPF.

International Documentation Network on the African Great Lakes Region
CD-Rom no. 6
Paris, 1998.

Once or twice a year, this network produces a CD-Rom containing original documents (1,250 documents, 27,000 pages) of exceptional value. It contains, among others, many documents and reports by or about André Sibomana. The summary of this bank of information can be found on the Internet (www.grandslacs.net).

Journal of Refugee Studies, Volume 9, no. 3, special issue:
The Rwandan emergency: causes, responses, solutions?
Oxford, Oxford University Press, 1996.

A selection of articles by different writers, with a focus on refugee and humanitarian issues.

Klinghoffer, Arthur Jay
The international dimension of genocide in Rwanda
London, Macmillan, 1998.

A study of the genocide in Rwanda in the broader context of events in Africa and other regions of the world with a particular focus on the reactions of the international community.

Misser, François
Vers un nouveau Rwanda? Entretiens avec Paul Kagame
Paris, Karthala, 1995.

The author interviews the historic leader of the RPF and the current Vice-President and Minister of Defence of Rwanda. The book is very enlightening on the successives stages of political and military victory but not very explicit on aspects of the new regime, particularly in the field of respect for human rights.

Newbury, Catharine
The cohesion of oppression, clientship and ethnicity in Rwanda, 1860–1960
New York, Columbia University Press, 1988.

An informative analysis of the social and political factors which shaped a century of Rwandan history, covering the changes which led to the social revolution and independence in Rwanda and the impact of colonial policies.

Peres, Gilles
Le Silence
Paris, Scalo, Fondation de France, 1995.

Gilles Peres's discreet and sober presentation of the photographs he took during the genocide. A book without any text which, as the title suggests, should be consulted in silence.

Poincaré, Nicolas and Maindron, Gabriel
Un prêtre dans la tragédie
Paris, Les Editions de l'Atelier, 1995.

Nicolas Poincaré, the special envoy of France Info in Rwanda, met Father Maindron during the genocide. Once peace had returned, he asked him to describe his daily 'life' during the three months of fighting and massacres.

Prunier, Gérard
The Rwanda crisis: history of a genocide (1959–1994)
Hurst & Co, London, 1995; New York, Columbia University Press, 1995.

One of the most brilliant syntheses of Rwanda's recent history. This French academic – writing in English – was very familiar with the RPF, having followed its evolution from its creation in 1987 to its accession to power in 1994. He manages to retain a critical perspective, which makes his analysis especially relevant.

Les politiques de la haine, Rwanda, Burundi, 1994–1995
Paris, *Les Temps modernes*, no. 583, July–August 1995.

This issue contains several articles by known specialists.

Reyntjens, Filip
L'Afrique des Grands Lacs en crise. Rwanda, Burundi: 1988–1994
Paris, Karthala, 1994.

This experienced and well-informed Belgian academic presents a very well-documented overview. In *Rwanda: Trois jours qui ont fait basculer l'histoire* (Paris, L'Harmattan, *Cahiers africains* no. 16, 1996), the author tries to identify the perpetrators of the attack of 6 April 1994.

Segev, Tom
The Seventh Million: the Israelis and the Holocaust
New York, Hill and Wang, 1993.

Steering Committee of the Joint Evaluation of Emergency Assistance to Rwanda
The international response to conflict and genocide: Lessons from the Rwanda experience
Steering Committee ...(as above), 1996.

An international evaluation of aid to Rwanda in four parts (plus a synthesis) covering a historical perspective, early warning and conflict management, humanitarian aid and effects and rebuilding post-genocide Rwanda.

Ternon, Yves
L'Etat criminel: les génocides au XXème siècle
Paris, Le Seuil, XXème siècle, 1995.

A comparative history of genocides.

Uvin, Peter
Aiding violence: the development enterprise in Rwanda
Connecticut, Kumarian Press, 1998.

An analysis of the role of development aid in Rwanda in the periods before and during the genocide of 1994.

Verschave, François-Xavier
Complicité de génocide? La politique de la France au Rwanda
Paris, La Découverte, 1994.

A polemical book which had the merit of opening the debate.

Vidal, Claudine
Le génocide des Rwandais tutsis: trois questions d'histoire, in *Afrique contemporaine*, no. 174.
Paris, La documentation française, April–June 1995.

A very clear synthesis of the main stakes. Researcher Claudine Vidal is one of the best French specialists on Rwanda.

Willame, Jean-Claude
Aux sources de l'hécatombe rwandaise
Paris, L'Harmattan, *Cahiers africains*, no. 14, 1995.

An analysis of the causes of the genocide.

Human Rights in Rwanda

Many governmental and non-governmental organizations have been closely involved in monitoring the progress of human rights in Rwanda. Below is a summary of the work of a few of them, chosen among those whose authority is recognized.

United Nations

The Office of the United Nations High Commissioner for Human Rights had, until recently, a Human Rights Field Operation for Rwanda and a Special Rapporteur for Rwanda, the Ivorian lawyer René Degni-Ségui. There is still a UN Special Rapporteur for the Democratic Republic of Congo (former Zaire), Roberto Garreton. The reports of these Special Rapporteurs and of other UN bodies involved in monitoring human rights in Rwanda and the DRC can be obtained from the UN office in Geneva.

Contact: Office of the UN High Commissioner for Human Rights, Palais Wilson, Geneva, Switzerland.

ADL

Created in 1991 in Kigali, the *Association rwandaise pour la défense des droits de la personne et des libertés publiques* (Rwandan Association for the Defence of Human Rights and Public Liberties) is one of the main independent Rwandan human rights organizations. It published two substantial annual reports in 1992 and 1993. Since 1994, it has published occasional reports which can be requested by writing to the ADL office.

Contact: ADL, BP 1932, Kigali, Rwanda.

Amnesty International

Based in London, the International Secretariat of Amnesty International publishes an annual report, one chapter of which is devoted to Rwanda, as well as high-quality specialized reports on the human rights situation in Rwanda. Amnesty International also produces campaigning actions on behalf of Rwandans who are victims of human rights violations.

Contact: Amnesty International, International Secretariat, 1 Easton Street, London WC1X 8DJ, UK.
Web: http://www.amnesty.org

Human Rights Watch

This US-based organization publishes an annual report, one chapter of which is devoted to Rwanda, as well as occasional detailed reports, often produced jointly with the International Federation of Human Rights (FIDH). A major report on the genocide was published in March 1999 (see bibliography).

Contact: Human Rights Watch, 485 Fifth Avenue, New York, NY 10017-6104, USA.
Web: http://www.hrw.org
Or: FIDH, 14 passage de la Main-d'Or, 75011 Paris, France.
Web: http://www.fidh.imaginet.fr

Reporters sans frontières

André Sibomana was one of the correspondents in Rwanda of Reporters sans frontières, the main organization campaigning for freedom of the press. Its annual report regularly denounces violations of the right to inform and to be informed in Rwanda. The organization has also published reports on the role of extremist media before and during the genocide of 1994 (*Rwanda: les médias du génocide*, Paris, Karthala, 1995) as well as more recent forms of pressure experienced by journalists (*Rwanda: L'impasse?*, Paris, RSF, 1995), in particular André Sibomana (*La désinformation au Rwanda: enquête sur le cas Sibomana*, Paris, RSF, 1995). In 1998, it published a report on his death (*Enquête sur la mort d'André Sibomana*, Paris, RSF, 1998).

Contact: Reporters sans frontières, 5 rue Geoffroy-Marie, 75009 Paris, France.
Web: http://www.rsf.fr

Index

ADL (*Association rwandaise pour la défense des droits de la personne et des libertés publiques*) 28–31, 113
  and CLADHO report 114
  determination of 169–70
  interim report 1996 142–3
  and public executions 167
  raising awareness 30, 43–4, 52
  setting up 28–9
  Sibomana's death 171–2
  team of investigators 30
  women's rights 30–1
African Charter for Human and Peoples' Rights 110
African Rights 134
AIDS/HIV 145, 146, 156
AJR (*Association des journalistes du Rwanda*) 44, 47
AJRE (*Association des journalistes du Rwanda en exil*) 116
Akayesu, Jean-Paul 166
akazu (little house) 36, 149
Amizero 116
Amnesty International 25, 72, 103
Angola 164n
Arafat, Yasser 151
Arbour, Louise 111
ARDHO (*Association rwandaise pour la défense des droits de l'homme*) 28, 113, 170
arms supply 38, 58–9, 150, 165
army, corruption 36, 40–1
Arusha *see* peace agreement
AVP (*Association des volontaires de la paix*) 113

Bagaragaza, Michel 36
Bagosora, Colonel Théoneste 111
Bakiga (mountain people) 81
Bakonde (land-clearers) 81

Bamwanga, Jean-Baptiste 49
Banyamulenge 81n, 148
Banyanduga (people from Nduga) 81, 89
Bazimaziki, Obed 46
Belgium 60, 74, 88–9
Bemeriki, Valérie 47
Benaco 61, 147
Berthelo, Bishop 129
birth control 93–4
Bisesero 73
bishops
  silence of 129
  supporting Habyarimana regime 122
Bizimungu, Pasteur 107
Blanchard, Father 125
Bonnet, Martial 19
Bouchet-Saulnier, Françoise 104, 114
bourgmestres 58, 59, 66
Boutros-Ghali, Boutros 54
Braeckman, Colette 21, 40
Brauman, Rony 77
Bugarama 141
Bugesera 48, 102
Bujumbura 149
Bukavu 74
Burundi 8, 38, 39, 88, 147, 149–50
Butare 57
Byumba 40

Catholic Relief Services 130
CDR (*Coalition pour la défense de la République*) 101, 102
CECI 113–14
censorship 143, 168–9
  see also press
Centrale, La 26, 36
Centre Saint-Paul 62
Chad 164n

children
  as killers 103
  mass killings of 57
Chollet, Lieutenant-Colonel 41
Christian Workers' Youth 131, 19
Christianity
  and caring for oppressed 110
  conversion to 81–2, 96
  and genocide 96
Christians
  effect of genocide on 126–7
  as killers 124, 126
Christus Centre, Remera 29, 123
church *see* Roman Catholic
  Church
churches, massacres in 65–6
Citizens' Network 106
civilian self-defence groups 56–7
CLADHO (*Collectif des ligues et
  associations de défense des
  droits de l'homme au Rwanda*)
  46, 172
  report on human rights
    violations 113–14
Classe, Archbishop 89
CNN (Cable News Network) 59
colonization 78–9
  oppression 89
  and racial stereotypes 87
Committee of Public Salvation,
  Butare 8
Committee for Social
  Communication 24, 25
Committee to Protect Journalists
  25, 71
communion 126
conciliation 154–5
confession 126
corruption 36, 40–1
cows, importance of 5
Curic, Father Vjeko 159, 165–6
Cyangugu 73, 74

Dallaire, General 51
de Saint-Exupéry, Antoine 12
de Schatzen, Pierre 11, 12
death squads 36
  see also interahamwe
Democratic Republic of Congo
  164–5
demography, and geography 93–4

Des Forges, Alison 30
detainees 166
  amnesty 112–13
  death rate 109
  living conditions of 43, 108–9
  screening committees 106–7
  statistics 108
Division spéciale présidentielle
  (Special Presidential
  Division) 41
Dodo, Colonel 107

Echo des Milles Collines, L' 47
economic growth 35, 93
Eid, Bassem 151–2
Etchegaray, Cardinal 122, 124,
  129
ethnic groups
  hierarchy 85, 86
  mobility between 87
  percentage of population 85
  similarities and differences
    83–4, 86
ethnic hatred 47, 69, 84

famine 22, 35, 54
FAR (*Forces armées rwandaises*)
  former soldiers 140–1, 163,
    165
  and genocide 58
  and Hutu population 41
  and Tutsi population 41–2
  unprepared 40–1
Flambeau, Le 51
food aid, diverted 54
France
  intervention 41, 61
  motives 73
  and safe humanitarian zone 60,
    61, 72–3, 147
  support for Habyarimana
    regime 37–8, 53, 73
Franche, Dominique 83, 88n

Gahigi, Gaspard 47, 116
Gahamamyi, Bishop Jean-Baptiste
  9
Garreton, Roberto 148n
Gasabwoya, Bishop Innocent 21
Gasasira, Gaspard 23, 26, 134
Gatabazi, Félicien 51

gendarmerie, and genocide 58
genocide
  causes 77, 92, 96–7, 137–8
    see also Rwanda, history of
  comparisons 119–20
  declared unlawful 98, 105
  drugs and alcohol 69
  effect on Christians 126–7
  end of 60–1
  evidence destroyed 70
  historical record of 120
    see also memory, duty of
  incitement of civilians 57–8,
    64, 71
  as justification for criminal
    actions 118
  and looting 69
  methods 59
  perpetrators' responsibility
    101–5
  planned 50–2, 55–6, 70, 101
  resurgence of violence 163–4
  soldiers involved 58
  spectators 101, 103–5
  timescale 97
  visible 97, 98
    see also ethnic hatred;
      massacres; murder
Germany 74
  administration 81
  understanding of problems 88
Gikongoro, memorial 114
Gisenyi 163, 164
Gitarama Prison 108–9, 130–1
Goldstone, Richard 111
Golias 132, 134
Goma 61, 74
government of national unity 61,
  139
graves, mass 30, 59
guilt and responsibility 31, 101–5

Habimana, Kantano 47
Habyarimana, Jean-Baptiste 57
Habyarimana, Jean-Pierre 37, 47
Habyarimana, Juvénal 8, 80
  assassination 54–6, 61–2
  and death of Sylvio
    Sindambiwe 21
  and democracy 28, 38, 42
  drug trafficking 24, 25

embezzlement 25
hostile to Muvara 11
and Mitterrand 37
opposition to 28, 35–8
and Pope's visit 28
Habyarimana regime
  creating confusion 42–3, 52
  incitement to murder 48–9
  killing of opponents 149
  preparing for war 48, 50
Hakizimana, Appollos 168
Hakizimana, Célestin 63
Hategekimana, Jean-Baptiste
  45–6
Hilberg, Raul 97, 113, 119
history
  falsifying 78, 80–1, 119
  Hutu portrayal 80, 94
  lack of coherent 94
  learning from 155
Hitimana, Noël 48
holocaust, political exploitation of
  118
Hugeux, Vincent 72
human rights 25, 51, 103, 109
  not negotiable 154
human rights organizations
  168–71
  difficulties 171
  divisions 169
  investigators 164
  politicized 170
  self-censorship 170
Human Rights Watch 25, 30,
  71–2, 103
Hutu
  in army 41
  and Church 92, 122–3
  demonised 112, 132, 169
  and education 90
  extremist ideology 80, 91, 94,
    102
  guilt 68
  and Habyarimana's
    assassination 55–6
  identity 82–3, 86
  inferiority 86, 91
  moderate 111–12
  moved into camps 164
  new elite 90, 91, 92
  percentage of population 85

portrayal in history 80, 94
resistance 67, 68
saving Tutsi 67–8, 104, 111–12
social revolution 94
under Belgian administration
	89–90, 92
Hutu-Tutsi problem 91, 94–5
manipulated 152

Ibyitso 43
ICRC (International Committee
	of the Red Cross) 59
ICTR (International Criminal
	Tribunal for Rwanda)
	110–11, 166
identity booklets 87
Imboni 145
impunity
	culture of 105
	effects of 107–8
Imvaho 20
incitement 57–8, 64, 71, 116
independence 80, 90, 92
'infiltrators' 163
innocence, presumption of
	109–10
Intego 168
intellectuals, and genocide 102–3
Interahamwe 47
interahamwe militia 58, 65, 104,
	163
	preparations 50–1, 57
	roadblocks 56
international community
	future role 156
	lack of assistance 60–1, 74,
		96–7, 98, 116, 148
International Covenant on Civil
	and Political Rights 109–10
International Federation of
	Human Rights 25, 103
International Monetary Fund 35
ipuzamugambi militia 50
Israel 117–18
Iyakaremye, Jean-Bosco 114

Jeunesse ouvrière chrétienne
	(Christian Workers' Youth)
	19, 131
Jews, and genocide 77, 96–7,
	117–18, 153–4

John Paul II, Pope 27–8, 76, 121,
	123
journalists/journalism
	and Christianity 31
	and code of ethics 47
	and political involvement 23,
		25
	threats to 45–6, 143–4, 168
justice 104, 105–13, 166–8
	and duty of memory 115–16
	executions 166–8
	of hearts 127–8
	magistrates' fears 106
	obstructed 106–7
	officials murdered 106–7
	and revenge 167
	see also detainees; ICTR;
		prisons
Justice and Peace Commission
	129

Kabgayi
	health care 130
	massacre 75–6
	occupied 64
	orphans 130
	policy of dialogue 127, 131
	rebuilding after genocide
		129–31, 133
	reconstruction work 131–2
	Tutsi-Hutu working together
		132
	young people 131
Kabila, Laurent-Désiré 148, 164
Kabuga, Félicien 47, 103, 116
Kaduha 65
Kagame, Alexis 80, 84, 94
Kagame, Paul 40, 61, 150, 151
Kamarampaka 47
Kambanda, Jean 166
Kameya, André 46
Kanama 142, 164
Kangura 47, 116
Kankindi, Cécile 6
Kansi, minor seminary 8–9
Kanyarwanda 113, 167
Kanziga, Agathe 24, 26, 35, 116
Karamira, Froduald 166n
Karekezi, Father Dominique 162
Kayibanda, Grégoire 14n, 80, 90
	and democracy 95

deposed 8, 29
as editor of *Kinyamateka* 20
end of regime 148
and genocide 8
Kayibanda, Louise 46
Kayiranga, Marcelin 46
Kesenne, Father 124
Kibeho 129,140, 142, 164
Kibungo 30
Kibuye 59, 65, 73, 74
killers, types of people 124
Kinyamateka 12, 20–7, 144
   financial independence 24
   and Habyarimana regime 21,
     24, 36–7, 44
   internal conflict 22–3
   photos of murdered detainees
     43
   and Pope's visit 27, 121
   role of 27
   and Roman Catholic Church
     23–4
   and RPF 44–5
   Sibomana's contract renewed
     25
   support from international
     organisations 25
   taking risks 25
   trial 25–6, 36
   and truth 22–3, 24
   under new leadership 162
Kinyarwanda 81, 83
Kirambo 51
Kirundi (language of Burundi) 83
Kirwa 4
Koloni, Placide 106

Lanzmann, Claude 119
Lavigerie, Cardinal 82
Leader, Joyce 53
Lee, Amadou 52
LIPROHOR (*Ligue rwandaise
   pour la promotion et la défense
   des droits de l'homme*) 113,
   167
Locatella, Antonia 48, 98
Lyell's Syndrome 12–13, 159
Lyon, Catholic Institute of 19

Maindron, Gabriel 71, 121
Majyambele, Silas 21

Manifesto of the Bahutu 14n, 90,
   91
Marcel, Gabriel 12
Masango 4, 143
massacres 48, 59, 65–6, 102,
   163–4
   in churches 65–6
   refugee camps 140, 142
Massada 161
Matata, Joseph 114
Mbanzamierera, Innocent 106
Médaille-Nyiramacibiri, La 47
Médecins sans frontières 104, 109,
   142, 156
media, incitement to murder
   48–50
memorials, using corpses 114–15
memory
   collective 153–4
   duty of 113–20
Messager, Le 143
Mibirizi 65
militias 50, 63, 155
   preparations 50–1
   returning with refugees 163
   roadblocks 62
Mitterrand, François 28, 37
Mitterrand, Jean-Christophe 37
mixed marriages 85, 145–6
Mobutu, Sese Seko 41
Mounier, Emmanuel 12
Mpayimana, Elie 46
MRND (*Mouvement révolutionnaire national pour le
   développement*) 20, 24, 93,
   101, 102
Mugabo, Manasse 144, 168
Mugabo, Pie 124–5
Mujawamaliya, Monique 61–2
Mukamihigo, Cécile, Sibomana's
   mother 3, 4, 6
Mukamurenzi, Marthe 130–1
Mukaragagi, Antoinette 107
Murambi 59
murder, normalization of 49,
   57–8, 70–1
Murenzi, Michel 18
Musangamfura, Sixbert 46
museums, as memorials 120
Mushenyi, Sibomana's father 3, 4,
   6

Mutangana, Innocent 49
Mutsinzi, Edouard 46, 143, 168
Mutura 51
Muvara, Félicien 11
Muyunzwe 16, 29, 64
mwami 82, 86, 89

Nahimana, Ferdinand 8, 47, 81,
    116
names 3, 4
Namibia 164n
Nasho, graves 30
'national synthesis committee' 38
Ndaberetse, Sylvestre 15
Ndadaye, Melchior 149–50
Ngeze, Hassan 47, 116
Nicodème, Sibomana's
    grandfather 6
Nkezabaganwa, Vincent 28n
Nkubiri, Sylvestre 23, 26, 43, 46
Nkubito, Alphonse-Marie 28, 46,
    139, 170
Nkuliza, Amiel 168
Nsabimana, Colonel 56–7
Nsabimana, Sylvain 57
Nsanzuwera, François-Xavier 114
Nsengimana, Joseph 85
Nsengiyumva, Archbishop
    Vincent 21, 24, 74, 121, 122
Nsengiyumva, Thaddée 25, 74
Ntahobali, Father Pie 125
Ntarama, 66, 114
Ntaryamira, Cyprien 54, 55
Ntezimana, Emmanuel 28–9
Ntihinyurwa, Thaddée 167n
nuns, killed 123
Nyakibanda, major seminary
    10–11
Nyamata 66, 98
Nyamirambo 26
Nyarubuye 66

Olympic Games, Albertville 19
Omaar, Rakiya 134
Operation Noroît 41
Operation Silver Back 60
Operation Turquoise 60, 61, 72–5
    petition to 75
opposition, political 169
ORINFOR (Office rwandais de
    l'information) 44

orphans 130, 144
overpopulation 39, 93–4

Palestine 151
PARMEHUTU (Parti du
    mouvement d'émancipation
    Hutu) 14n, 91
Partisan, Le 168
peace agreement, Arusha 138, 150
    and assassination of
        Habyarimana 54, 55
    ceasefire July 1992 48
    control of airwaves 47
    sabotage of 52
    UNAMIR's role 50
peasants, and responsibility 31
Péguy, Charles 78
Perraudin, André, Bishop of
    Kabgayi 13, 14–15, 16, 18
Pharaohs, civilization of 79, 85
Pinard, Father Guy 125
PLO (Palestine Liberation
    Organization) 151
poverty 4, 144
power, unwillingness to share
    148–9, 152
'Power' faction 101–2
préfets, and genocide 58
prejudice, of explorers 78–9
Presidential Guard 58, 64
press
    freedom of 20, 143–4
    international 29–30, 31, 156–7
    predicting disaster 102–3
    and propaganda 46–7
    self-censorship 168–9
    and struggle for democracy 46
priests
    carrying arms 124
    criticism of Roman Catholic
        Church 121–2
    killed 123, 125, 130
    responsibilities 127
prison conditions 107, 108–9,
    130-1
Prisoners, Standard Minimum
    Rules for the Treatment of
    110
propaganda
    against Hutu 169
    of denial 116

power of 48
pressure 71
see also incitement
Prunier, Gérard 74

Radio Rwanda 47
Rakotomanana, Honoré 111
Rangira, Adrien 46
Ransoni, Philibert 21
Rawson, David 52
Rebero, memorial 114
recession 35
reconciliation, national 139–40
refugees
    in Centre Saint-Paul 62–3
    as human shield 61
    Hutu camps 147–8
    massacred in camps 140, 142
    militias amongst 163
    returning to Rwanda 146–8,
        163
    temporary migration 95–6
    Tutsi 146–7
Relève, La 20
Reporters sans frontières 72, 116,
    133, 159
republic, declaration of 92
réseau zéro (network zero) 36
resistance 31, 67, 68
Resistance Forces for Democracy
    169
revenge 114, 117, 167
RFI (Radio France
    Internationale) 73
Rilima prison 107
Rillieux-la-Pape 19
roadblocks 56, 59, 62, 63–4, 87
roadbuilding 88
Robinson, Mary 171
Roman Catholic Church
    and Belgian administration 89
    and birth control 94
    clergy politicized 135
    complicity 121–2, 135–6, 165
    criticized by priests 121–2
    and education 7
    future of 135
    rebuilding after genocide
        127–8, 130
    religious officials killed 123
    responsibility in genocide 102,
        121–36
    saving Tutsi 124–5, 126
    and Sibomana's death 160
    taking sides 82, 122
    training for seminarians 135
    unfair criticism 124–6
RPA (Rwandan Patriotic Army)
    in the Democratic Republic of
        Congo 164
    human rights violations 140,
        163-4
RPF (Rwandan Patriotic Front)
    38–43, 102
    achievements 138
    arms sales to 74
    casualties 40
    defeat of FAR 60
    first incursions 23
    and Habyarimana's assassina-
        tion 55–6
    human rights violations 117,
        143
    and Kagame 40
    killing Hutu and Tutsi 42
    monopolizing power 149
    murder of bishops 74–5
    offensive 38, 39–40, 102, 138
    parallels with PLO 151
RTLM (*Radio Télévision Libre des
    Mille Collines*) 47–8, 61, 62,
    150
Rudahigwa, King 89, 94
Ruggiu, Georges 48
Ruhengeri 163, 164
Ruhorahoza, Judge Gratien 106
ruralization 93
Rusatira, Colonel Léonidas 64
Ruzigana, Jean-Baptiste 18
Rwabukumba, Séraphin 26, 36
Rwabukwisi, Vincent 46
Rwagahilima, Antoine 26
Rwanda
    democracy 117, 169
    discovery of 78–9
    and future 154–7
    history of 78–92, 151
        see also history
    national identity 83
    north-south divisions 81–2
    official history 80–1

population 80
problems today 140–9
traditional borders 81
Rwangabo, Pierre-Claver 107
Rwigyema, Major Fred 40

safe humanitarian zone 60, 61,
    72–3, 147
Sagatwa, Elie 54
Sartre, Colonel 73
Save, minor seminary 7
Segev, Tom 117, 119, 153
Sendashonga, Seth 139, 169
Seruvumba, Anastase 21
sexuality, of ethnic groups 84
Shumbusho, Daniel 106
Sibomana, André
    accusations against 132–5
    and celibacy 13–14
    childhood 4–6
    and church hierarchy 160,
        161–2
    criticizing Church 122
    death of 159–61, 168, 170, 171
    determination/optimism 9, 12,
        13, 14, 25
    education 6–8
    escaping arrest/ambush 63–4,
        74, 134
    and executions 167–8
    faith 14, 71–2, 128–9
    family 3, 5, 10, 13
    as head of *Kinyamateka* 21–2
    helping survivors 29
    in hiding 64, 72
    as human rights activist 28–31,
        51–2, 129, 133
    illness 12–13
    influence of Perraudin 15
    and injustice 7–8, 9
    journalism course (France)
        18–20
    as journalist 18–27
    in Kabgayi 15–16, 75–6,
        129–32, 133
    and literature 12
    meaning of name 5
    meeting Habyarimana 36–7
    newspaper articles 12
    ordination 14, 15
    pacification work 129

pessimism 117, 137–8, 153
    as priest in Muyunzwe 16–17
    reaction to publication 158–9
    reconciling different roles 31–2
    religious vocation 7, 10, 13, 14
    Roman Catholicism 6, 13
    saving Tutsi 68
    threatened 45–6
    training as priest 10–11, 13
    on trial 25–6
    and truth 16–17, 21–3, 24, 133
    visits to Rome 128–9
    'wild animal' 16
Simard, Father 125
Simbikangwa, Pascal 36
Simburudali, Théodore 21
Sindambiwe, Father Sylvio 20–1,
    25, 45
Sindikubwabo, Théodore 57
social revolution 1959 80, 90, 92
sons, need for 4
South Africa, arms sales 74
state, role of 155–6
stereotypes, racial 84, 87
stories, traditional 6, 83–4
Stuhlmann, Franz 78
succession, order of 80
Superior Council 90
survivors 115, 118

Taba 51
Tanzania,
    mass exodus to 61
    refugees in 147
Ternon, Yves 101
Terras, Christian 134
Tomko, Bishop Joseph 129
torture 69
Tutsi
    and Belgian administration
        88–9, 91–2
    and Church 122–3
    demonisation of 14–15, 70–1,
        102
    driven out of schools 8–9
    in exile 38–9
    extremist ideology 94
    fears exploited 8
    growing resentment towards 89
    identity 82–3, 86
    murdered at roadblocks 56

passive attitude 66–7, 98
percentage of population 85
political monopoly 91
portrayal in history 80
saved by Hutu 67–8, 104,
    111–12
superiority 86
war poetry 84
see also RPF
Twa
executioners 84–5
identity 82–3, 85
percentage of population 85
portrayal in history 80
Twagiramungu, Faustin 117,
    138–9
Twagirimana, François 68

UDPR (*Union démocratique du
    peuple rwandais*) 23
Uganda 23, 38, 95, 164
Umusemburo 134, 145
UNAMIR (United Nations
    Assistance Mission for
    Rwanda) 54, 130
lack of action 50, 51, 60, 142
withdrawal 60, 138, 150
UNDP (United Nations Develop-
    ment Programme) 52
unemployment 35
UNESCO 116
UNHRFOR (United Nations
    Human Rights Field
    Operation for Rwanda)
    150,170–1
United Kingdom 74
United Nations 90–1
human rights observers 130,
    141
investigators 59
United Nations High
    Commissioner for Refugees
    61
United Nations Human Rights
    Commission 116, 148n
United States, support for
    Kagame 150
Universal Declaration of Human
    Rights 51, 109
Urayeneza, Tharcisse 20–1

Vallmajo, Father 124
Vermeersch, Father Leopold 62
Victoria, Lake 59
Vie Nouvelle, La, Chambéry 19,
    21
villagization 164

war
causes 39–40
fake battle 43
French intervention 41
and human rights 41–2
political consequences 42–3
progress of 40–1
and truth 44
war criminals, asylum 116
weapons used 58–9
White Fathers
changing attitude 90
killed 124
leaving Rwanda 124
not learning from mistakes 127
spreading Christianity 81–2, 88
whites, influence on Rwanda 79,
    85, 86–7
widows 144–5
Wimana 4
women
future of 144–5
as killers 103
and rape 145, 146
rights 30–1
victims of war 144–5
wood sculpting 3–4
World Bank 35
World Food Programme 54

Xaveri Movement 131

Yad VaShem Memorial,
    Jerusalem 77, 96, 114
young people 131, 146

Zaire 5, ,61, 74, 81, 147–8
Zigiranyirazo, Protais 36
Zimbabwe 164n
Zionist ideology 118

Index compiled by Sue Carlton